Steps in Time

Fred Astaire
Steps in Time

Foreword by Ginger Rogers

 PERENNIAL LIBRARY

Harper & Row, Publishers, New York
Cambridge, Philadelphia, San Francisco, Washington
London, Mexico City, São Paulo, Singapore, Sydney

Library of Congress Cataloging-in-Publication Data
Astaire, Fred.
  Steps in time.

  Includes index.
  1. Astaire, Fred. 2. Dancers—United States—Biography. I. Title.
GV1785.A83A3 1987   793.3'2'0924 [B]   87-25830
ISBN 0-06-091481-5 (pbk.)

87 88 89 90 91 MPC 10 9 8 7 6 5 4 3 2 1

To my cousin HELENE, *and* OMAHA, NEBRASKA

Contents

Illustrations

Foreword

"'Mr. A'!, when will you be ready? We're all set up for the dance stills. 'Miss R' is putting on her gown! Can I tell Johnny Miehle ten minutes? or what is your pleasure?" Eddie Rubin, who was the Astaire-Rogers personal publicity man, was standing outside Mr. Astaire's portable dressing-room, awaiting the answer to his question. That "Mr. A" business started with Eddie, and soon the whole RKO lot referred to him in like manner.

The one pet bore to each of us—in our own grumbling way—was "dance stills." After an "okayed take" by the director, to have to return to the stage and reenact the dance routine piece by piece ... that was heavy! Johnny Miehle, realizing this, would cautiously praise and encourage us, knowing well how hard it is to reheat a soufflé. Little by little, an hour would be consumed—hitting positions, hand actions, toe matching steps—that in the filming of the routine had marked only four minutes of film time. Unfortunately, these photos were taken when Mr. A and I were quite tired and more ready to be comfortably seated with our feet up and a cool lemonade by our side. Frequently, we'd talk about which "take" the other one favored as the posing continued—and once I recall he excused himself and vanished for about ten minutes, to come back to the "still taking" telling me his mother had just arrived for a look at the dance, and now had to be content seeing it in sections of stills instead. His lovely mother was a gracious and dignified lady and Mr. A's affection for her was genuinely understood by me, as I too cared a great deal for *my* beautiful and intelligent mother.

Mr. A's tastes and reactions were very closely allied to mine. His desire for perfection was a quality not unknown to me in my outlook toward performance. I've always agreed that the best actor, dancer, singer, is the one who recognizes quality and looks to that as his target in every department of his theatrical efforts. That is just what Fred Astaire does. Mr. A's target has always been quality, with a capital "Q"! That is why his talent has captured the entire spectrum of the viewing public—even of this generation—and they are continually bemoaning the fact that "They just don't make them like that anymore."

This book, *Steps in Time*, was his first writing and touches on some of the most tender and sensitive moments of his growing into a new field—"the movies"—from his previous childhood devotion to "the stage." For example, his account of seeing himself for the first time "on film" is the story of most of us who loathe the early glimpses of ourselves as we walk, talk, dance, sing—or even quietly react. "Do I really look like that?? Take it away!! Couldn't they just cut to my fingernails—they're at least even, polished, and symmetrical!" No, viewing oneself on film doesn't "go away" but, as the song says, one merely has "grown accustomed to her face."

Mr. A makes one comment that I feel obliged to correct. He tells of a script that was being presented to me by my studio. In all honesty, I felt it wasn't right for me, so I wrote a letter telling the "powers that be" of my disenchantment. But I was contractually forced to do the film which, to my dismay, turned out to be a hit movie, entitled *Bachelor Mother*. The report Mr. A makes in this book is right, up to a point. He quotes me as saying, "If only I had not written that note," but in the line preceding the quote, Mr. A says, "She never did agree she was wrong!" Well, I must reject the implication that I am unwilling to admit I could be wrong. *Yes, I was wrong!* There is no stolid core within my makeup that would let me disclaim the truth in the face of plain evidence to the contrary. *No, never!* Proud am I of individuals who, seeing their mistakes, admit them! I verbally and happily admitted my mistake then and now. My evaluation of the script was wrong, and thanks to all concerned—Pan Berman, Garson Kanin, and David Niven—it worked successfully. And, Mr. A, by the same token, didn't the feather dress turn out superbly, contrary to your "on the set" evaluation when I first wore it? Guess we all make snap judgments!

But the judgment I care to make here, now, is not "snap." It has been a lingering theme of rejoicing—for having had the privilege of working in films with the gentleman who wrote this book. Ten films! Doesn't sound like a lot, does it? But it was quite a few more than Nelson Eddy and Jeannette MacDonald made together, or Judy with Mickey . . . and one more than Kate made with Spencer. And for each one of those ten films, I can't think of any performer of the screen or stage I would rather have performed alongside than *You*, Mr. A!

GINGER ROGERS
Eagle Point, Oregon
November 1980

Steps in Time

Chapter 1 Forethoughts

As long as fifteen years ago I was very kindly asked to write my story. They wanted a sort of saga of the song-and-dance theatre. However, even back there in 1943 I said, "I can't do it. I can't remember a whole bookful."

Starting in again now, fifteen years later, of course there's a lot more to remember, including fourteen more movies. I've come to the conclusion that as far as this job is concerned I belong somewhere or other "in the rhythm section."

My status as an amateur writer is certainly taken for granted, and this can give one a complex.

When I find myself blocked by a sort of mental impasse, I seek out my friend Cameron Shipp for advice and guidance on the project. I ask: "How does that sound?" or "Can I say it like this?"

Mr. Shipp says, "No you can't," and I do it anyway.

Cam and I are not strangers to each other. Not at all.

Here's how it happened:

Through the years at various studios I would get an occasional call from the publicity department and someone would say,

"Mr. Astaire, Cam Shipp called in. He wants to see you about an article for . . ."

To which I'd reply, "Oh, no! What? Again?"

Now we have a different deal: *I'm* to write the story. What a switch! And Cam says, "Oh, no! What?"

Anyway, I am indeed grateful to Cam for his aid and personal interest in this book.

Now, as far as career stories, biographies and things like that go, one is supposed to have had a fabulous life, a tale to tell. Well, maybe mine wasn't fabulous, but as I look back it certainly was active. I never realized it so much until this writing job came along.

What about the present position of this career?

I'm not nearly finished. Or am I? I don't know.

I don't think anyone familiar with my work feels that I am, although the press makes a habit of blasting out my age every time they review a job of mine. It's sort of a newspaper gimmick these days to be age conscious.

Frankly, it amuses me to read it, but it also gives me a big fat headache. Oh, not really.

Worry? Yes, this I do, always, about my work.

"They went that way"—the years, I mean. I don't know what happened to them, they just went. I wasn't aware that this could happen, and I think no one can be unless he gets that sudden, jolting awakening, as I did.

People do not really think about the age of an actor unless they have been briefed by the press. There's the "He's-been-around-ever-since-I-can-remember" line. Then, "The fifty-something-year-old-Fred-who-doesn't-look-it" is of course a compliment, but it also acts as a theatrical kiss of death. One becomes a freak attraction.

What is this age bit that goes on about actors and athletes, anyway? You read it all the time, but no one ever hears a word about the balding racehorse trainer, the wrinkling magazine writer, or the graying hi-fi album executive!

The truth about me is, however, that for some years I've been looking for the quitting signal. Seeing themselves on the screen is usually a chore for most performers. In my case, it's frightening because I've always thought that I looked rather peculiar.

I've had my eye out for the time when the years would simply show too much, even if they photographed me through three lace curtains.

Right now, all I can detect in the way of a menacing change is an occasional close-up which reveals an unusual number of creases under the chin. This happens when I hold my head down a bit.

I am fifty-eight as I write these lines. What I'll be when the book comes out I don't know. In this assault on basic English, Mr. Shipp claims that I am aging him the way you antique furniture, at the rate of several years per week.

But it's nice to hear, "How does the old boy do it . . . why isn't he falling apart?" And all that jazz.

These things sound odd to me because I don't feel any different. In fact, I feel a lot better than when I was belting around at eighteen.

A teen-ager, no less! Oh sure, and working in the New York Winter Garden in *The Passing Show of 1918*. And I teened my way through many professional years before that, too.

Of course, those were "the good old days"—we must say that. But these are better. To me, *these* are the good old days, theatrically speaking.

In trying to think of a title for this book. I ran into difficulties, of course. Titles are not always easy to find. But I thought up a few, my dear Cam.

How about: *A Hoofer Sounds Off?—Too Many Words—Hooray for Bookmakers?*—No?

All right, I'll get one.

I considered some of those nifty concoctions you dream up sometimes, such as the one you tagged on a magazine story about

Ginger Rogers and me a few years back: *How to Dance Like Four Antelopes.* Liked that one.

I snaffled my son, Fred, Jr., and asked him if he had any suggestions.

"I've got it," he said, *"Gone With the Dance."* Fred was in the service at the time, home on leave for the day.

My daughter, Ava, who is sixteen, called from the next room: "I know! Call it *With No Hair on My Head.*"

I was caught in a vise.

"Oh, very pretty, Ava," I said. "Except that it's untrue. I have lots and lots of hair on my head. It just so happens that on top it's the kind of rare hair you don't see too well unless you make a very close inspection."

"Of course, Daddy," came the faint reply.

When the teen-age and the Air Force ribbing starts swarming over me I have to prop myself in almost helpless defense. But it's a lot of fun and sometimes I hold my own.

Now, about this "fabulous" career thing.

Lucky? Sometimes. Unlucky? Sometimes.

In my opinion, luck is not most essential. My sister and I had to saw our way through. It wasn't easy.

What counts more than luck is determination and perseverance. If the talent is there, it will come through. Don't be too impatient. Stick at it. That's my advice.

You have to plug away, keep thinking up new ideas. If one doesn't work, try another.

My most recent pictures were made at Paramount and Metro-Goldwyn-Mayer, and both of these were happy vehicles. It has not always been so. As far back as I can remember—even in the remote vaudeville days—there were seemingly insurmountable obstacles.

I have worked in a number of stage and screen productions that offered problems from the start. Some turned out very well. A few never got off the ground. When this happens and you sense that the show isn't working out, you feel trapped. You wriggle and writhe your way through the best you can, but something fundamentally wrong, which you can't fathom, seems to prevent your getting the results you want.

Every time I have begun a picture or a stage show I've been convinced that it was a potential smash hit. Otherwise I would never have started it. Some shows give you a grand feeling of satisfaction, some leave you with a "Well-that-worked-out-all-right-after-all" sensation, some are hits, and some just give you a pain in the neck.

I've had the flops, danced myself to a frazzle to no applause—and in vaudeville when we needed the work, my sister and I were fired a number of times and once we were replaced by a dog act.

What keeps all performers going is the belief that the next try will surely be a wow.

The only way I know to get a good show is to practice, sweat, rehearse and worry. Adele used to call me "Moaning Minnie." She retired to get married in 1932. There were many people who said she would have retired anyway because I made her work too hard. That is not true. I never made her work too hard because she simply would not do it. Delly hated to practice. She didn't need to.

We made a habit of enjoying ourselves in private life. I don't mean that the work wasn't enjoyable, but we were fortunate enough to know how to live off stage.

My private life was No. 1 with me from the time of my marriage on. Before that, I suppose my career did come first. Everything changed when I married Phyllis in 1933. That was the point where I first made my step into the movies. The work was tough. The success was unmistakable. It was so perfect, the whole life. I often woke up in the morning saying to myself, "I must be the happiest fellow in the world."

This went on and on and suddenly in 1954 a stone wall loomed in front of me. I refused to believe that I, or rather Phyllis and I, could not break through. I was wrong. After five months of an indescribable ordeal, I lost her. It simply never occurred to me that she could ever be ill.

Phyllis was an extraordinary girl. We were always together other than in my working hours. She seldom came to the studios.

At the completion of a film, we would travel abroad or go on shooting and fishing trips here. I usually managed three months off between pictures. Weekends during productions we spent at our Blue Valley Ranch, which she loved so much. We established that in 1950.

It is still difficult for me to realize what happened. Sometimes I feel that if she walked in that door right now, I wouldn't be too surprised.

When working on my own choreography I am not always receptive to outside suggestions or opinions. I believe that if you have something in mind in the way of a creation, such as a new dance, a sequence, or an effect, you are certain to come up with inaccurate criticism and damaging results if you go around asking for opinions. It is the easiest thing in the world to become discouraged by a well-meant suggestion which may throw you off your original train of thought. Your idea can be so completely distorted that it never gets back on the beam.

It takes several negative reactions to my own work, while rehearsing and getting it ready, before I decide on a serious change. If the reaction keeps nagging me, I usually go into a "revision trance," whether it concerns one insignificant dance step that no one but me might notice, or the whole thing.

I concur with what Howard Dietz once told me: "When I write something, or produce anything, I do it for myself. If I like it—that's it."

I find this is the only way I can get anything started. Of course, I realize that the audience must like it too. And I try to put myself in their place.

But I do nothing that I don't like, such as inventing "up" to the arty or "down" to the corny. I happen to relish a certain type of corn. What I think is the really dangerous approach is the "let's be artistic" attitude.

I know that artistry just happens. Believe it or not, there is even an artistic way to pick up a garbage can.

I have been known in the past as very difficult interview copy. In other words, just a dull assignment.

At one time I was mentioned in the first ten of a list of the most unco-operative actors in Hollywood. This was exciting, but I always thought it rather unfair on the part of the group of women writers who dreamed up that particular idea.

I tried hard to please them, but they asked the damnedest questions!

Such as, "How many miles do you dance in a picture?"

"Why have you never married one of your dancing partners?"

"What is your favorite hate?"

"What goes through your mind in the middle of a spin?"

"Have you any broken toes?"

It's like being on one of those quiz programs. Even if you know an answer, it won't come out when you're on the spot like that. So they became very tired of me. Probably they expected a totally different character from the one they found, and the shock was too much.

I hate to disappoint people, but there's nothing I can do about it.

I'm sure there is a big misunderstanding anyway, about what sort of a guy I am.

I'm convinced the general idea is that I'm a suave Joe who just dances from here to there.

A grinning goof and kind of a sucker for anything.

Too lightfooted and lightheaded to know what it's all about.

Well, the answer is that I am not that way at all. I am really bad-tempered, impatient, hard to please, critical; and as Jimmy

Cagney said to me years ago, "You know, you so-and-so, you've got a little of the hoodlum in you."

At the risk of disillusionment, I must admit that I don't like top hats, white ties and tails.

I am always arriving at dinner parties not wearing a dinner jacket when I should, or vice versa.

Also, invariably, I don't know how to get there or what time to arrive. Things are always spilling on the tablecloth in front of me. Not always my fault, but nevertheless, there it is. Take beet sauce or beet salad. I have had some devastating experiences with beets.

The carefree, the best-dressed, the debonair Astaire! What a myth!

My hats are too small, my coats are too short, my walk is loose. I am full of faults. I have a sense of humor but it won't always work for me. I am always blowing my top over the wrong things.

I tell you, I am a very annoying guy.

But I'm mighty grateful for my chance at the theatre and all of its offshoots: night clubs, radio, television, movies—show business is a terrific job—it's great work if you can get it.

It has a way of grabbing people, enslaving them. The theatre is a medium of great mystery, or at least it used to be. I dare say in present days it's much more of an open book, with all the disclosures of how a show is made, produced, conceived.

Everybody hears how much it costs to produce one, how much business it's doing, and naturally how much salary the actors get. With all the backstage stories that have appeared on stage, screen and TV, there isn't much that people don't know about show business right now.

How different in comparison to the days when an actress was advised by her manager not to be seen in public.

"If they are to see you, they must pay to do so," she was told.

Nevertheless it's everything Irving Berlin said about it in that certain song of his.

I've had some of my most interesting and memorable moments

on an empty stage in an empty theatre, by myself, alone. I would usually have a light dinner about five-thirty and be in before the ushers or stagehands arrived, so that I could run through some steps and concentrate on what I had to do that night.

I like an empty theatre.

Except when the show is going on.

Chapter 2 Omaha

Being born in a Midwestern city has its advantages. Omaha was just right for a home town. Although it was a city, population a little over 100,000 as I remember, it had the flavor, the neighborliness, and that small-town feeling without actually being one.

We lived in a wooden frame house on North Nineteenth Street, about twenty minutes' walk to the business district and not much faster by buggy. My father used to take me to town on Sunday afternoons, riding beside him in the two-seater to visit his friends at Saks' Cigar Store. Father was in the brewery business. He was a lively man with a sense of humor and an Austrian accent. A favorite quip of his was "There are two kinds of Austrians— musicians and rascals—I, of course, am a musician!"

Another thing I remember about Omaha is the rumbling of locomotives in the distance as engines switched freight cars in the evening when we sat on the front porch and also after I went to bed. That and the railroad whistles in the night, going someplace. I used to imagine that I was riding on a train. Aside from these few impressions I have almost no memories of my earliest youth.

Of course, I played with other boys and had the usual childhood adventures. I recall, too, having scarlet fever, with a quarantine sign on the front door.

My sister played with paper dolls (she played with them for a surprisingly long time). Adele had a yen for paper dolls, somewhat the same as I had for railroads. She told me recently that she remembers trying to get me to play paper dolls with her and that I would have none of it. This I was pleased to hear.

Like most girls of her age, Adele went to dancing school. She was a little more than a year older than I and attended Chambers' Dancing Academy on West Farnum Street. I did not.

I remember the school only because at various times I went with my father or mother to deliver or to pick up my sister. I saw little girls hopping, whirling, learning how to dance. Perhaps I should have been inspired by this, but the truth is I cannot remember that I had any reaction at all. Dancing was merely something my sister did, something that all little girls did. I let it go at that and the hell with it.

They said Adele was good. She was featured in school recitals and was a local prodigy. Looking back at family scrapbooks now, I can see that she was a charmer at the age of six, but I can't say that I was aware of it then.

The story goes that one time when I had gone with my mother to fetch Adele, I put on a pair of ballet slippers. I found them in a corner while I was dawdling around the place, killing time, waiting for Adele to finish her lesson. I had seen other children walk on their toes, so I put on the slippers and walked on my toes. It was as simple as that.

I don't recall that this created any particular excitement. In fact, I am not certain that I recall the incident. It may be one of those childhood tales so often told that you begin to think you remember it yourself. At any rate, it seems to be true that I walked on my toes, aged four, showing off, probably, but certainly not inspired by any ambitions to dance.

Adele was the dancer of the family, and the time soon came when our parents decided that she ought to have her chance.

"Adele has real talent," my father said. "And maybe Fred will come around to it someday too."

My sister's ability was apparent to everybody. She deserved her opportunity.

Adele was stage struck. And in a sense so was my father. He did not long to perform himself, he had never acted or danced, but he played the piano and he enjoyed the theatre. My mother had no stage aspirations whatsoever. In fact, her parents were inclined to oppose any suggestion of theatrical ambitions in the family.

My father was born in Vienna. He came to New York in 1895, stayed only a few days and headed west. He went directly to Omaha, where friends had arranged a job for him in the leather business. He didn't care for the leather business. He switched to beer—a trade he was bound to know something about inasmuch as he came from a long line of brewers.

Vienna in the early 1890's was undoubtedly as romantic and waltzy as the motion pictures often made about it. And Father belonged to that colorful Franz Josef era. He was a subaltern in the Austrian Army. His two brothers, Otto and Ernest, were his superior officers.

One day he ran into a snag with the eldest brother, Ernest, which caused quite a hassle, as I understand it. It seems my Dad and Ernest met on the street and Dad failed to salute Ernest. Well, this was apparently something you could not do in those Austrian days and get away with it, no matter whose brother you were. So there was trouble.

Now I don't know that my uncle Ernest was an unreasonable martinet. (I found him a most delightfully charming man when I met him, years later.) Nor do I know whether it was customary to throw subalterns into the guardhouse for failing to salute their superiors. But the fact stands that my father's brother threw him in, and that was just too much for Dad.

It would be fun to relate here that my father escaped from the guardhouse in some feat of daring, turned his back on imperialism, and fled to the country of democracy. He talked very little to me about this adventure so I do not know. But I imagine that he behaved like a soldier, took his reprimand, and then took off from Austria as fast as he could. From the fact that he seldom talked about it, I suppose he never considered the incident amusing.

At any rate, he came to New York, moved to Omaha and went to work for the Storz Brewing Company. He liked the business and prospered at it.

He married my mother in 1896.

I recently asked Mother what she was like in those early days but she shyly avoided the issue. I can recall that she was pretty, and she was usually ready to play with us, but she was also strict. I don't remember any spankings but I think we got a slap or two occasionally just to level things off a bit. And why not?

I can truthfully say without reservations that we have a sensational mother. Married in her teens, she was in her early twenties when she took on the challenging job of carting her two brats to New York in search of a career. She was and still is gentle, soft-spoken and retiring. I don't know how she ever penetrated some of the barriers that must have confronted her in the maze of the Broadway theatrical world.

Mother went to a parochial school in Omaha where students finished their courses academically well educated and spiritually enlightened. Thus equipped she was able to, and did, teach Adele and me our first reading, writing and arithmetic. It came in mighty handy too, that private tutoring, with the work schedule we found ourselves engrossed in.

Mother was in her late teens when she first met my father at a party. He was about ten years older. They were married after a brief courtship.

In 1904, when I was about four and a half years old, I remember being aware of rumblings around our house—conversations about New York—a railroad trip being discussed. I heard my father say it would take two days and two nights with a change of trains in Chicago. Naturally, I was curious but I didn't ask any questions—just listened. This went on for some months. It was obvious that something was up—I didn't know what. I kept hearing "New York" until that name was firmly imbedded in my mind. Quite suddenly one day, I was told that we were going there.

Almost before I knew it, we were on our way.

Father drove my mother, Adele and me to the railroad station in the family buggy. He put us on a train and waved good-by. I looked back at him as he stood there waving. It was not a sad parting.

There had been a good deal of preparation for the journey. Something new was about to take place. What it was was not clear to me. It concerned Adele and I was going along for the ride.

Anyway—there we were, headed for the big city. My father was to stay in Omaha and send money to keep us going. He would join us from time to time.

As I learned years later, this trip was really a stab in the dark. We were going to New York without so much as a letter of introduction to somebody's aunt. My mother had never been there, and she knew no one, theatrical or otherwise. She had not even written ahead to enroll us in a dancing school. So none of the Astaires could have known what was in store for them.

As for me—I just went along for the ride.

As we boarded the Pullman I remember announcing quite loudly, "I don't care if anybody else goes to New York as long as I do!"

I thought I had made an impressive noise and was surprised when no one paid any attention to me except Adele and she said, "Oh, shut up."

I must have been a tiresome little boy.

Everything about the trip intrigued me, of course. The conductors, brakemen, Pullman porters, upper berths—everything about railroads. They literally sent me.

Soon—too soon it seemed—we were in New York.

Chapter 3 New York

We arrived at the Pennsylvania Station on a gray day. It was unusual for us to see so many people, all in a hurry. The New York attitude as ever was to hurry whether you had to or not. We soon found that out, so we hurried too.

Mother parked us by the information booth in the middle of the vast station and told us to stay there while she saw about baggage and transportation. We did.

I said to Adele, "This is a big city."

She gave me a flat look and replied,

"This is only the depot."

Mother arrived with a porter in a red cap and I asked him, "Which way is the business district?" He grinned, "Yassuh." I didn't realize, of course, that New York was nothin' else but.

We went to the Herald Square Hotel through jams of street cars, hansom cabs and beer trucks.

There were a few days of sight-seeing and staring at new things, such as elevated trains, the Flatiron Building and the subway. But we had come to town to work, as I soon found out, and the work, to my surprise, included me.

I can't say that I protested. I simply did not get the idea that dancing was for me. However, I took it as a matter of course. It seemed natural enough to go with Adele and do what she did.

Claude Alvienne's dancing school was in the same building as the Grand Opera House on Eighth Avenue at Twenty-third Street. To get to the dancing school we climbed a dark flight of narrow stairs to a small door which opened, surprisingly, into a big ballroom. Rows of folding chairs lined three sides of the room and at one end was a stage.

This was a school that our parents had selected through a small advertisement they saw in a theatrical trade paper, the *New York Clipper*, to which my father subscribed. There we were. Alvienne was a kindly, fatherly man with white hair, quite the picturesque dancing master. We liked him at once and we liked Mrs. Alvienne. She was known as La Neva and had been a well-known toe dancer.

I can't remember much about my first dancing lessons but I know I didn't mind them. I think I did simple exercises along with other children. That phase is all quite vague to me.

What I do remember vividly is Mr. Alvienne beating time with a stick on the back of a wooden chair. On one side of the ballroom a lady played the piano. Mr. Alvienne stood in front of us, his right foot on a rung of the chair, that stick in his right hand, beating out the time. This got me.

When we made a mistake he would stop, lay his stick on the chair and say, "Now, we do it like so," as he demonstrated the step. He never scolded. He patiently showed how to do it "like so," then returned to his stick.

I still had no urge to dance, but I loved that stick.

Then there was acting, too. We were being trained in the drama.

Alvienne's was a good school and he was significant in the start of some very successful performers. Of those in our class, one to earn fame was Harry Pilcer, who became noted as a partner of the French star, Gaby Deslys, and also for his solo dance which he concluded by falling down a flight of stairs.

We usually hurried home after our classes to get at our grammar school work, which, as I mentioned before, Mother taught us. (We did not attend public school until several years later.) Between times we played, out in the street, with the kids in the neighborhood.

A part of Mother's curriculum also was to see that we went to the theatre occasionally. There were always many great stars appearing on the stage in New York. Lilly Langtry, Laurette Taylor, Maxine Elliott, Ethel Barrymore, DeWolf Hopper, Maude Adams, E. H. Sothern, William Collier, Weber and Fields, John Drew were known and loved everywhere not only on Broadway but in great and little theatres across the country, and in small-town opera houses. They were familiar names to us, of course, in a sort of oblivious kind of way.

We saw one musical comedy twenty-eight times, *The Soul Kiss* with Adeline Genee, the celebrated Danish ballet star. Mother hoped that some of Genee's dancing would rub off on us. This was the first really great dancing I ever saw. We all studied it intensely.

Adele and I danced from time to time in the school recitals. However, dramatic work was stressed just as much as the dance for these affairs and our first plunge in that direction came with Edmond Rostand. We were going to do *Cyrano de Bergerac*.

We asked who *he* was.

"A brave and gallant man in a famous play," Mother explained. "He has an enormous nose. In the play, Cyrano wears an artificial nose, made out of putty or something like that, and he fights anyone who makes fun of it.

"He is in love with a girl named Roxane," Mother went on. "She is beautiful and has long blond hair. This is a good part, too. Freddie, you will play Roxane."

This was news. Me play the girl?

But that's the way it turned out. I became Roxane in a blond wig, which tickled the back of my neck, and a satin dress rented from a costume company which kept tripping me up. There was logic in the arrangement: I played the girl because I was three inches shorter than Adele.

My sister wore the pants, and swashbuckled in the balcony scene—only we had no balcony. We spoke Rostand's great poetry almost as if we understood what it meant.

Adele proclaimed:

> Roxane, adieu! I soon must die!
> This very night, beloved, and I
> Feel my soul heavy with love untold.
> I die! No more, as in days of old,
> My loving, longing eyes will feast
> On your least gesture. . . .

If I made any gestures they must have been from distress.

I was plagued by the wig, annoyed by the long dress, and embarrassed by the female impersonation. But Adele and I both looked on *Cyrano* as just another of those things we were supposed to do, like spelling. I didn't object. I was merely surprised that we did it at all. Why weren't we dancing?

Our *Cyrano* had a run of one night only, along with other dramatic and dancing skits by the various pupils, and was on stage seventeen minutes.

The next recital brought two large prop wedding cakes. This was actually a vaudeville act planned by Professor Alvienne, and he decided to give it a dress rehearsal at the recital. Mother bought all the props and effects for the act, most of which were built to order, not to mention the elaborate wardrobe and costumes. The wedding cakes were rather remarkable electrical and mechanical contrivances, about six feet in diameter and two feet high. They could be danced on and were equipped with musical bells which could be played with hands and feet. Electric lights were built into the structure so that at the proper moment they flashed on and off.

The purpose of these wedding cakes was to provide a background for a novelty miniature bride-and-groom number, Adele being the bride and I the groom. The costumes were fancy. Adele was in white satin and I was in full evening dress—black satin knickerbockers, white tie and tails. And naturally—a top hat.

There it was. The evil idea was planted way back there.

This was the first appearance of the top hat in my life. I've been trying for years to dispel the idea that I was born in one, but I guess I did come close to it.

Our act was "crazy." We not only danced on the cakes but up and down the musical stairs leading to them, while playing "Dreamland Waltz" with our toes.

After that specialty the cakes lit up, we made an exit, and Adele returned for a solo. Then I appeared in my solo, a buck and wing on my toes, bowed off in a hurry, and returned as a lobster. Adele, meanwhile, made a quick change and became a glass of champagne.

In these costumes we did an eccentric dance duet—then played more tunes on the musical cakes with our hands and feet. The act ran twelve minutes in full stage.

Actually, after only about a year at Alvienne's we were preparing to make our professional bow. And this was the act that did it.

I can remember being aware of coming up to the big event. It was not a nervous approach by either Adele or me. I don't think child performers are ever nervous.

We made our pro debut in Keyport, New Jersey. I remember our arrival there quite vividly.

Our crates of props and wardrobe trunks, sent ahead, were already on the stage awaiting the Monday-morning rehearsal. We arrived at the theatre about 8:30 A.M. and it was not yet open. It was on a pier, and there was an extended portion over the water for some one hundred yards, and a place reserved for fishing at the end. There were a number of anglers on hand that morning. I immediately brought up the idea that we could do a little fishing ourselves while waiting for the stage door to open.

I was quickly reminded that we were not there to fish. This was our professional theatrical debut and it was necessary to concentrate on the work. So we ambled on back to the theatre and, finding it still closed, Mother decided to sit on the beach near the stage door where she could watch for the doors to open while her children played in the sand.

That suited me all right. We had been there only a few minutes when I found a dime. I showed it to Adele and she started scratching around a bit herself. I moved away a few feet and soon was able to shout, "Look, a quarter!" That brought Adele over closer to me and she found a dime. Within a half hour we had forty-five cents, and now I was hoping the doors of the theatre would never open. But they soon did and we had to leave our bonanza.

On that early Monday morning after a heavy weekend of seaside visitors the men who raked the sand and cleaned up the beach hadn't arrived; I had hopes of getting back there soon while the hunting was good.

"Come on now," Ma said, and off to the stage door we went and into the chore of unpacking our crates and trappings. This was done mostly by Mother and one of the stagehands, who was not too happy about the whole thing.

He said, "Hey, Mamma, how much of this freight have you got anyway?"

We cluttered up the stage with our complicated equipment.

There were three other acts on the bill, and they all arrived within half an hour. They watched while we worked out our lighting cues with the electrician and rehearsed the four-piece orchestra.

During rehearsal I kept running over to get a peek at the place on the beach where we had found the money. Up to 11:30 it was still untouched and I figured I could get out there soon and have another crack before time to get ready for the matinee at three o'clock. We finished our rehearsal shortly after twelve noon and were to go for a bite of lunch. I steered us in the direction of our private beach only to discover five men were raking, cleaning away, picking up things. What a horrible sight that was!

When we went on we were the opening act, the worst spot on the bill, placed there because it took so much time and made so much noise to set up our props.

Adele and I stepped out just as we had been taught. I think on the whole we did pretty well. I remember Mr. Alvienne's coming back after the matinee to comment favorably and give us encouragement. He told us we showed promise and just needed to keep working and practicing to become smoother and more professional.

My father, waiting hopefully in Omaha, was pleased to learn how we made out. The Keyport newspaper proclaimed: "The Astaires are the greatest child act in vaudeville." I think if two words had been added, "In Keyport," this might have been more accurate.

Chapter 4 Professionals

The step between amateur and professional can be a short, quick one. We received fifty dollars for that first split-week engagement. All of a sudden, there we were—pros.

My father had a lot to do with our progress from then on. He was an active and talented man and he took a keen part in our early struggles. He came East as frequently as possible to be with his family. He adored New York, the theatre, the cafés, and show people. We always had a swell time when he arrived.

"Luchow's!" we'd suggest, naming the famous German restaurant on Fourteenth Street. Or it would be Café Boulevard at 156 Second Avenue, one of his favorites, a big gay place with an orchestra—Hungarian. Or it might be the old Hofbrau House. We went to the expensive restaurants when Father came to town.

But these expeditions were not all for fun. They had a practical purpose. Father made friends easily. In no time he knew a lot about Broadway and his knowledge included producers, agents and booking offices.

We played the wedding cake act in Keyport, Perth Amboy, Passaic, Paterson, Shamokin, Lancaster, and a few other small cities—along with the inevitable dogs, the acrobats, the monologists and the illusionists.

We worked on the act through these weeks, improving with the aid of Mr. Alvienne, and got it as near perfection as we could.

When all this was done, Father brought off a coup. He got us an engagement on the Orpheum Circuit. He waited until our act looked in tiptop shape and then brought one of his friends, a prominent official of the Orpheum Circuit, over to Paterson, New Jersey, to see us perform. I wondered who Dad's friend was, sitting in the audience with him. He turned out to be Frank Vincent, head booking man of the circuit. They never came backstage to see us, but Mr. Vincent was sufficiently impressed to give us a route of some twenty weeks at $150 a week and railroad fares paid for Mother, Adele and myself. It sounded mighty big! This was "The Big Time"! The travels began, wedding cakes and all, and we became an important child act.

We played Pottstown, Pennsylvania, at the Opera House, with W. E. Whittle, the ventriloquist. In Philadelphia we met English pantomimists and their "London Fire Brigade." At Union Hill, Joe Cook. At the Majestic in Des Moines we worked alongside of Jwan Teschernoff and his trick ponies. In Sioux City, at the Orpheum, we stood in the wings to watch Jesse L. Lasky's "Piano-Phiends."

We hopped from Pittsburgh to Dayton, Sioux City to Des Moines, and on to Denver, Butte, Seattle, Oakland, and San Francisco, Los Angeles, Salt Lake City, St. Paul, Minneapolis, Lincoln, Milwaukee, and, also, on a note of triumph, Omaha. All the way round we had a successful tour.

I loved California and was fascinated by the orange groves and the Angel's Flight in Los Angeles. That was the famous "funicular" which, incidentally, is still running. Mother took us riding up and down that thing as many times as we wanted. The weather was always fine and clear. We saw Mt. Lowe, the Cawston Ostrich Farm, but no movie studios because there weren't any then. We played the old Orpheum Theatre and people made a fuss about us—such small children on the big time.

The long train trips and the observation cars on the Overland Limited and other scenic routes were exciting. I envied the brakemen and made friends with them, but most of all I liked the time when we were snowbound.

This occurred between Butte and Denver. We ran into a snowbank and were marooned for twenty-four hours waiting for the sweepers to come and rescue us. Another storm struck that night and the snow piled up in some places higher than the windows. The heating went out. There was food, but how long would it last if this kept up? Some passengers were displeased and some were panicky: I couldn't understand why. I was sorry when rescue crews arrived to shovel us out. We were two days late for our engagement at the Orpheum in Denver.

When we reached Omaha the old home town gave us a memorable welcome. We were billed tremendously and flowers overflowed the stage at every performance. One huge basket of roses for Adele contained a live white poodle. But we couldn't stay in Omaha to take bows. We had to move on.

We were in fast enough company on the road. We watched and learned.

We could now be classed as more or less seasoned vaudevillians, even though we were barely nine and seven years old.

At the conclusion of the tour we returned to New York and went to Asbury Park for a vacation, but we did not lose touch with our theatrical connections. We had been a hit on the Orpheum Circuit and so were in line for another tour. This time we eliminated the heavy props because we were told it would be easier to fit us into more spots if we didn't require full stage and all that equipment.

We cut the act down to size, retaining the dances and songs. My father and a friend of his helped, and by that time I was beginning to ham it up a little and toss in a few suggestions myself.

The return tour was as good as the first, and Adele and I were more experienced performers. Now we were "with it." We made some good friends here and there, and all in all we were coasting from coast to coast.

It all seemed to come pretty easy now that we were launched. There was only one disconcerting thing: I started to grow a bit, but so did Adele. She still topped me by three or four inches.

There were interesting acts on this tour. I was particularly taken by a troupe called the Kita Banzai Japs, tumblers and jugglers. There was a boy about my age in this act—a son of one of the men. His name was Zenzo Hashimato and we became pals. We were together for many consecutive weeks as the show traveled intact as a unit much of the way. I admired Zenzo and envied him as a great performer in a big headline act. At one point in their performance the older Japanese would lie on their backs on a specially built thing and juggle my pal back and forth with their feet. As a climax they tossed Zenzo from father to uncle and back again a number of times across the full length of the stage with a few double flips thrown in. I stood in the wings every time they did that.

The Japanese also swung jugs of water, using a long rope with a jug at each end, never spilling a drop. Theirs was a standard act, as many a vaudeville fan may recall. I haven't seen such an act for years. If there were any extant and available it's a cinch Ed Sullivan would have them.

Zenzo and I wrote to each other for a year or so, then I lost track of him.

My other good friend was a contortionist, Bobby Aitken of the Aitken Whitman Trio. Bobby and his father and mother dressed like frogs and did marvelous, impossible things. I loved watching that act and Bobby became a good friend. I never saw him after those vaudeville days but I heard from him and his dad several years ago. He's doing fine in business.

I used to hang around the theatre a lot. A kid can pick up quite a bit of worldly wiseness hanging around backstage. But Mother usually whisked Adele from the theatre as soon as our act was over. Adele returned to her paper dolls while I tried to further my ham education.

Now I don't mean to give the impression that Adele didn't have a little ham in her. She liked applause and worked for it. So did I—who doesn't? But at that stage, I didn't fret when we didn't get it. Adele didn't like coping with a cold audience. Backstage where she couldn't be seen, she'd stick her tongue out at them.

It was about this time that we began to have trouble with a kindhearted gentleman named Elbridge Thomas Gerry. Mr. Gerry was a New York lawyer and philanthropist, about seventy years old then, who had good intentions.

Among his many accomplishments, he organized the Gerry Society, which acquired affiliates in many other cities for the prevention of cruelty to children, which meant that child actors coming under this category were not permitted to perform on the stage professionally.

He designated an age limit. A child had to be fourteen or sixteen, according to the local Gerry rule in various cities. The law allowed us to perform in New York, if we were not paid for it. And this we did once on Christmas Eve at a benefit—for the Gerry Society.

We did not like the Gerry Society's works at the time. Their laws made it tough for us to succeed, so we followed the pattern of countless other theatrical-minded parents and juveniles. We lied about our ages for some years and danced across the country nevertheless.

I was still not tall enough and had to do something to make me look older if possible. I switched to long pants a few years ahead of time. All boys wear long trousers now, but it was not so in those days. A kid stayed in knickers until he was ready to shave.

I walked into a Western hotel one morning with my new long pants on and a traveling salesman clapped an eye on me, pointed to his bags and beckoned, "Here, boy!"

I answered, "Yessir." I was taken for a bellhop. Incidentally, bellhops were always my friends. I used to sit on the bench with them in hotel lobbies and enhance my education. And I don't necessarily mean theatrically.

Los Angeles was one of the Gerry Society cities and we ran into trouble there. We were informed after our opening performance at the Orpheum that we could not continue to appear. This was a shattering blow. The act had been a big hit. The newspapers carried articles sympathizing with our plight.

Mother met with the Gerry Society man in a long session and argued so eloquently about our studious habits and learning that the officials permitted us to continue.

Chapter 5   *Awkward Age*

Looking back many years now, I think that for performers of our age, Adele and I must have been pretty good. But the appeal of our act was that we were a pair of amusing youngsters with a novelty. Maybe they thought we were cute kids or something like that. But whatever we were, we didn't stay that way.

I was approaching the awkward age. Adele grew and blossomed, but I spoiled the act by refusing to grow fast enough, remaining plainly a kid not quite tall enough to be the partner of a pretty girl in a dancing act.

Then another problem. Adele not only outgrew me but we outgrew our material.

Success stopped—we could not get bookings.

I can remember our agent sending Mother a report from one theatre manager to show why he could not get work for us. It was a routine procedure for the local manager of each theatre to send in his report to the main booking offices after the first matinee, pointing out the strength or weakness of the various acts. This report on our act read as follows:

"The girl seems to have talent but the boy can do nothing."

This puzzled me for a long time because I not only danced and sang, but played the piano in the act as well. I thought I was doing something.

Our parents wisely rescued us from embarrassment. Father came to New York. There was a conference and a decision.

My father, as I have said, got around and knew people. One of his friends was T. B. ("Bernie") MacDonald, of the Mac-Donald Construction Company, which built scenery for Florenz Ziegfeld and most of the big shows of the day, and incidentally the wedding cakes for the Astaires. Mr. MacDonald considered our problem and solved it with a happy thought.

"Highwood Park," he suggested.

Highwood Park was the residential district of Weehawken, across the river in New Jersey. He knew of a good house there which could be rented, near the grammar school, and anyway it was high time that we went to school with other boys and girls. We had no idea of retiring, but we took one look at Highwood Park and decided to postpone stage activities for the time being.

There was talk about returning to Omaha, but Adele and I prevailed upon the family to let us stay near New York. We wanted to continue with our work at a more opportune time.

Attending public school in Highwood Park proved to be a pleasant change. Our private schooling had put us a year ahead of our contemporaries. I entered fourth grade, where my age group belonged, and inside a week was promoted to the fifth.

The tutoring in boardinghouses, hotels, theatres, and aboard the Union Pacific was paying off. Incidentally, geography on a moving train is a good idea: the lessons are less painful when you see the geography moving by.

I got my first punch in the nose the first day.

There was a boy named Cyrus whom I played with before we were fully settled and entered school. On that first day the kids were gathered on the grounds, talking, fooling around. Cyrus and I were discussing nothing in particular when I threw him a verbal curve.

"You're a liar," I said.

This infuriated Cyrus and all of sudden he turned on me. I hadn't thought it was so unusual to call a guy a liar.

"Don't you call me a liar," Cyrus said.

I thought he was joking so I promptly repeated: "You're a liar."

"You can't call me a liar."

"I can too," I came back, still not taking this seriously.

We bandied this point back and forth a few times.

"All right, put your hands up then," said Cyrus.

I put them up.

"You hit me first," Cyrus said.

"No," I replied. "You hit me first."

And he *did*.

He let me have it right on the nose. The blood flowed and the kids laughed. I didn't understand why my friend Cyrus suddenly hated me. I must have been pretty dumb. At any rate, Cyrus taught me a lesson: never ask a guy to hit you first.

We shook hands a few days later. The rest of the kids tried to have us go at it again but I thought that wouldn't be so good. Cyrus and I were friends after that and convinced each other that we didn't mean it.

All of us enjoyed our stay in Highwood Park. Adele and I found many boys and girls to play with. You could see the New York skyline across the Hudson River but Highwood Park itself was like a small town.

On cold, snowy winter nights our crowd organized sledding parties for the rides down the long run called "The Valley," all the way to Jersey City.

After studying and resting for two years, we were ready to go to work again, enrolling at Ned Wayburn's dancing school on West Forty-fourth Street in New York. Wayburn was a tall, heavy-set man who didn't look like a dancer, but he operated one of the most outstanding theatrical dancing schools in the country and was a stage director for Klaw and Erlanger, Ziegfeld, and the Shuberts. I looked upon him as a giant. He was a fine showman.

We were not under Wayburn personally. He had teachers who took charge of us. But he was kind to us, and I recall that he came in and showed me some buck-and-wing steps. I was surprised that such a big man could dance.

We picked up quite a lot of theatrical knowledge at that school during our six months there. Wayburn wrote us an act for which my mother paid $1,000.

In an old scrapbook I find a receipt, dated February 20, 1911. It says: "Received of Mrs. Anna Astaire the sum of two hundred and fifty dollars, being the third payment on account of vaudeville vehicle for Freddie and Adele Astaire."

But on June 8, Wayburn was apologizing for not having completed the act. He wrote to Mother:

I have just returned to New York and am feeling like my old self. You perhaps don't know that I completely exhausted my *nerve force* and experienced a case of *brain-fag* of the worst kind. My health alone has occasioned the delay in getting the act ready, but it was simply impossible to grind it out like a *sausage machine.*

I have been obliged to use your voice off stage occasionally *to make the situations* but you do not have to appear unless you wish *to at the finish.* I am depending upon Adele accompanying Freddie's song for the *finish* and playing for his dancing later.

I want Freddie to wear a grey baseball uniform the same as the N. Y. Giants. It is grey with a faint black stripe in it. . . . Across the breast of the shirt have them put THE LITTLE GIANTS. . . . Adele should be dressed in a dainty little summer frock with her hair in a single braid. The title of the act is A RAINY SATURDAY, the idea being that Freddie is obliged to stay indoors against his will. Adele is practicing her music lesson. She finally coaxes him to play house and he has a little scene showing how her first beau will act. . . . They lead into a number after a proposal scene. The next scene shows how "Father" comes home late from the club and with a slight "jag." . . .

In that scene I want Freddie to wear a silk hat large enough to come down over his ears and an old prop dress coat. . . . I have the act boiled down to about *18 minutes* now and by Monday I will get it down to *12 minutes,* including the two numbers.

That was what we called the "Baseball Act."

Meantime, we had moved back to New York City to a boardinghouse on West Forty-fifth Street because of the difficulty in making the ferry trip back and forth daily from New Jersey. It was one of those typical brownstone-front houses in the block between Times Square and Eighth Avenue on the south side of the street, and could be a pretty tough neighborhood at times. Kids would come through from below Eighth Avenue in gang fights and other pastimes.

Recently, out of curiosity, I went by the exact spot where I used to live and figured that my old room in the boardinghouse must now be about the third-row balcony of the Royal Theatre.

Most of the boys and the neighborhood characters there were nice guys and I ran across some of them in later years. Jack McPartland was one I saw a lot of. He worked for Charles Dillingham at the Globe Theatre, on the office staff, when Adele and I were under contract there.

It was good fun playing on the street in front of our boardinghouse. We played baseball, stoop ball, all kinds of tag, hide-and-seek, marbles and kat. Adele seldom took part in street activities. She had a few girl friends in the neighborhood but they stayed away from the sidewalks.

In general our daily routine was simple. After school, which was Wayburn's for me, we gathered at about 3:30 and started the games. We also played after supper. There was no sign of juvenile delinquency in that particular block, as I remember it, but there was plenty of mischief. I had one special treat through the kindness of Bernie MacDonald. He arranged a season pass for me to the Yankees' ball park. I spent many an afternoon there.

We stayed on Forty-fifth Street for one year, then moved to West Fifty-seventh Street and lived at the Calumet Hotel between Eighth and Ninth avenues. I liked the neighborhood. It was a wide street, pleasant and residential when we were there.

We practiced our dancing constantly and I began to grow out of the awkward age. There was a YMCA at the Eighth Avenue corner where I attended gym classes. New friends were Dick and Herb, the two sons of Dr. Henry Moeller, prominent physician, whose house was just across the street from our hotel. Also Mahlon Beakes whose father owned the Beakes Dairy Company. The four of us found plenty to do.

The Calumet was a residential hotel next door to the church of Zion and St. Timothy where I met the Rev. Randolph Ray, then the curate. He was transferred later to the Church of the Transfiguration (the Little Church Around the Corner) at Twenty-ninth and Fifth Avenue, where I was confirmed.

I'll always remember Dick Moeller shooting tomcats off back-yard fences that ran between Fifty-seventh and Fifty-eighth streets. Those cats kept the whole neighborhood awake until Dick blasted them. I think he used a .30-.30.

Another pastime of ours was to get up on the roof, four stories high, and throw handfuls of pebbles down on pedestrians. Then we filled paper bags with water, twisted the necks tight, and dropped them on the sidewalk, timed so they would explode about ten feet in front of a passerby. They made a "plop" noise and scattered water in all directions but our aim was good and we never made a direct hit.

From the roof we also shot bulbs out of electric signs with a .22. The signs were half a block away on an Eighth Avenue building roof.

One day out on Fifty-seventh Street, Dick and I were batting a tennis ball back and forth from a long distance up and down the block. Along came a half a dozen roving juveniles from Tenth Avenue, looking for trouble. One, when he saw Dick with the tennis racket, went over to him, reached for it, and yelled, "Hey, you! Gimme that!"

Dick did. He smashed the racket down over the kid's head, breaking through the gut strings. The kid took off with it wrapped around his neck like a horse collar, running back toward Tenth Avenue, followed by his gang.

I was retreating to my hotel for cover but I took a quick look back. When I saw what Dick had done and that our guests were on their way, I picked up a baseball bat and chased them down the street.

So it was not all dancing. The fun-on-the-street days ended abruptly, however, when Ned Wayburn completed "A Rainy Saturday," the baseball act, and we were ready to open again. But it was difficult for us to get an agent to look at our act. We could not get any bookings. It was some months before a break came.

Ned Wayburn arranged for us to appear on a benefit program he was sponsoring at the Broadway Theatre. At last we were to play before a New York audience.

Our act did well at that benefit. There was even some mention in the *Morning Telegraph* about it. The *Telegraph* at that time specialized in theatrical news. It said: "Fred and Adele Astaire are a clever singing and dancing team. . . ."

Another notice read: "Credit a sure-fire hit to Ned Wayburn and those Astaire children, Fred and Adele. . . ."

Possibly these comments were written by Mr. Wayburn himself. We never knew. At any rate it was pleasant to read and we were much encouraged. Was the awkward period over with? We thought maybe we had arrived on Broadway.

One week later we opened at Proctor's Fifth Avenue.

Chapter 6 The Big Time

Proctor's Fifth Avenue, on the corner of Broadway and Twenty-eighth Street, was an important engagement. It was our very first booking in a New York big-time theatre. We were well aware of the seriousness of this, and approached it with caution and fear. We had outgrown the unconscious, nerveless stage.

A big show was booked in for that week, headlined by Douglas Fairbanks, Sr. In those days he was starring in such legitimate stage hits as *Gentleman of Leisure, Hawthorne of the U.S.A.,* and *Show Shop,* and was making a short vaudeville tour between plays in a sketch called "A Regular Business Man." This was several years before he went to Hollywood and the movies. I was quite awe-struck at seeing him during the Monday-morning rehearsals, but he noticed neither Adele nor me. I do not remember one other act on that bill.

We rehearsed our music carefully, then waited until it was time to get dressed for the opening matinee. We were surprised and disappointed to find that our position on the bill was number one—opening the show.

Our act was partly a sketch with all dialogue for the first five minutes. I knew the audience would be coming in on us and that the dialogue would suffer. We had the most dreaded spot on the bill. But Adele and I got together and decided to let nothing upset us. We hoped we'd be good enough at the matinee so that the manager would give us a later spot for the evening performance and the rest of the week.

We were limbering up as we heard the overture, and curtain time approached. Because this was a long show the usual newsreel was eliminated at the beginning, which meant that we would go on cold, right after the short overture. We were very nervous. Before we knew it we were on. The curtain went up and there was—to use the old vaudeville jargon—"nobody in the house." We were dismayed to see rows and rows of empty seats on the lower floor. Upstairs in the balcony and gallery the customers had arrived earlier, but they were paying little attention to us. Line after line of our comic dialogue went by without a snicker.

Our opening number got practically no applause and the "flop sweat" started to come out. All this time the orchestra-seat patrons were arriving and making considerable noise as they did. We gave everything we had, but it wasn't any good.

I had a solo, "When Uncle Joe Plays a Rag on His Old Banjo," in which I sang first and then danced and played the piano simultaneously. This was the number that had murdered the benefit audience at the Broadway Theatre, but it sure did lay a big fat egg at Proctor's.

As Adele and I went on with the act there was no enthusiasm whatsoever from the audience. They were now arriving in droves, with ushers slamming down seats. At the final exit of our closing dance number we received a sparse, sympathetic kind of hand, and returned to steal one bow.

To make a horrible story more agonizing, what little applause there was stopped while we were out there, leaving us hanging. We had to get off in complete silence.

Of course we were not good, that's all, but it was hard to take. We had not been prepared for any such disaster. As boy and girl prodigies from coast to coast a few years before, Adele and

I had been fondly and even affectionately received. We couldn't understand, having lost that spark, the thing that happens to so many growing child performers.

We had a crying spell when we got to our dressing rooms. But after we pulled ourselves together we decided to go down and watch some of the show from the wings. I wanted to see Doug Fairbanks. We saw him in his act and at the end taking numerous curtain calls to tremendous applause, but that was all. He never saw us. We stood by hoping he would but Doug didn't give us a tumble.

Many years later, Doug and I became close friends. I brought up how he had snubbed me at Proctor's Fifth Avenue. He said, "Don't be silly. I never snubbed you. I never even knew you were on the bill."

When we returned to the theatre that Monday evening about seven o'clock, after a walk and a light dinner, we had new ambition. I said to Adele, "Maybe we'll be put down later on the bill tonight. It's no good opening the show with a sketch."

And sure enough, when we looked at the board where the order of acts was tacked up, our names no longer opened the show. We were delighted as we looked slowly down the bill to see what better spot we had drawn.

Then a cold sweat set in when I couldn't find our names anywhere at all!

Confused, I went to the doorman and asked him what this meant.

"Sonny," he said, "I heard the manager say they had to make a change. Why don't you run out to his office and see him? He's there now."

We went out and got the story from the manager. He said simply, "I'm sorry, kids—your act wasn't strong enough. You've been canceled." That was it. There is no worse blow to a vaudevillian than that word, "canceled."

We talked it over for days and weeks, having little else to do. Why had we been such a hit at the Broadway? The kindness of that benefit audience had been sincere, but it was misleading.

And so that's how it was with our Broadway opening. We tried to pick up the pieces, soothe our pride, and get going again. We did. We got going, smack into a long series of flop engagements.

Looking back on that act now, I'm sure we must have been awful, unbalanced and plain dull.

On top of that, my voice began to change.

We went on working where we could, a bit confused and bewildered. We managed to get a few engagements at small-time theatres. These places played three performances daily and four on Saturdays.

At the Monticello Theatre in Jersey City we ran into a new experience. Opening-day matinee we were out there doing our stuff—the dialogue part of the act—and a clinking noise at my feet distracted me for a moment. Adele and I looked at each other and went on. In a few minutes two more noises. They were pennies—and not from heaven. Well, we looked up and I almost got hit by another coin. In addition, the restless galleryites were making occasional noises like cats. I longed for my old friend Dick Moeller and his .30-.30. However, the noise soon subsided, stopped by theater attendants, I guess. We ignored it all and finished to some mild hand clapping from a few downstairs patrons. We weren't bothered after that performance. The rest of the engagement went off fairly well. That theatre, I found out, was noted for its roughhouse opening matinee gallery.

We also played three days at the Hudson Theatre, Union Hill, New Jersey. This was the business section of Highwood Park. Some of our Highwood Park friends came to see us and we wished they hadn't. We were still not good, and furthermore we were now becoming self-conscious about it. We didn't get the razz there. We didn't get anything.

A number of weeks passed by with occasional bookings in small towns and at private parties and clubs. We played a New Year's Eve party where everybody was so loaded that they never even looked at us.

We knew we were not getting anywhere, but as the weeks went by ambition seemed to grow in spite of the lack of encouragement. There was no enthusiasm for our act or our work from any source except from one man named Lew Golder. He was an agent with offices in the Palace Theatre building. Lew caught our act at Proctor's Fifth Avenue, of all places, and remembered something about us that interested him and that he thought was worth while. In fact, he predicted a brilliant future if we would just keep on working the smaller circuits, developing our act. He was at that time primarily interested in booking what was called the small-time United Booking Offices circuit. There were many split weeks all the way from New York to Chicago. In the Chicago area, Western Vaudeville circuit predominated.

Lew was affiliated with another agent in that territory who handled any bookings his acts required out that way. Consequently, there was a good deal of work to be had on the so-called "split pea" circuit. The Gus Sun circuit or the "Sun Time," as it was referred to by vaudevillians, was not a United Booking Office unit but we did occasionally slip into a Gus Sun house. This was the small small time.

The outlook was pretty grim. We were ambitious enough, but overcoming discouragement was the real problem.

It didn't take much to persuade us to start out on the long small-time trek because, among other things, we were running out of money from home, and we had to make some to live on. Father's resources were diminishing. His job with the Storz Brewing Co. was in danger because the state of Nebraska was going Prohibition, and he would have to find a new livelihood.

We played every rat trap and chicken coop in the Middle West for about two years. One place—oh, it could have been Coffee Cup, Indiana—we had to climb a ladder to get to our dressing rooms because the trained seals on the bill had the only downstairs dressing room. The seals were talented in almost every respect, but they couldn't climb a ladder going straight up the side of a wall. So we had to climb or dress out in the alley. It was a little bit of a wooden theatre and we were the only two acts on the bill.

In another town, in Missouri, the manager of the theatre played a sextuplet role. He was also the orchestra (piano only), the ticket seller, stage manager, and prop man, and he announced the acts from the orchestra pit. He did this to save program printing expenses. In addition he was a hell of a nice fellow and took personal pride in welcoming his acts.

On the other hand, there were many large and well-appointed theatres on that small-time circuit. Our activities were confined to the United Booking Office theatres. We never played the Loew Circuit. That was considered "opposition" and usually acts that played one circuit could not play the other. They operated largely in the same cities.

I would say that we were fairly successful on that small-time tour, but I was still a detriment to my sister. She practically had to "carry me on her back" all through that period. I don't think she ever realized it, and if she did she never let me know it. I was in a sort of blank stage and it took several years before I came near showing anything like form.

We seldom worked in the summer. We spent our vacations at Delaware Water Gap, Pennsylvania. Although we didn't get much money, Mother managed to save a bit so we could have these summer resort vacations and live at the best hotels. Our standard joint salary was $150. Sometimes we'd split the summer between the mountains and the seashore, going to Atlantic City for a month.

It was at Water Gap that I first learned to play golf, swim, and ride.

I was so crazy about golf I couldn't sleep nights. It was a tough little nine-hole course at Water Gap—big rocks in the middle of the fairways, not long, but very sporty. I used to tour it in about forty blows, and sometimes under. The second summer we spent there, my friend the pro let me work in the golf shop cleaning clubs, winding grips, etc. He paid me off in old golf balls. I liked that.

Mary Pickford came through on location for the film *Fanchon the Cricket* and the company stayed at Water Gap House, where we were. This was of course an event and I used to watch what went on and wish I could be in the movies. They were a gay company and very attractive. Mary's brother, Jack, came to visit. We met them all and they were nice to us but we were too young to really associate with them. Jack was about fifteen then and all over the place. I watched him dance at night. He was a good ballroom dancer. James Kirkwood played opposite Mary in *Fanchon*. He, too, was always most kind to us youngsters who hung around watching. Peter Arno was also vacationing there.

One summer at Water Gap we rented a bungalow for the whole season and Father spent some time with us. It was about then that we decided to sum up our situation again. We were tired of being small-timers and were outgrowing the baseball act. What could be done?

Father had the solution. He came up with a man whom I consider the most influential, as far as dancing goes, of any man in my career—Aurelia Coccia. He and his wife had a well-known vaudeville musical flash act called "The Apple of Paris." Mrs. Coccia (Minnie Amato) was starred in this act and it was a standard big-time attraction of headline caliber.

Mr. Coccia took great pains to teach us a tango and a waltz and other rhythms and to instill some showmanship into both Adele and me.

I overheard a conversation between him and Mother one day in which he said, "They need training and coaching. There's a lot of talent there. If they'll promise to work I'll take them on but they must have the heart, the incentive, the will to practice and do as I say. It means that they'll just have to make up their minds that it will take quite a long time. They'll have to forget what they know and start all over again."

That last sentence dropped me flat.

"Start all over again!"

I told Adele what I had heard and she too was sunk. The old ambition flew temporarily out of reach, and for a while we hated the stage, show business, Mr. Coccia and all his ideas. However, we did go to work with him for a period of about six months. We soon found out that his remark about having to forget all we knew and start over again was just a figure of speech. It was only in the nature of a pep talk. He wanted us to attack this new phase with interest and renewed ambition. I've never been much for pep talks—they knock me down more than key me up, and I've always been annoyed by them. I don't think I've ever really needed this sort of prodding.

Mr. Coccia advised eliminating the entire baseball dialogue. He devised an idea for a straight song and dance act and staged some new dances, reconstructing the ones we already had, and added several songs, two with me playing the piano.

This act developed after a time into a streamlined show stopper but it took time, plenty of time, and patience which we did not have. We went through agonies finding the right songs and keeping them up-to-date, revising and improving the dances.

We managed to get a few tryout weeks at summer resorts, such as the Brighton Beach Music Hall and Young's Pier, Atlantic City. These were big-time, two-a-day engagements, and although we occupied an unimportant position on the bills reports were favorable. Lew Golder advised us to work the act up on some better-class Eastern small time. Pretty soon, he thought, he could get us a big-time route.

So off we went up New England way. We hit Manchester, N.H., Biddeford, Maine, Attleboro, Massachusetts, the small outlying suburban Boston theatres, the Poli Circuit, consisting of Bridgeport, New Haven, Hartford, Worcester and so on.

We played Woonsocket and Pawtucket, Rhode Island, and other places, including the Opera House in Newport. We went pretty well in Pawtucket but died the death of a dog in Woonsocket. Here Adele ran into a snag with the manager of the theatre.

At the opening performance, we finished our last dance and rushed out to take an unwarranted bow, acknowledging applause which amounted to the least. When we got off stage Adele (here we go again) stuck her tongue out at the audience. That did it.

What she didn't realize was that about one quarter of the people out there could see her. The manager came rushing back.

"What do you mean by sticking your tongue out at my audience?"

Adele, totally surprised, replied, "They were a terrible audience and anyway they couldn't see me do it."

The manager answered furiously, "Well, I saw you."

And Adele said, "Where were you?"

He pointed: "Right out there, young lady," which drew an "Oh!" from Miss Brat Astaire.

His highness then said, "Well, don't ever do a thing like that again. I'm going to have to put that in my report," and he stalked away.

Adele was generous and understanding, though. As he turned his back she didn't want him to be slighted so she stuck her tongue out at him, too.

In Newport the audience was somewhat more cosmopolitan than in most small-time theatres. It was, of course, the summer colony of the super sort, and we were interested to see the famous residences and many young people driving sports cars and such. There were plenty of sports cars.

The Opera House drew the colonists and they usually made a good audience. One night Mother was sitting out front to watch a new number in our act and happened to hear a very high-toned lady and gentleman discussing us at length.

The gentleman said, "I wondah what sort of people they are?" Mother turned around and answered, "They are very nice people!"

When she told us about it later we roared with laughter.

In New Haven we were entertained by a good number of Yale students who admired my sister and hounded me for an introduction. They showed us all over the place and gave us a rush. We lived at the Taft Hotel. I remember so well Alderman's, the men's furnishing shop across the street. Sammy Alderman had a fleet of Mercer sports cars that he rented out to the students. They were great. I longed to have one—but I was a bit too young and also could not afford it. However, I did get one several years later and, oh yes, a raccoon coat, too!

Around Boston we were similarly entertained by numbers of Harvard men. They all took a big shine to Adele. As usual, I went along for the ride, although they were swell to me too. Those college audiences could really whoop it up if they liked you. They'd arrive at the theatre in masses of hundreds.

All through these years we were "creeping up on it" so to speak, gaining in general theatrical knowledge but unable to get ahead substantially. We were a small-time act and Lew Golder, much as he tried, could not get us booked on the big time. I would keep after him, trying to find out why, and he would say, "Don't worry —everything's going to be o.k."

This was a favorite phrase of his and we used to tease him about it, "Oh yes, Lew—we know everything's going to be o.k."

We played in Canada—we played in the South, East, West and North of the U.S.A. and then along came a vaudeville actors' strike led by an organization called "The White Rats." We did not belong to the White Rats or to any other group, but scabbing was not for us, so we were out of work for several months.

This reduced us to a financial bust. All the money saved for the coming summer vacation went right there. Things were rather tough for a while.

We were in Detroit—stranded—and that is where Mother did the pawning-of-the-jewels bit. She hocked her engagement ring, sold a fur coat and a few trinkets to be able to feed her two out-of-work hoofers. Actually though, this was not a sloppy or beaten-down sequence.

We knew we'd outlive it—in fact, it might have been an incentive.

While marking time in Detroit I spent a good many hours at Jerome H. Remick's music publishing branch offices.

Songwriting was a serious hobby of mine. At one point I really wanted to give up every other side of show business to concentrate on composing. I also wrote lyrics, but they were not my real goal. I'm afraid they were pretty bad. My music was not much, either, but I was trying, and it rather jarred me that I couldn't prove something. Oh, I've had lots of songs published. I even had a hit, "I'm Building Up to an Awful Let-Down," written with a Johnny Mercer lyric in '38. That one made the *Hit Parade*. I've had others that were played around a bit.

One, "Hello, Baby," I liked. It was considered a possible hit but never made it. "Just Like Taking Candy from a Baby" also got a play but no sales.

The song business is a hard one to crack. I've been an ASCAP member for many years but I am the lowest—the dregs of their rated members list.

In Detroit I made friends with Dick Whiting, a favorite composer of mine who was working at Remick's local offices then. He was very kind to me, trying to help with my songwriting. Dick was even then a renowned songwriter of such standard numbers as "Japanese Sandman," "Till We Meet Again," "Beyond the Blue Horizon," "Sleepy Time Gal," "She's Funny That Way," "Louise" and others. My general theatrical knowledge was enriched by my friendship with him.

Incidentally, Dick was the father of the present-day singing stars, Margaret Whiting and her sister Barbara. His sense of humor and the fun we had were a big help through those lean, idle months. That was the way I passed my time. I don't know what

Adele did but I guess she got those paper dolls out and worked them to a frazzle.

Finally that White Rats strike broke. We had a wire from Lew Golder that he had some good news, would let us know soon, and that "Everything was going to be o.k." This time it was so. It seems the recent reports that came in on our act were consistently good and Bob O'Donnell of the Interstate Circuit in Texas wanted to give us a route which meant bookings in Dallas, Fort Worth, Houston, San Antonio, Waco and Galveston. This was the big time and we would get $175 a week. Lew Golder had placed us in the hands of a big-time agent, Max Hayes, who worked with him for us.

Things began to move from then on. But while we were an accepted big-time act, we were still an unimportant one, and were usually assigned the lousy number-two spot on the bill. This was the worst, with the exception of our other prize position, number one, and that misery would fall upon us every now and then, too.

Occasionally, we would for some reason find ourselves in a very good spot and when we did we would score. The audience would be in their seats. We could hardly believe it—no ushers rushing down the aisles with streams of people. I still have recurrent nightmares that I am going on the stage to a half-filled house performing to the banging-down of seats.

I'll never forget the innumerable times that our act was ruined on the first matinee because the theatre orchestra would play our music wrong—the fast numbers too slow or the slow numbers too fast. Slippery stages were the terror of my life, and many times the stage manager would bawl me out as I tried to put rosin down.

I used to sneak in in the dark before the show started and attempt to sprinkle it through a little arrangement I had invented. That was a thin stocking with a few small holes in the bottom so the powdered rosin could filter through. Sometimes I got away with it, but often I'd hear, "Hey, son, you can't do that."

I fought the "Battle of Rosin" from Maine to California. A

manager would send in a mediocre or even a bad report and that would hinder our progress. If you made a hit you got credit for it and if you flopped, regardless of the cause, you'd be reported that way.

The booking office wanted good news, *not* "This act didn't get over very well with my audience. They seemed to need rehearsals because the boy tripped the girl a couple of times and once nearly fell into the footlights. Mild applause."

The Interstate Circuit was an excellent tour, very well equipped and managed and when we finished that route we were booked on the Orpheum Circuit at $225 a week. It was on this tour that I met Eduardo and Elisa Cansino. They were headliners with their magnificent Spanish dancing act. Adele and I were a small act on the bill and occupied the number-two spot. I watched Eduardo at almost every show. He was a marvelous dancer and together he and his sister were exciting performers. We worked with the Cansinos for a number of weeks. Eduardo spoke enthusiastically about our dancing and we were flattered and encouraged. We became good friends. Some thirty years later I made several pictures with his beautiful young daughter—Rita Hayworth.

The most important acts on the Orpheum route played San Francisco and Los Angeles. Adele and I were not booked there. We went to Oakland and turned back to Salt Lake City, Denver, Des Moines, Lincoln, Sioux City. This hurt a little. We were longing to play San Francisco and Los Angeles and it embarrassed us not to be booked there.

In Salt Lake City, which was noted in those days as a "cold" audience, the orchestra was a good one but not too painstaking with the smaller acts on the bill. Our music was on the complicated side and I had to keep after the leader all the time during the week.

I would go to him and say, "Please—the second number was a little too fast last night. Would you please take it a little slower?" or "Please, would you mind keeping the brass down a bit during the first song? I'm afraid we can't sing loud enough to be heard."

Several times I had to say, "Faster please." It was a miserable week and we didn't go well. When I picked up my music books after the last show Saturday night, I scanned through, giving them the usual checking over to see if all parts were there and ready for the next stop. As I went through the trumpet part I was amazed to read across the top of the page of the first number— in big black marking pencil: THIS FELLOW THINKS HE KNOWS SOMETHING BUT HE DON'T.

We played a number of the smaller cities on the way back East to break the jump.

In Davenport, Iowa, at the Opera House the show consisted of only three acts: Bill Robinson, the celebrated Negro tap dancer, was one. The great Bill interested me, not only for his incomparable dancing but for his good nature and likable personality—in addition to his ability as a pool player. He often watched our act. His first words to me were "Boy, you can dance!" That meant a lot to me. We discussed dancing and compared steps.

I played pool and billiards now and then, not that I was much good at them, but I liked the games and would spend quite a bit of time after the show in pool parlors. I was discussing pool with Bill one night and he asked me to go with him and play. He was a shark, and of course there was no match between us, but I had a lesson. He put on a stunt for me that night.

There were some fellows hanging around acting wise and talking too much to suit Bill, so when we finished one of the frames he said, "I'll tell you what I'll do with you fellows—you see this setup?"

He then placed the black ball against the cushion in the middle of the rail at one end of the table—a yellow ball at the other end of the table in a similarly impossible position—and then put the cue ball in another impossible position in the middle of the table between the other two balls. As he leaned over, poised to hit the cue ball in another direction, away from either ball, he said, "Now I'll bet you guys a buck apiece I can pocket the yellow ball!"

Most of them—about eight or ten—held their money out and Bill went to the yellow ball and shot it straight into the pocket *with his cue.* Of course, the fellows all started screaming, "Hey— now wait a minute—you said you were going to pocket the yellow ball with the cue ball—nothing doing."

Before they were through yapping Bill said, "Take it easy, take it easy now, I'm not going to take your money. You guys stand around with a lot of wise talk. I just want to teach you to listen a bit. I never said I was going to pocket the yellow ball with the cue ball. I said, 'I bet a buck I'll pocket the yellow ball.' Get it?"

They mumbled and grumbled and we resumed. Bill winked at me.

Chapter 7 Take a Giant Step

We worked our way back to Chicago and were having a week of rest when we got a call to jump down to New Orleans. It was an emergency. Some featured act was unable to make it at the Orpheum there and they needed a quick replacement. We fell into the spot and were to get $350 for the week.

That salary seemed tremendous to us, although the extra money was intended only to pay the railroad fares. In no way was it meant to establish a permanent raise for our act.

Anyway, this engagement was a big break for us. We had the number-five position on that big-time bill and stopped the show at every performance.

This report was valuable. It proved our act could hold up in an important spot.

Soon came news from Lew Golder that we were booked at the Palace, Chicago; Orpheum, Milwaukee; and the Columbia, St. Louis. All important dates. We were still assigned the horrible number-one position at the Palace Chicago, but we were performing like clockwork now, and besides there was a newsreel on first which meant that the audience would be seated by the time we got on. We felt we had a chance to knock 'em over.

This was a strong bill.

We had a good rehearsal with the orchestra Monday morning. The conductor was an extra-fine musician and we had confidence in him from the start—he instinctively knew what we wanted and required. This was the real big time and I sensed a positive atmosphere.

I got hold of the stage manager and told him I wanted to put some rosin down and he replied, "Sure—go ahead, but don't put too much and don't let anybody see you." This was a relief.

The floor was right, the music was almost sure to be perfect, and we were waiting for our turn as the newsreel went on. Then came the slight pause after its conclusion and the opening bars of our introduction music to "Love Made Me a Wonderful Detective."

This was a number we found quite by accident at the Waterson, Snyder & Berlin publishing house. It was written by Ted Snyder, was not a plug song of the day, but a special-material sort of thing that nobody was using, and it suited our purpose perfectly. My first lines in the song were shouted from off-stage:

"Stop! Stop! Don't you dare to move, you're under arrest!"

Adele replied in song, "What have I done to you?" and then I continued, "Stop! Stop! I've got you covered, see that badge on my chest." Then I pulled Adele on stage as an amber spotlight uncovered to reveal us to the audience.

We proceeded without any faults through the song, topped by a short dance, at the conclusion of which a crash of applause, starting from 'way upstairs, hit us like a thunderclap. I thought to myself, "If they do this now what will happen when we get to our best numbers?"

Well, everything went perfectly. After our last dance exit we had to take six long-drawn-out bows.

The music for the next act started. They had to stop it, and we were called by the stage manager from halfway up the stairs to our dressing rooms to take another bow.

We had "stopped the show."

We almost fell downstairs to get out there for that extra bow and Adele made a short, breathless speech: "My brother and I thank you from the bottom of our hearts."

That was it. We were back in business now. All the other acts on the bill heard about this unprecedented opening-the-show panic and one by one they congratulated us. That night we were switched from opening the show to number three, just ahead of the team of Cantor and Lee. The same thing happened—we murdered 'em again. As we were taking our bows at the end, Eddie Cantor walked up and down waiting his turn to go on, saying, "What is this? The Gans-Nelson fight?"

That Palace Chicago week gave us the first real feeling that we were finally catching on. We were in demand by the booking offices, and we were shaking off the opening-act status, although it still did occur now and then because of earlier commitments or top-heavy bills.

We met big-time performers, many of whom went out of their way to put in a good word where it might help us.

Billy Halligan and Dama Sykes were a standard act and they kindly spoke to one of the Keith Circuit executives in our behalf. Wilbur Mack and Nella Walker were a standard attraction. They too gave us a valuable boost.

The many famous vaudeville names with whom we appeared on the same bill included Diamond and Brennan, Bayonne Whipple and Walter Huston, J. C. Nugent and the Gus Edwards Song Revue.

Arthur Freed, who has produced many of the pictures I've made at M-G-M in recent years, was a member of the Gus Edwards act at that time. It was a cast of juvenile entertainers.

Morris Brown was also with that act then. "Brownie" has been with me as a genius of wardrobe handling for many years at Metro. In the Gus Edwards act he was noted for his amazing singing voice. He had a very high and piercing soprano as a kid and he absolutely killed the audience. He sure hasn't got any soprano now. I've had great times with Brownie—a wonderful friend and always a big help. I often delight in the fact that Arthur Freed, Brownie and I, as kids on a vaudeville bill, should be thrown together like this in later years.

There were also the famous Nat Wills, tramp comedian; Rock & Fulton; and the Charlie Ahern Troupe. In that well-known act of comedy trick bicyclists was a lad named Freddie Sweeney whom I used to pal around with. He was about my age and we ran into each other on a bill at Keith's Boston. Freddie was a clever boy and later went on to make one half of the famous team of Duffy and Sweeney. Their sojourn was legendary in vaudeville. The nut comics to end all nut comics.

There were Bert Fitzgibbons, Al Herman, Charles Irwin and Kitty Henry, Cross and Josephine, Ruth Roye, Belle Baker, Sophie Tucker, Van and Schenck, McKay and Ardine, Rube Dickinson, Sam and Kitty Morton, Trixie Friganza and many others. I wish I could put them all down here.

We were constantly trying to keep our material fresh and in shape, and now that bookings were coming in more satisfactorily it was our ambition to play the Palace in New York. We never could make it. For some reason they would not book us at the Palace. We were trying to get a good spot on the bill there and told our agent that we would not accept the number-one or two position. Perhaps that is what kept us out. The Palace, as almost everyone acquainted with vaudeville knows, was the prize vaude house in the country and it was every act's ambition to play there.

We still worked very few summer engagements, preferring to go to the mountains in Pennsylvania for vacations during the hot months. We spent several summers at Galen Hall, Wernersville, Pennsylvania.

After our summer relaxation, playing golf and enjoying life in general, we would return to New York a few weeks in advance of our vaudeville engagements to practice and get new songs, if necessary, for our act. It was in this way that I first met George Gershwin.

I would go to the various music publishers looking for material, and George was a piano player demonstrating songs at Jerome H. Remick's. We struck up a friendship at once. He was amused by my piano playing and often made me play for him. I had a sort of knocked-out slap left hand technique and the beat pleased him. He'd often stop me and say, "Wait a minute, Freddie, do that one again."

I told George how my sister and I longed to get into musical comedy. He in turn wanted to write one. He said, "Wouldn't it be great if I could write a musical show and you could be in it?" That thought materialized only a few years later when Adele and I were in *Lady, Be Good!* at the Liberty Theatre, New York, music by George Gershwin, lyrics by Ira Gershwin. I was fortunate later on to do several pictures with scores by George and his brother, Ira.

I often went to the Waterson, Snyder & Berlin Music Publishing Company for songs, too. Irving Berlin was not always there and I didn't meet him until later years, when I had the privilege of introducing the wonderful material, much of which he wrote especially for me for the motion pictures *Top Hat, Follow the Fleet, Holiday Inn, Blue Skies, Carefree* and *Easter Parade.*

In those vaudeville days I also sang Irving's popular songs. "I Love to Quarrel with You" was a very useful one for me.

This tour coming up (1915-16), which I didn't realize was to be our last in vaudeville, was carefully planned. I combed the song market for special material and went into the musical-comedy field for my final choices. One was "They Didn't Believe Me" by Jerome Kern from *The Girl from Utah* and the other a Cole Porter song, "I've a Shooting Box in Scotland"; the latter was from a show of Cole's called *See America First,* which lasted a very short time. It was one of Adele's and my most successful numbers. We had to get special permission to use these songs.

I didn't meet Cole Porter until some years later and eventually did a number of vehicles for which he supplied the music and lyrics: *The Gay Divorce* on the stage, *Gay Divorcee* on the screen. Also *You'll Never Get Rich, Broadway Melody,* and *Silk Stockings.* My association with Cole has, of course, been one of the highlights of my career.

Our tour consisted of a route covering the large cities, such as Pittsburgh, the Temple Theatres in Detroit and Rochester, Shea's Buffalo and Toronto, Dayton, Toledo, Grand Rapids and St. Louis, the Palace, Chicago, again, and also the Majestic, Chicago.

We played a week at the Great Northern Hippodrome in Chicago. That was known as a "shift" house. It worked two separate units of shows on shifts of four performances each, daily. One unit worked from ten in the morning until five in the afternoon and the other from five in the afternoon until midnight for the first three days of the week, then the two units changed positions for the latter part of the week. It was an interesting engagement and many big-time acts played it, even though it was a hard grind. They paid top salaries. Jack Benny was on the opposite shift from ours doing his violin act.

At Keith's Washington, D. C., we had a bit of difficulty. Mr. and Mrs. Carter De Haven were the headliners and they were using our song, "Love Made Me a Wonderful Detective." We were entitled to it because we rehearsed first, but the De Havens as headliners won out and we had to cut the number from our act. That was a blow.

Only recently, I met a young man named Carter De Haven who was assigned as assistant director on a TV film of mine called *Imp on a Cobweb Leash.*

I was talking to young Carter one day and brought up my experience with his father. He was amused but added, "Mr. Astaire, that was not my father—that was my grandfather."

We played Syracuse at the Opera House on the bill with Eddie Foy and the Seven Little Foys. We made a big hit there and the Foy kids made us very happy by complimenting us after the first matinee. They watched our act from the wings at many performances, as we did theirs.

The Foys were the headline attraction and it was a great act, very popular all over the country. Their dad, Eddie, the famous comedian, was making this tour between his musical-comedy shows.

When we came off the stage that first matinee, the kids surrounded us, forming a circle, shook our hands, and patted us on the back.

The press treated us kindly on that tour. For instance:

Boston *Record*: "Fred and Adele Astaire, brother and sister, gave a fine exhibition of whirlwind dancing, although it could be wished that the young man give up some of the blasé air which he carries constantly with him. He is too young for it and it deceives no one."

Now listen here!

Washington, D.C.: "One of the best brother and sister acts seen here in a long time is given by Fred and Adele Astaire. . . . The girl is superior to the boy."

Detroit *Free Press*: "Every once in a while there comes along a performer who is really exceptional. For sheer personality and charm Adele Astaire who, with her brother Fred, make up a song and dance team, outshines anyone who has appeared at the Temple in months. Anyone who can watch Adele for ten seconds and not like her had better get terms from the nearest undertaker. . . ."

It was in the spring of 1916 that we hit our vaudeville peak. We were given a route in all the Eddie Darling-booked houses in New York City—the choice metropolitan circuit. The Colonial, the Alhambra, the Royal in the Bronx, the Orpheum in Brooklyn, the Bushwick in Brooklyn, and Keith's Washington again.

We still didn't get the Palace, although we were featured on all those other bills.

Press notices were good. I took a full back-page ad in *Variety,* publishing the newspaper clippings.

The next week Rufus LeMaire, a prominent agent, offered us a contract for a Shubert musical show. At last! After one second of consideration we accepted the offer and stepped out of vaudeville—never to return.

Chapter 8 Broadway

Adele and I were two mighty happy ex-vaudevillians. We had "had" vaudeville and were all keyed up to tackle the Broadway musical-comedy stage.

Rufus LeMaire took us to meet Lee Shubert, one of our new bosses. "Mr. Lee" said he was pleased we had signed with them and that our first show would be with a new star he was introducing, the former Ziegfeld beauty Justine Johnstone. He described the venture glowingly.

It was to be a revue for the new roof theatre atop the Forty-fourth Street Theatre, just west of Broadway on Times Square —where part of the Paramount Theatre Building now stands.

This revue was to have T. Roy Barnes as the featured comedian and a cast made up of prominent names, some from vaudeville: Joe Laurie and Aileen Bronson, Ray Conlin, the Sharrocks, Mary Eaton, Pearl Eaton and Craig Campbell.

We devoured all this news with great interest, but rehearsals were not due to start for several months. In the meantime we stayed in New York and could hardly wait to get at the job.

Justine asked us to dine with her and we were charmed by her kindness and beauty.

Rehearsal time finally arrived. The first day went well. We were given several opportunities in the show with numbers together and also parts in comedy skits. The show was intended as a special new ultra-chic idea—to start at nine o'clock. It was to be called *The Nine O'Clock Revue* with no matinees—or possibly just a Saturday matinee—they hadn't decided.

After about six weeks of much confusion and indecision during rehearsals we opened in New Haven at the Shubert Theatre for the tryout.

It was a hectic opening night.

The show was ragged but didn't go too badly, because the theatre was loaded with about seventy-five per cent Yale students. They whooped it up for all the girl numbers. Delly and I went fine, which made the ordeal easier. We were quite relieved to get this first test out of the way. After the show, the students stormed the stage door. A bunch of them trapped me as before and wanted introductions to my sister.

Busy as we were with a new show, we found some time to be whisked off to all parts of Yale University, the various fraternity houses and the outlying sections of New Haven.

After that break-in, consisting of revisions, pep talks by the stage director, bawlings-out by the stage manager, and all that goes with the technique of building a stage show, the "opera" was as ready as they could get it for New York.

So away the company went in the special train, on a Saturday night, with hundreds of college lads to see us off. We were to open the following Tuesday in New York. This of course meant a grueling set of dress rehearsals on the stage of the new theatre, which, naturally, was not nearly ready as yet—so more complications set in. We couldn't move in and get to work without scenery, and the opening was delayed. After our final dress rehearsal, lasting all night, we were sent home exhausted about two o'clock in the afternoon to rest up as much as possible for the night's opening.

The final title was *Over the Top*. The opening, a swanky affair, was not too well received. It turned out to be just a mediocre show—not so ultra chic. However, there was applause at times and Adele and I were lucky enough to get some of it.

The press remarked:

God's in his heavens and all's well with the world, for we have a new theatre in our desolate midst. Right over Raymond Hitchcock's unique and devoted head, the place once called Castles in the Air—where we used to have the privilege of paying 50 cents at least for at least 10 cents worth of drink and food—has been converted by the Shuberts into a regular playhouse. Or perhaps I should say an irregular playhouse, as it is unusually pretty and comfortable.

. . . One of the prettiest features of the show is the dancing of the two Astaires. The girl, a light, spritelike little creature, has really an exquisite floating style in her caperings, while the young man combines eccentric agility with humor. . . . I admit that I am rather prejudiced in favor of the show because it begins at 9 o'clock—which is soon enough after dinner for any entertainment to begin. For the sake of the customers, I also hope it ends at 11 in the future.—Louis Sherwin, New York *Globe*.

After a few weeks the Shuberts decided to change the policy of the theatre from the nine o'clock starting-time to eight-thirty and a more normal style of Shubert revue. But the swells did not go for the show as hoped for. Business was not too hot. An important change was made in the cast. T. Roy Barnes was a top comedian but he was not happy in this show. So he stepped out and Ed Wynn replaced him. That was the beginning of a more successful run. Ed brought many of his own stunts and the whole thing got a much needed face lifting.

Business went up and we had a fairly good New York run, and also a good run on the road. It was in Washington at the Garrick Theatre that Charles Dillingham saw the show.

This was during World War I, and Washington was buzzing with activity. All shows were selling out in advance and we were jammed at every performance of the two-week run.

Charles Dillingham sat in the left upstairs front box one night and looked rather interested. His presence caused quite a flutter among the cast.

Adele and I were signed by him after that visit but we still had another show to do for the Shuberts, *The Passing Show of 1918.* Lee and J. J. did not like our signing away from them for the future years, but Mr. Lee was kind and understanding about it. I never had much contact with J. J.

On this, our first legit tour, business was bound to be pretty good, with Ed Wynn as our star, so we had nothing to worry about. It was an education. Ed and I played golf nearly every place we went. I had many enjoyable times with him.

I always pestered Ed to tell me jokes. He could make them up on the spot, ad lib, about anything, an object, a name or a place. He can still do it, too: just take this book to Mr. Wynn and he'll put a joke in it for you, right here:

Joe Laurie, Ted Lorraine and I usually had a dressing room together and we raised hell most of the time with crap games, poker and gags on each other.

One day I left my watch and some cash—about twenty dollars—on my make-up shelf and put a sign on it, "Anybody who steals this is a son of a bitch." When I returned to the room the watch and cash were gone and a message was added to my sign as follows: "I'm the son of a bitch who stole it—what are you gonna do about it?"

They made me stew for three days before I got it back. Good old Joe Laurie, of course. He was a mighty clever little guy and was encouraging to me about my work.

That tour ended in the spring of 1917. It was a useful experience. Adele and I managed to hold our own throughout and I think we gained some recognition.

I didn't do any solo dances in those days. Everything was with my sister. I subsequently did several dances leading a large chorus but didn't tackle any real solo spots until years later.

After *Over the Top* we were assigned to *The Passing Show of 1918* at the New York Winter Garden.

This was to be the customary extravaganza type of revue known as "Another Winter Garden Show," and rehearsals started in May pointed to an out-of-town tryout opening in Atlantic City at the Globe Theatre around the middle of July. That gave us a chance to go away for a few weeks and rest if we wanted to, but we didn't.

It was exciting, looking forward to that Winter Garden show, and we could hardly wait. At this point we would have preferred being invited into the *Ziegfeld Follies,* which was well above the Winter Garden in importance and stature, but we had not been approached by Mr. Z., although we had heard rumors that he was interested in our work.

Rehearsals for *The Passing Show of 1918* started about June 1, 1918. World War I was raging and I had just reached draft age. I was expecting to be called but never made it. My classification card arrived but the war ended before I had to report for duty.

Adele and I went at the job of putting on our dances and rehearsals in general. It was an enormous show—lots of people, big chorus numbers, many beautiful girls. Nita Naldi was a show girl—a striking personality. She went on to become a star in silent pictures.

Another beautiful girl, Jessie Reed, was also with us. I developed a crush on Jessie and would stand gaping at her like a dope. She was always pleasant to me but my crush got absolutely nowhere, I can tell you that. Jessie had many beaus—she was a much-pursued young lady. She went over to Ziegfeld the following year and became one of the most famous of Ziegfeld beauties.

Willie and Eugene Howard were the main stars of *The Passing Show,* and powerful they were, too. Willie, the clever comic, and Gene, the straight man and singer. They had a tremendous following.

I always remember their opening lines in this show. As they made their entrance, Eugene preceded Willie, who came on about five steps behind carrying two supposedly limp dead geese by their necks.

Eugene said, "Come on—come on—now what are you doing with those geese?"

Willie shot back, "I'm gonna make myself a pair of white duck pants."

There were many skits and specialties in the show and Delly and I had several good opportunities both together and working separately. One of our stunts together was a bird number. We were supposed to be bird aviators and the lyric of the song went "Twit-twit-twit-twit-twit-twit-twit—you'd better do your little bit bit bit. . . ."

We were in bird costumes and had a big chorus of chicks behind us. I hated that costume but I was stuck with it and had to flit all over the place in the number staged by the dance director, Jack Mason.

Frank Fay had an important part in the show—so did Charlie Ruggles.

About ten of us principal fellows had the famous Dressing Room 18 together at the Winter Garden. It was an enormous room on the ground floor by the stage door and things went on in there. A million laughs.

Willie and Eugene, although they didn't dress there, spent most of the time with us. It was like a club. Crap games, bets on horses, fights. There were Sammy White and Lou Clayton, Charlie Ruggles, Frank Fay, David Dreyer, George Hassell, Roger Davis, Edward Basse and me. Roger Davis had a small part in the show but offstage he was, and still is, one of the funniest.

J. C. Huffman, the stage director, was a very capable man for this type of show and he really screamed and ranted to get his points across. One day during the dress rehearsal in Atlantic City, Adele and I were doing our tango specialty, the one we used in vaudeville, and the spotlight wasn't the right color or something to suit me, so I stopped the orchestra and tried to explain my worries.

This caused a volcanic eruption from J. C. He bawled me out
—I had no right to stop anything unless he said so— if I wanted
to direct the show he would step out—I was just a punk kid with a
swelled head—I wouldn't last long on Broadway if I was going
to run the show every minute and I don't know what all not.
Adele came to my rescue.

She said, "Mr. Huffman, you don't understand. We've been
doing this dance for years in vaudeville. My brother knows how
it should look. This dance is sacred to us."

There was a silence of about a half a minute and Huffman
bellowed, "All right, young lady, may we now go ahead with *The
Dance of the Sacred Cow?* Music please!"

At the dress rehearsal in New York before the opening, we
were rehearsing the bird number and I slipped and stopped again.

Huffman yelled, "What's the matter now, Astaire, is there a
feather in your way?"

J. C. knew what he was doing, though, and we liked him a lot.

After a tough rehearsal period we got to Atlantic City in time
to open on schedule. It was a cumbersome thing, an ornate extravaganza. This throwaway advertisement card, typical of its day,
best describes it:

THE PASSING SHOW OF 1918
It is a whale—Without Jonah
A HUGE WHIZZING ENTERTAINMENT!
A brilliant array of talent with
The Winter Garden's famous
WIGGLING WAVE OF WINSOME WITCHES!!!
150 PEOPLE   2 ACTS   25 SCENES!

I had a dance number with Sammy White and Lou Clayton
in which we portrayed waiters in a Childs restaurant scene.

We slid all over the long tables serving pancakes and coffee.
It was an amusing number which the audiences liked.

As I said, this was a usual Winter Garden show. It was sure
to be a draw—they all were. Some were outstanding—this one was

not, but it was o.k. There were many things that scored in Atlantic City. Adele and I came through well. It was a step ahead. The press notices were good. The Garden Show was always accepted in those days—it was part of the yearly theatrical routine.

After our week in Atlantic City we went right back to New York by special train and opened on time at the home base.

We had been given the usual pep talks and lectures about giving our best. We were all told we were awful after the opening in Atlantic City. We knew it was coming here, too, after dress rehearsals and nobody minded. We just lined up like a lot of schoolchildren—or maybe buck privates—when told to, and took it. Stage directors or producers dearly loved to bawl out the company in those days. A principal never dared talk back. Not so in the movies. Very often I've heard a small bit player sock it into a director.

Recently while I was making the picture *Band Wagon* at M-G-M director Vincente Minnelli was telling a very tall character woman bit player how he wanted her to do this bit, which was in one of my scenes. He kept acting it out for her over and over again, as he often likes to do, and as he started one more demonstration of how to do it, she suddenly yelled:

"Well, how the hell do you expect me to do it if you don't give me a chance to try it once myself?"

Vince looked at me and then at her and said, "All right, honey —go ahead."

Then he whispered to me, "You know, the worst of it is, she's absolutely right."

Getting back to *The Passing Show*:

We had a smooth opening night. Mr. Huffman knew how to get that. It was not exactly a fashionable or social event but still drew the important mob of Broadway sophisticates.

Heywood Broun said:

"The Passing Show" has a gorgeous setting, good songs and a rather dull book. In an evening in which there was an abundance of good dancing, Fred Astaire stood out. He and his partner, Adele Astaire, made the show pause early in the evening with a beautiful loose-limbed dance. It almost seemed as if the two young persons had been poured into the dance. . . .

We appeared at the Winter Garden Sunday Night Concerts too, throughout the season (for which we did not get paid). That fact, however, did not concern us. Contracts called for those extra appearances and we liked them. They were big shows. It was fast company.

The Shuberts would draft all of their stars from different productions in nearby cities as well as New York to appear at these concerts. Here is a typical Sunday-night program:

AL JOLSON

WILLIE & EUGENE HOWARD	FANNIE BRICE
IRENE FRANKLIN & BURT GREEN	CHARLIE RUGGLES
FRANK FAY	FRED AND ADELE ASTAIRE
BEN BERNIE AND PHIL BAKER	WHITING AND BURT
HARRY ROSE	HARRY CARROLL
HALE AND PATTERSON AND ORIGINAL DIXIELAND JAZZ BAND	
SAM HEARN	RATH BROTHERS
GORDON AND BILL DOOLEY	ROY CUMMINGS

THE WINTER GARDEN BEAUTIES

The Passing Show ran about five months in New York and then hit the road, which was par for those Garden opuses except the Al Jolson shows. They usually ran longer.

Our general education and Broadway experience were well furthered by this engagement. It was a prominent showcase, and brought its performers to the notice of the show world.

Adele and I had our fun away from the theatre as well as in our work. We kept meeting people, going places, and seeing things.

One beautiful fall day, I was standing outside the stagedoor of the Winter Garden minding my own business when along came a couple of friends of mine, Gordon Dooley and Charley Foy.

Gordon of the famous Dooley family, Johnny, Billy, Gordon and sister Ray. Charley of the famous Foys.

The boys had come by the Winter Garden on their way to the races at Belmont Park, and Charles asked me if I wanted to go along. I had never seen a horse race. It was not a matinee day and I said I'd go. Dooley had a Stutz Bearcat and we all piled into it and went to Belmont Park. I was at once fascinated by this racing business and the first horse I had a bet on won quite easily at four to one. Its name, Tiger Rose. I finished the day a winner and thought to myself what a pleasant sport it was. It hardly occurred to me then that I'd want to be an owner or breeder of horses. All I knew was that I liked it.

I went again, soon after that—had another winning day and became more engrossed in the excitement of it all. It seemed kind of easy, too, to win a bet. I didn't bet much but I collected and it was nice.

In the dressing room at the Winter Garden I was now qualified to chime in the conversation with Sammy White and Lou Clayton, discussing this horse or that one. Also, our stars, the Howard Brothers, would count me in on their talks too and that made me feel pretty big.

I had a few bets occasionally, with the bookie who hung around just outside the dressing-room door. Sometimes successfully, but I gradually began to realize that it wasn't so easy to pick winners. However, that too fascinated me.

When we went on the road, Frank Fay left the show and I inherited his role. Up to then I did not have any speaking part in the sketches.

That tour took us to all the big cities, sold out everywhere in advance. It was a seasonal event in those days.

In Detroit I had a horrible scare—for an actor—when I went to my hotel room for a little nap late one afternoon, after a matinee performance, and never thought about leaving a call.

I awoke suddenly and saw that the time was 8:15 P.M. Here I was on the eighteenth floor of the hotel, about six blocks from the theatre, and due on the stage in full make-up in eight minutes!

I cannot describe the panic I was in.

The curtain usually went up after an overture of five minutes. I was due to make my entrance three minutes later with comic Roy Cummings. We had some business, chasing two girls, right after the opening chorus number.

The thought flashed through my mind that it would take me at least five minutes to get to the ground floor of the hotel.

I grabbed my hat and coat and ran for the elevator. It was nowhere near the eighteenth floor. I spotted some fire escape stairs and ran down four flights about five or six steps at a time and managed to catch an elevator standing there. I reached in my pocket, grabbed a bill, handed it to the elevator boy and said:

"Mac, get me downstairs now—fast—don't stop even if Mr. Statler rings."

He got me there. The panic was mounting. I had never been late or absent. Would they hold the curtain?

I now had five blocks through heavy theatre-time traffic, no taxis available, so I ran zigzag like a crazy man. Reached the stage door of the theatre, crashed through the reception hall just as the first chorus number was finishing.

I had to rush right on stage as I was without changing clothes or putting on make-up. I was completely out of breath. Everyone wondered what on earth was the matter with me.

Nobody knew I hadn't arrived as usual, several hours before curtain time, to practice and get ready. The overture was sent in and the show started without checking.

I'll never forget the look on Roy Cummings' face when he saw me. We made our entrances from opposite sides of the stage and met in the middle.

He took one look at my pale skinny face and said under his breath, "What the hell's eatin' you?"

It was about an hour before I could get time to change clothes and slap on some make-up. There was no other chance.

I managed to get into that damn bird outfit for the "chicken number" in time. It would have been a fine sight, me hopping about in a Brooks suit amidst all those feathered cuties. This number was my first meeting point with Adele in the show. She took a gander at me and said out of the side of her mouth, "Hey— your hat's on backwards. Are you drunk?"

During intermission Delly decided she'd get temperamental and bawl out somebody for not missing me. She said to the stage manager: "It seems to me that somebody could at least hold the curtain for my brother. He has so much work to do, and after all he's one of the stars of the show and the least you could do would be to find out if he's in the theatre before you send the overture in. My poor brother was taking a nap after the matinee."

They listened.

This episode left an imprint on me. One of my collection of nightmares.

We wound up with a summer run starting May, 1919, in Chicago, at the Palace, the scene of our memorable (to us) vaudeville triumph of a few years back.

It was now a legit house. We had a pleasant time staying at the Edgewater Beach Hotel, which was very lively, and there were many young people. I bought myself a used Mercer sports car and had me a ball. Sold it when we left town.

Chapter 9 Dillingham

The Passing Show faded out about the end of June, 1919, and *Apple Blossoms* faded in. This was the Charles Dillingham show starring John Charles Thomas and Wilda Bennett, with music by Fritz Kreisler and Victor Jacobi. Featured members of the cast were Percival Knight, Roy Atwell, Rena Parker, Juanita Fletcher, Florence Shirley, Harrison Brockbank, and us.

Our salary had come in for another boost. In *The Passing Show* we received $350, a raise of $100 a week over the previous *Over the Top*, and now we were to get $550 a week with Mr. Dillingham.

This prompted us to move to the Hotel Majestic on Seventy-second Street and Central Park West. So Mother, Adele and I leased a suite overlooking the park and made that our new permanent residence.

We were taken up to meet "C. B." (as we later called him), and he was in a fine humor. C. B. was full of fun, always joking and ribbing with his office force of Vera Murray, his secretary, and Murray Lachman and Jack McPartland, his two office assistants.

Headquarters were one flight up over the Globe Theatre in

Times Square at Forty-sixth and Broadway. The outer office, where Vera Murray sat at her desk, was done in red carpet and mahogany furniture.

Mr. C. B.'s office was a long room with the same kind of red carpet, his desk at the extreme end so that he could give his visitors a lengthy once-over as they came to him on their arrival. I'll always remember that delightful smiling face as we entered and walked toward him with Rufus LeMaire, our agent.

He got up and came to greet us and right away started in with his ribbing.

Suddenly he frowned and said: "Now what's all this about $550 a week? That's a funny figure, 550. I can understand what the 50 is for but what's the 500 for?"

Our agent didn't say anything, but I came back with: "Oh, we tacked on the 50 so we could pay him his ten per cent" (pointing to Rufus) "and keep the whole 500 for ourselves."

C. B. said, "Say, that's a damn good idea!"

Then he put his arms around us both, gave my sister a kiss, and said, "Now when are you kids going away for a rest? I won't need you until late August."

We stayed with him for about half an hour enjoying his jokes and teasing.

I brought up a couple of times that I'd like to know something about the show we were going to do but he changed the subject and finally said, in a sort of confidential whisper: "I can't tell you anything about the show because I don't know a thing about it. Nobody tells me anything around here. But I'll let you in on a little secret."

Then he looked around as if to be sure nobody was eavesdropping and said: "There's a rumor going around that if I behave all this week, Vera is going to let me know what kind of a show she is producing for these Tin Pan Alley guys, Kreisler and Jacobi, whom I just got off the Loew Circuit."

C. B. was a very attractive man, about five feet ten, stocky of build and an extremely good dresser. He had a great personality with that roundish face and gray mustache.

"Now listen, kids, when we do get this show going we must be sure not to make it too good, because if it's a big hit Ziegfeld won't like it.

"He hates it when I get a hit! You know, he's very jealous of me. When you see one of those shows billed 'Dillingham and Ziegfeld present'—I only do that to keep him quiet."

Adele said, "What about the Shuberts, Mr. C. B.?"

"Oh, hell—they don't count," said the boss. And then he really had a good laugh, as we all did.

We told him how we remembered the night he sat up in the box in Washington for *Over the Top* and that we and all the company got a big kick out of his being there.

He replied, "Well, you got a bigger kick than I did. That was a terrible show!"

He was loving every minute of this but I finally suggested that perhaps we'd better go and leave him to his work.

He said, "Oh, no! When I want to get rid of people, I just push this little buttton here" (and he pushed it), "then Murray comes in and empties the office." Just then Murray appeared.

"See?" said C. B. "There's nothing to it." And he got up from his chair.

"Say—we're gonna have a lot of fun around here, you kids and I. Anything you don't like, you just tell Murray, and he'll tell Vera, and she'll tell Jack and between them they'll make you more miserable than ever."

He walked us through Vera's office and stopped to say, "Now be careful of her—she eats too much candy."

We all shook hands and he told us to take his car any place we wanted to go.

"It's that big new Rolls standing down there in front of the theatre. I stole it from my wife for the day. I've got one of my own but I like hers better. Just tell the chauffeur that Mr. Ziegfeld says it's o.k."

We took the car, all right, and enjoyed it a lot. It was the first time we had ever been in a Rolls-Royce and after a little while Delly said to me, "Say, I like these things. We ought to get one."

That was our introduction to C. B., and we were of course elated to be working for such a wonderful person.

We went to Galen Hall, Wernersville, for our vacation and my usual golf spree. Wernersville was a beautiful summer resort in Pennsylvania. It was there I first ran into Jimmy Altemus and his sister Liz (Mary Elizabeth) from Philadelphia. Jimmy was several years younger than I and Liz only about fourteen. Their mother, Bessie Dobson Altemus, was a stunning woman, prominent socially and politically. They lived on the outskirts of Philadelphia in a huge wooden mansion at Falls of Schuylkill.

The kids had an affectionate nickname for this residence and estate. They called it "The Dump." It stood rather high on a hill and the dirt roads to it were tricky and winding.

I spent many a weekend out at The Dump, in later years, always looking forward to my crazy visits with Jimmy. I'll confess many of them were primarily designed so that I could hang around that knockout sister Liz. She was a great horsewoman then as she is to this day—at present maintaining one of the most powerful racing stables in the world, Llangollen Farm.

When we all met at Wernersville that first time, they looked at us in a strange way. Someone had told them that Adele and I were on the stage, and they were curious. It didn't take long, however, for us all to understand each other.

Jimmy whipped out his new Hudson Super Six four-passenger open car with special wire wheels and the two of us went for a ride. He started out by shifting the gearstick with his foot instead of his hand. He had a knack of kicking those gears around which intrigued me.

Jimmy was the last word in dressing. The first one I knew to enamel the outer edges of his shoe soles black.

We had a splendid vacation those weeks, one of the highlights being the escape of Liz's pet raccoon. It got out the window of her bedroom and onto the adjacent roof. This raccoon would have none of being rescued. We all tried for days and I finally gave up. Liz, I might add, was as hard to approach as that raccoon.

We were soon off for New York again to pick up our obligation to Charlie Dillingham, and reported in about a week ahead of schedule, eager to get back to work.

In *Apple Blossoms*, which was an operetta, we had no speaking parts, just two dances, one in the first act and one in the third act. They were important spots, however, and we had to deliver a knockout punch both times. This is always a frightening thing to anticipate.

One of our numbers we had planned previously. It was to be a version of the "Sacred Cow" dance we had done before. Inasmuch as this was our main attraction it was all right to use it— disguised somewhat—and with the added value of doing it to a Fritz Kreisler melody. Also, the audience would be totally different from those who patronized a Winter Garden show.

The other number had to be a whole new thing, and that was our worry. That worry soon disappeared, however, when we met the dance director, Edward Royce. He was a fine choreographer and put on an excellent number for us. The music for this was written by Victor Jacobi.

The scene was a girls' school and Adele, seated on a bench under a tree, was knitting as I peered over the garden wall.

She dropped her ball of yarn, and as it rolled out on the stage I jumped over the wall à la Doug Fairbanks, retrieved the yarn, and we pantomimed our way into a dance. It scored.

When it came time to go at the "Sacred Cow" dance we met Mr. Kreisler and he asked us what kind of music we wanted. I sat down at the piano and played our tango that we had used in the past. Mr. Kreisler asked, "Would this fit your dance?" and proceeded to play his famous "Tambourin Chinois" on the piano.

Lyrics were written to this melody and it was sung elsewhere in the show by Wilda Bennett.

We were happy about this, as it was the perfect music to give the new touch we wanted. Worries were over as far as our two stunts were concerned.

The rest of the company worked with Fred Latham, the stage director, and we were all finally thrown together.

John Charles Thomas was a lot of fun, always having a laugh about something except when he lost his temper; then he'd get very mad indeed. Wilda Bennett was beautiful and Percy Knight a fine actor.

Fred Latham was an English gentleman of about sixty-five, and he had all the tricks of the old-time stage director. He would rant and rave and bawl everybody out at the slightest provocation and most of the time they took it. One day he took me completely by surprise and lit into me in front of everybody. I was about one minute late for a full run-through rehearsal and wasn't even concerned with the opening scene, but he let me have it anyway.

I lost my temper and yelled back at him louder than he could himself, which brought about a dense silence. Most of the cast sitting around were holding their sides and stifling their desire to laugh out loud.

Latham just stood there, doing all he could to keep from busting out again.

I felt bad about it afterward and went to C. B. to explain.

He said, "Now you'd better go right over and apologize to that kid [Latham]. He's very hurt."

I went to Latham and told him I was very sorry, etc., etc.

"My dear boy," he replied as he stood there with his arms folded, towering over me. "You don't have to apologize. I'll be bawling you out enough between now and the time this show opens so that you'll get rather used to it. And I warn you—don't you dare bawl me out back again, either."

I said, "Nevertheless, Mr. L., I'm sorry," to which he paid no attention whatsoever.

We got along very well after that.

C. B. brought his young and attractive wife, Eileen, backstage one day soon after rehearsals started. He said: "Kids, I want you to meet my mother."

Mrs. Dillingham asked to design Adele's dancing dress for the last number. It was a lovely one.

Many interesting things occurred during rehearsals. For instance, I don't think any other dancers in the world can boast of having had Fritz Kreisler as rehearsal pianist—yet that actually happened to Adele and me when we were measuring out our dance to fit the music of "Tambourin Chinois."

He insisted on playing for us, on the piano in the orchestra pit, and seemed to enjoy it, glancing up intently from time to time to see what was going on.

C. B. enjoyed this little episode and said to Adele and me afterward, "Why don't you get a decent piano player? I told that guy to bring his fiddle but he won't do it."

On another day when the regular rehearsal pianist was not available to us, George Gershwin, who was still working at Remick's, came over as a favor and we found ourselves rehearsing to George's playing.

He called up from the orchestra pit, "Hey, Freddie—you didn't expect to find me here, did you? We'll be doing that show together yet."

Adele and I stopped for a minute to thank him for coming and he told us that his first musical comedy, *La La Lucille*, had done pretty well and that he'd be doing another one soon.

After about five weeks we took off for the tryout in Baltimore.

The show was an immediate success. It was welcomed as a happy relief from the jazz period that had been going on.

Jimmy and Liz were around and we had time to go to a few parties since the show was in excellent shape and there were no changes to be made as far as we were concerned. Business was at capacity. We all got our bawling-out pep talks, as expected, and Latham could really do it, too.

The preliminary tryout over, we returned to New York to open at the Globe on schedule, October 17. It was one of the very fashionable and ritzy opening nights for which Dillingham was noted.

He said to me that night with his usual twinkle, "You know, there are a lot of millionaires out there who won't like this show because I wouldn't let them put their money in it. I want all the profits for myself so that you and Adele and I can go away on a long trip."

It was a very successful opening night. They loved the show. You could sense it in the atmosphere. It had that important feeling.

John Charles Thomas hit them with "I Love the Girls, Girls, Girls Just the Same." His duets with Wilda went beautifully; the comedy of Roy Atwell and Percy Knight registered, and the Astaires' two spots did what they were meant to do.

Next morning some of the press were picky, but it had no effect on business. The show was called a "Top Ticket" by all agencies and the scalpers were cleaning up.

Charles Darnton said in the *Evening World*:

> . . . Relief from the jazz of Broadway musical comedies came last night with Charles Dillingham's "Apple Blossoms." . . . John Charles Thomas did the finest singing of his notable career. . . . Fred Astaire and his pretty sister, Adele, danced as though they were twins and scored the biggest hit they've ever made. . . .

And Alexander Woollcott in the *New York Times*:

> . . . A pleasant unexciting evening at the theater is assured for those who go to the Globe to see the new operetta called "Apple Blossoms" which was presented there for the first time last evening with all the familiar lavishness that characterizes Mr. Dillingham when he feels the urge to do another musical piece. The polite, agreeable and mildly diverting libretto is by William LeBaron while responsibility for the score is pretty evenly divided between the wonderful Fritz Kreisler and the not-to-be-sneezed-at-Jacobi. . . . Much of it has the advantage of being sung by that buoyantly healthy Prince Charming of light opera, the ever reliable John Charles Thomas. . . .

. . . There should be a half a dozen special words for the vastly entertaining dances by the two Adaires [Mr. Woollcott's spelling] in particular for those by the incredibly nimble and lack-a-daisical Adaire named
Fred. He is one of those extraordinary persons whose senses of rhythm
and humor have been all mixed up, whose very muscles of which he
seems to have an extra supply are downright facetious. . . .

Our work in the show was what I called a sort of "dream job."
There we were in one of the biggest of Broadway hits with only
two dance spots to worry about. We killed 'em in the first act and
"panicked 'em" in the third (to use the vernacular). We had
nothing to do in the second act so I always put on my dressing
gown and went down to the basement under the stage to play stud
poker with the stage crew (25¢ and 50¢ limit). They were a swell
bunch and I looked forward to that time. My cue to cut out of
the game was when John Charles knocked 'em in the aisles with
his singing of "You Are Free."

That gave me just enough time with the short intermission to
get ready for our dance in the last act.

I don't know what my little sister did during these spare moments. I got her in the poker game once but she didn't care for
it. I know she was fed up with paper dolls by this time. I think
she took to knitting things.

That season we were in "theatrical heaven" and took full advantage of it all. We went to many parties—night clubs. In fact,
all through those Broadway stage years, we did the night club
thing a-plenty. Perhaps that is why I can't stand the sight of
one now. My arrival in California was the end of any night life
I may have enjoyed previously.

C. B. often would take Adele and me to a restaurant on Long
Island called Pavilion. He'd say, "How about some crêpes Suzette
this Sunday?" We looked forward to these invitations. He seldom
brought anybody with him when he picked us up in the Rolls.

At Christmas he sent a note written in his own handwriting,
accompanied by a small package, also an envelope containing a
check made out to me for $200. Here's the note:

Dear Freddie:—

I am sending you and Adele a little Christmas present.

Sister can have the ring and you can get yourself just what you want.

Thanking you both for being such a success in Apple Blossoms, I am

Sincerely,

C. B.

One great satisfaction came my way during this particular period.

We were in a position to try and induce Father to come East and forget his business worries in the Middle West. But Father declined the idea of accepting any monetary aid from his children. He would always bring up that it was a man's undying duty to provide for his family. The fact that he had found it impossible to do that in recent years worried and depressed him.

He wrote, "I'll come back as soon as I can straighten out my affairs here. Don't worry about me. I'm happy that you and my little Adele are advancing in your work. I'm longing to see you all. Take good care of Mamma. . . . "

In those days it was still a big event to take a trip to or from Omaha. Two days and two nights on the train.

We kept after him and finally convinced him that there were more business opportunities in New York than out there. He joined us shortly after that.

It was a happy occasion, this family reunion. He was thrilled with our work in *Apple Blossoms* and gloated over the fact that the music was written by Austrians.

He attempted several business ventures but nothing much materialized.

The show continued its successful run.

When the hot weather arrived, business began to drop off a bit. There was no air cooling in theatres in those days and *Apple Blossoms* was not exactly a summer-type show, so C. B. decided to close down and reopen on the road in September. We had had a good long run for those times.

One day just before the New York run ended, he came to us

and said, "I'm taking a floor at the Ritz in Atlantic City for a few weeks as soon as we close and you two are coming down for a weekend. Freddie, you can have the east wing and Dellie can have the west wing.

"We'll ride up and down the boardwalk and hang around the beach and raise the devil!"

It turned out just like that.

The rest of the summer—back to Wernersville we went, after which we reported for our tour with *Apple Blossoms* in September.

This tour had an added interest to us. Our salary went up to $750 a week as per contract. The year was 1920.

All through the vacation we had letters from C. B. I had written him that I was studying Percy Knight's part. He sent me this note:

Dear Fred:

I was glad to learn that you were up in Percy Knight's part. It is good experience and I will try to get one just as good for you next year in a new play.

Will your aunt Adele be dancing with you next season?

Come in and see me when you get back to town and I will let you know what you have to do for the rest of your life.

Yours very truly,
C. B. D.

Here's one he sent to Adele:

Dell Dear:

How's Galen Hall?

I mailed you some magazines today so you can read and not have to talk with Freddie all the time.

Let me know if you are laying out the new dances and if you want me to work them out here with Anne Caldwell to demonstrate them.

That's the cat's cuffs—

C. B. D.

That road tour was successful. The press enthused and particularly appreciated the lack of jazz.

John Charles Thomas and I played a lot of golf. Usually I'd meet him early and he would drive us out to the country club in his car. In Cleveland one morning when I showed up, there stood John with his arm in a sling.

What the—?

He explained, "When I asked the garage attendant to get my car, he was slow and snotty and I didn't like his attitude, so I had to flatten him." John's wrist was broken.

We had no golf together for a month, and what's more, John was a pretty sight playing the romantic lead in the show with his arm in a sling.

I used to laugh at two of his pet sayings which he would throw in frequently. "I don't want to meet any more people," and "I'm going to give this fellow a thousand-dollar tip."

Apple Blossoms went out of our lives about April of 1921. C. B. assigned us to another operetta with John Charles Thomas as solo star. Music by Victor Jacobi, lyrics and libretto by William Le Baron. This one to be called *The Love Letter*. It sounded fine as explained to us but turned out to be quite the opposite of the "dream job" experience of the last one.

The Love Letter was one of those cumbersome vehicles, very well meant and planned, but it had a concept that couldn't be conquered for musical purposes.

It was an adaptation of a Molnár story, the original of which promised many opportunities for the star.

Both Mr. Dillingham and John Charles were confident when they agreed to do it, but somehow the thing did not come off. The comedy was weak, which made it all the more difficult.

Edward "Teddy" Royce again choreographed the show and was a tremendous help to Adele and me. He gave Adele one of her greatest comedy dancing bits.

One day at rehearsals on the stage of the Globe Theatre he asked her to put her arms in front of her as if she were on a bicycle holding the handlebars. "Now run around in a large circle like this, as if you're very intent upon getting somewhere," and he started singing "um-pah-um-pah-um-pah-um-pah" as he demonstrated what he meant. He then told the piano player to play a lot of um-pahs, "Just keep playing them until I tell you to stop."

Adele was jogging around a circle about twenty feet in diameter looking somewhat like a six-day bike racer. Mr. Royce started to laugh and asked me to join in with her, shoulder-to-shoulder, doing the same thing. He demonstrated what he meant by doing it with her, and then told me to try it.

Teddy stood there with his arms folded, chuckling away while we ran around in circles for about twenty or thirty laps.

He said, "I think we've got something here. This is the kind of thing that if you sustain it for three or four run-arounds and then make an exit, the audience will demand no end of encores." Then he stopped the um-pahs and wandered off by himself to think.

Royce was a brilliant showman, born in England. He had a wonderful sense of timing and comedy values in addition to his other type dancing work. He was a slightly built man, five feet seven, with gray hair, sixty years of age, and an accomplished dancer himself.

"What we need here," he said when he came back to us after about five minutes of thought in a remote corner of the stage, "is a 'nut' number. It should make no sense at all in lyrics and then the dance should be silly but tricky until you both drop into this run-around thing and then eventually you just run off stage. I think it'll bring down the house."

He explained to Victor Jacobi and Bill LeBaron what sort of song he wanted and they came back next day with "Upside Down." This was the ideal piece of material. We were certainly lucky to have had Mr. Royce to work with.

That run-around finish became a trademark of ours and we used it in five different shows over a period of about ten years.

In England that stunt actually became a fixture. We did it in our first show over there in 1923, *Stop Flirting*. It was nicknamed, "The Oompah Trot" and was taken up as a sort of crazy romp when people felt like whooping it up in night clubs. As only the British can.

It was like striking oil—that little stunt handed to us by Teddy Royce. In *Love Letter,* it stopped the show cold "next to closing," a big help for a vehicle which was having comedy troubles.

Rehearsals were tough, in fact everything was tough about *The Love Letter.* Although C. B. knew it, he was trying his best to laugh and joke as usual, but I could tell he was worried.

When we finally got to the out-of-town tryout stage, Philadelphia was our first stop.

The Forrest was a fine theatre and the opening drew a distinguished audience, what with Dillingham, John Charles Thomas and Victor Jacobi.

The show went only fairly well on opening night. It was not good, although there was some enthusiasm for various songs and numbers. Our "nut" dance cleaned up, and that was a relief.

The press, much to our surprise, was quite lenient, predicting that the show would most likely be pulled into shape for New York.

After that week of revision and rehearsals and a sort of hopeless effort to get the thing right, we went back to New York and opened at the Globe on time, October 4, 1921.

Strangely enough, the notices were not too bad but we knew we were in trouble.

New York *Herald*:

LOVE LETTER A MUSICAL TREAT;
JOHN CHARLES THOMAS STARRED

"The Love Letter" in which John Charles Thomas reached the top notes of a solo star for the first time last night, was Charles Dillingham's first sweeping gesture of the season. . . . Next to the star, the Astaires once more dancing about him like fireflies made the high score of the evening, getting four encores for their entertaining singing and nutty dancing to "Upside Down" and revealing in this and other whirlwind numbers they have developed a penetrating comedy touch with their lips as well as their always ambitious feet. . . .

Fred Astaire in a dancing school number at the age of five

Adele and Fred Astaire in some of their early vaudeville numbers

Mrs. Astaire in 1925

Fred Astaire's father

Fred's Uncle Ernest in Vienna

Adele and Fred at the ages of
eleven and ten respectively

In a vaudeville routine in 1912

A picture taken in Portland,
Oregon, in 1914

In London at the ages of nine-
teen and twenty

The "Whichness of the Whatness" number in *For Goodness Sake* in New York in 1922

In London in 1923 in the same show, now called *Stop Flirting*

Fred and Adele Astaire in *Funny Face* in New York in 1927

CULVER

The Astaires in 1927

HUGH CECIL

In *The Band Wagon*, 1931, their last show together

CULVER

Chapter 10 *Result of a Flop*

Life is not pleasant when you're in a flop. You are hesitant to go anyplace.

Adele and I were rather miserable and we seldom went out socially. No parties or night clubs. I even avoided going into shops for a while. I didn't want to hear any more opinions.

After a few weeks, however, I came out of hiding and happened to drop in to Finchley's men's furnishing shop. It was on Fifty-something Street then, just west of Fifth Avenue. I wandered in there to buy a tie.

The fellow who waited on me was a pleasant young man and, in the course of my visit, he mentioned the fact that he always admired Adele's and my work, and he thought we should do some sort of show like Jerome Kern's *Oh, Boy!* which had been a big success through the past year or so; something on the more intimate musical-comedy side, rather than the big revue or operetta type for a change.

This idea appealed to me right away. However, I was rather skeptical about this sudden new acquaintance of mine and I thought in the back of my mind that he was being a bit presumptuous telling me what kind of show we should do. So, I asked him:

"Mr.—what's your name, sir?"

"Aarons, Alex A. Aarons," he replied.

"Well, Mr. Aarons," I said, "I don't want to appear rude, but you seem to know quite a lot about show business—would you mind telling me what you're doing here selling ties?"

He laughed and quickly answered, "Oh, I own a part of this business, but I'm getting out. This is not for me. My father is Alfred E. Aarons. You know of him."

I did know of him as a main executive in the firm of Klaw and Erlanger, powerful theatrical producers and theatre owners. I nodded.

Young Aarons said he had a new fellow named George Gershwin tied up and that his music would be great for us to work with. He also told me that he had produced Gershwin's first musical show, *La La Lucille,* and while the show wasn't much of a hit, everybody was talking about Gershwin.

I explained that I hadn't heard much about *La La Lucille* because it was done while we were on the road with *Apple Blossoms,* but I did know Gershwin rather well from Remick's.

He brought up the fact that he didn't think *The Love Letter* would last much longer and wanted to know what my contract obligations were with Dillingham.

I told him we were tied up but would discuss the situation with him later.

He said, "I'm going in for producing on my own in a bigger way soon, and I'd like to get you and your sister for something."

We shook hands and I left.

I didn't take the whole thing too seriously because it wasn't easy to visualize working for anyone else but Dillingham at that point. I just forgot about it, although I did like Aarons. He impressed me.

One of the memorable instances in connection with *Love Letter* was our first introduction to Noel Coward, who came backstage one night with some friends. Noel, at that time in the early stages of his career, was the source of much encouragement to both Adele and me.

He was particularly insistent that we come to London.

"You two will be a tremendous success there—you must come as soon as possible," he told us.

We were bemoaning the fact that *Love Letter* was a failure.

Noel jumped in quickly with, "Good, then you can come to London at once."

We had no idea how we were going to get to London.

The show ran very few weeks in New York and then C. B. sent us on the road. It was just as well because the show did all right on that tour. Several cast changes were made. Charles Judels joined us and bolstered up the comedy immeasurably. However, it was too expensive a show to travel. Business was good but "the opera" was barely breaking even.

A few weeks before Christmas I received this telegram:

MY FATHER SAYS LOVE LETTER CLOSING. ARE YOU AVAILABLE PLEASE WIRE.

ALEX A. AARONS

Alex's father was right. The company had just been given notice.

I answered the wire:

CLOSING IN TWO WEEKS. WILL SEE YOU THEN.

I didn't want to hit C. B. with a request for a postponement of our other commitment with him until we got back to New York and could talk to him personally.

The rather unexpected short run of the show left us in a quandary as to what we would do next. We were temporarily through with C. B., since he hadn't anything ready for us at the moment. We wanted to keep active, so we decided to consider Aaron's proposition.

We called on C. B. when we got back to town and asked him

if we could do a show somewhere else and postpone our obligation to him until he could find something he wanted us to do. I told him of an offer that had been made to us and he agreed that we should consider it, but be very careful not to pick another lemon, and that he would only loan us out until August, 1922.

I convinced him that we didn't consider *Love Letter* a lemon at all. It was just one of those things and nobody really got hurt.

He was plainly disappointed and a bit upset about that one, though. It was easy to tell—he seemed embarrassed by the whole thing.

Actually, *Love Letter* was a flop, but not for Adele and me. We gained by it.

The next day I called Aarons on the phone and arranged for a meeting. We discussed the thing he had in mind and I liked the idea. It was a farcical-type musical comedy and we both would have good speaking parts.

One thing disappointed me and that was that George Gershwin was not going to do the music. I think he was engaged by George White for the *Scandals* just then.

Our music was by Bill Daly and Paul Lannin. Bill Daly was a prominent conductor and this was his first score. Paul was a fine musician and loved the theatre. This was his first show. It was an interesting setup and we were to start rehearsals in August. The title, *For Goodness Sake*.

Our salary was $800 a week, same as the Dillingham contract. The program was obliged to carry a line: "Fred and Adele Astaire appear by arrangement with Charles Dillingham."

Off we went again to Wernersville for the good old vacation. This one I think we appreciated more than usual. We were pretty tired. Flops have a way of doing that to you.

There were Jimmy and Liz again on schedule with Ma and the retinue, but no raccoon—thank goodness.

We had our customary relaxation and, after a few weeks, began to get fidgety for work. When there's a new production coming up I guess I must show it.

Jimmy Altemus used to tag it right away with "Well—what are you doing, getting ready to crawl back into that shell again?"

Back in New York, we went at the new show with a lot of zip. We liked everything about it. The cast: Jack Hazzard, Vinton Freedley, Marjorie Gateson, Charles Judels and Helen Ford.

It was a funny show, and of the more intimate type. Adele and I, with the help of Allan Foster, the dance director, worked out some useful dance specialties. It was around this time that I started to take hold at creating and choreographing our dances.

We patterned one number on the "nut" style again, thinking it had been somewhat wasted in *Love Letter,* which ran such a short time. This one was called "The Whichness of the Whatness and the Whereness of the Who." We retained the "nugget" runaround stunt from Teddy Royce for the finish of our main number and it again proved itself.

Aarons was fun to work with. He and his wife, Ella, became our close friends.

That show was probably the most potent hop forward in our careers up to that point. There were other factors of lasting importance:

Vinton Freedley, who was cast in the main juvenile role, subsequently became Aaron's partner. The firm of Aarons and Freedley produced many Broadway successes, some of which Adele and I were in.

For Goodness Sake developed pretty well in rehearsals and was ready for tryout in New Haven after about six weeks. We all felt that we had a potentially good show of its kind and possibly a good one to try out before an audience of college students. We were right.

The boys in New Haven went for the whole thing.

At the routine rehearsal call after the opening we again went through the bawling-out bit by the producer. The old pep talk.

Alex came to me first in this instance and said, "Don't pay any attention to what I say, it doesn't concern you two in particular, but there are a couple in this troupe who need a little waking up. It was a good performance last night and I'm going to tell 'em so but I want one tonight, too." (There was always that chance of a second-night let-down.)

Things went smoothly that week and business was at capacity.

There were a few revisions to make and the expected rehearsals were called, but we had time to relax and take a few little trips through Yale again. The lads, true to form, were swarming around my sister and she was loving it—kidding the ears off of 'em. I never saw any girl that could handle a bunch of men like she could. Young or old . . .

And that includes Bernard Shaw, whom she met in later years.

The show checked out of New Haven that Saturday night and played a week in Worcester and one in Hartford on the way to New York.

We arrived in New York early on a Sunday morning. The company was quite nervous about the opening Tuesday night, mostly because everything had gone so well on the road. We began to wonder if it was really so good. After all it was an unpretentious kind of thing—not at all on the Dillingham scale.

We had a wire from C. B. while in New Haven saying he had heard it was a great show and also adding at the end of his wire, "It better be."

Vinton Freedley, Charles Judels, and I had a dressing room together at the Lyric and we shared a valet, Walter Williams, a colored gent of great distinction. We knew we were in for a good season when we started dealing with Walter.

There were even more laughs in that room than in Room 18 at the Winter Garden. With Charles Judels that was a foregone conclusion. Walter became an important part of my life for many years after that, as my valet.

The dress rehearsal was pretty good and that made us all feel a little uneasy. Usually, if the dress rehearsal is too good everybody gets suspicious of his luck.

It was a different kind of opening night from a Dillingham première. Not so ritzy. The swells didn't turn out en masse but it was a snappy audience and a well-dressed one.

Adele and I felt that this was our biggest opportunity. We had so much to do in the show and we were nervous while the overture was playing.

The minute the curtain went up, I was fine. Never really nervous and thank heavens I never made any terrible mistakes on an opening night. Some of my second nights were pretty lousy—but not the first.

This was a good one. The show went great. Walter was happy. Charles Judels' comedy scored on the stage and in the dressing room as well. Vinton was pleased, being one of the backers.

Everything Adele and I did went over, and when we finished we were slightly numb from it all.

At the final curtain the cast all threw their arms around each other. Alex Aarons came back—he had been hiding in the men's room most of the time. Openings affected him that way. He used to say to me, "You know, I just feel like throwing up all the time the show is on."

We were all mighty festive that night and stayed in the theatre until about 1 A.M. with our visitors backstage. Dillingham came back, too, enthusiastically. He said, "Come in and see me soon as you can."

My father was delighted. Even though he had not been feeling too well of late, this seemed to bring him around.

He said, "You surprised me. I didn't know you two could do all those things."

We had a hit.

Alan Dale, New York *Morning American*:

The two Astaires are the principal assets of "For Goodness Sake." They can speak a little, act a little, and dance quarts. They are as nice a twain as one could wish to see. They pirouette through the mazes of this musical comedy with energy, yet restraint, and the dances they exhibit are always clever and artistic. Miss Astaire is a pleasant little body, with a sense of humor, and **Mr.** Astaire has the lank lissomeness necessary for his "line of work."

Life:

. . . There isn't much to say about "For Goodness Sake" that you couldn't say about most musical comedies except that the Astaires (perhaps late of 'Astaires and Down') are in it. When they dance everything seems brighter and their comedy alone would be good enough to carry them through even if they were to stop dancing (which God forbid!).—ROBERT C. BENCHLEY

A few days later we called on C. B. He had Adele sitting on his knee like a ventriloquist's dummy as he told us of his plans for the next venture, and ended up with: "Now I've got to star you two just because that silly Aarons boy gave you so much to do in that damn show."

Our activities in and out of the theatre that season were numerous. Everything was interesting as the careers were being stabilized.

I became a member of the Lambs Club, sponsored by my friend Percy Helton. This membership afforded me much pleasure through the years to come, as I was able to use the club frequently until moving to California in 1933. I spent many enjoyable hours participating in the bottle pool, the gin rummy and the bridge games with Percy Helton, Mal Williams, Wally Ford, Fred Hillebrand, Billy Gaxton, Harland Dixon, Frank MacIntyre, Johnny Gallaudet, Jimmy Gleason, Hal Skelly, Roger Pryor, Charles Winninger, Tom Meighan, Jack Whiting. And when everybody went to work on one of the celebrated Lambs Gambols—it was crazy.

I also had a weekly standing date with Marcus Loew for pinochle, his favorite game. These I always looked forward to with much pleasure.

We had a good solid run at the Lyric but when the summer heat hit us business faded. There were still very few air-cooled theatres then and the Lyric was not one of them. That sultry New York heat was almost unbearable. We went to Chicago for a few weeks and then folded up to get ready for the next Dilling-ham commitment.

It was a nice thing to look forward to—the most important theatrical test Adele and I had yet been given. We were probably the envy of most dancers in the world, stars in a Dillingham show. C. B. had written us that the title would be *The Bunch and Judy*.

He called Adele and me in for a meeting and, after the custom-ary kidding and jokes, we learned that we were to be co-starred with Joseph Cawthorn. We had seen and admired this noted com-edian many times. Once when Julia Sanderson and he were reign-ing favorites of the year with *The Sunshine Girl*, Adele and I saw it nine times. (Mr. and Mrs. Vernon Castle scored one of their first great hits in this show.) We told C. B. how pleased we were to be working with Cawthorn.

The music for the show was written by Jerome Kern and that, in itself, was inspiring. Anne Caldwell's book offered many novel approaches.

First day at rehearsal was businesslike with Fred Latham in rare fettle. Kern himself was there.

Adele and I were pleased with the outlook but I found one item concerning me which I didn't like, and it stayed with me through many months. I was obliged to wear a white wig with a knot hanging down the back, and it bothered me.

The whole number bothered me. Although it was Kern's, the song was too rangy and high in spots for me and I had a hard time with it. The lyric started out: "When my gondola glides on the blue lagoon . . . with the pale moon shining up above . . . " etc. It was a costume number in a show within our show. The rest was all modern.

Everything seemed to be working into fair shape. Adele and I had a rather tricky dance on top of a banquet table which, in the course of events during the number, was lifted high up above the heads of the cast by a dozen chorus men and a few girls. This was the climax of the first act. Adele, according to the plot, was to retire and marry an English nobleman and this was a farewell party, a strong story point.

The table was long and narrow, about four feet wide and twelve feet long. To lift it at an even level was not easy for the boys and girls, and many times during rehearsals we were dumped overboard.

All of us were nervous about that stunt, the chorus kids as well as Adele and myself, but I couldn't get the dance director to cut it out. I felt that it was not practical and that we were likely to have mishaps once in a while. I also thought there were a few other things in the show that wouldn't work, including a bagpipe number.

Little by little these hazards kept popping up but we finally took off for Philadelphia to try out. Walter was with me and Adele had Louise Lux as her maid. These two helped plenty at all times, not only in their work but in moral support and ever-ready good humor.

We were to open on Wednesday night, if I remember correctly, but on Tuesday afternoon our co-star, Joe Cawthorn, fell down a flight of iron fire-escape stairs and broke his leg. Poor Joe—he suffered so for himself and all of us and had to resign from the cast.

This threw everybody into a state of frenzy. Of course we had to postpone the opening. Jack Potter, the company manager for C. B., finally told us that Johnny Dooley was on his way over to replace Joe Cawthorn. Ray Dooley, Johnny's sister, was also engaged and this sudden decision to rewrite caused a further delay.

We considered ourselves mighty fortunate to get Johnny and Ray. They were solid comedians and it seemed we were off with a fresh and interesting new touch. A whole flock of starring brothers and sisters. However, the production needed much work and we were being pressed for time, with the company all there and on salary. It was not the most pleasant experience in the world for our first starring attempt.

We were worried and had reason to be. It was hard to get the show to feel right.

Things were rushed, and after about five days we had a perfectly awful dress rehearsal. Among other things that happened that horrible night, Adele and I were dumped off the table lifted by the boys. Instead of raising it evenly at a given note in the music, they tilted one end first and we went sliding off as if we were in a fun house at Coney Island. Delly got a little bruise but we weren't badly hurt. I was mad!

My sister hardly ever lost her sense of humor and even in this very annoying predicament, as we were lying there sprawled on the floor with the importance of the whole show hanging in the balance, she looked up at me and said: "This is a hell of a way to become a star."

I thought Latham would blow his beard off. He turned purple and screamed, "Music—stop!" Teddy Royce put his hands to his head and walked up the aisle of the empty theatre in an absolute rage. What a mess that was!

We were tired and nowhere near finished. Still another act to go. This was about midnight. They sent out for some sandwiches and coffee and then the second act started.

The rehearsal ended about four in the morning. We were to open that night. And we did.

The company managed to get some rest. Nobody was obliged to show up until late in the afternoon and the entire cast was told to be in the theatre by seven o'clock.

Adele and I lived at the Bellevue-Stratford just across the street. About five-thirty we ordered some light food sent to our rooms and ate a little of it. We were nervous and frightened about this show. Somehow it had never entered our minds that such a tangle could occur in an organization like Dillingham's.

Adele started to cry, and there was a thick gloom permeating the atmosphere. We couldn't find one thing to smile about. It was like being led to the slaughter and I called Adele's attention to the fact by saying:

"Come on, let's go over and stick our heads in the noose and get it over with. After all, it may not be as bad as all that. We've been saturated with this turkey and can't think clearly. No matter what happens, the run-around will get 'em if nothing else does."

Oh, yes—the old trade-mark was still with us in a new number called "Katinka."

We ambled over to the Forrest and worked out a bit before making up.

I was all ready and on the stage twenty minutes before the overture went on, walking around blankly nervous.

Walter was following me, pleading, "Sit down, Mr. Fred, you'll wear yourself out before the curtain goes up." This didn't help any and I said, "Leave me alone, will you? Stop mothering me—I can't sit down, get me some rosin."

Finally the asbestos fire curtain was raised and I could hear the buzzing of the audience, full of excitement as the musicians were entering the pit and tuning up. I thought, "Those poor, unsuspecting people—little do they know what they're in for!" Just about then the opening bars of the overture blasted out and I muttered to myself, "The old ax is about to fall." I started wishing people luck and, as Delly came toward me, I pulled the old cliché, "Well, it's too late to turn back now." This got a rise out of her. She said, "Oh, no—not that again. Stop moaning, will you—this is the biggest thing since *Ben Hur.* "

Just then C. B. came and put his arms around us and said, "There's nothing to worry about. We'll get this show in shape." The Dooleys and all of us were there ready for the fray, in a synthetically cheerful mood. Jack Potter came back to wish us luck.

With the overture over, the curtain went up and my nervousness was lost in the shuffle, as usual.

The show was ragged. We all did the best we could. The audience was tolerant—there were some laughs. The Dooleys scored in some things and Adele and I did, too. We were not dumped off the table. The run-around number came through again, but the entire vehicle did not succeed. That was obvious. Some of our friends who had come over from New York tried to reassure us but we knew what we were up against and decided that the only thing left was to go to work at getting the blasted "opera" right.

Liz and Jim, incidentally, didn't come to our opening nights. We prevailed upon them most of the time to wait until the show was in shape. The local press critics were quite tolerant and seemed to hope that we would get the thing fixed. They thought it had the necessary ingredients.

The test run in Philadelphia was extended to accommodate the emergency and a heroic attempt was made in every way to get a potential hit. New numbers were written and a few discarded. However, my white wig song remained with us, white satin knickerbocker costume and all.

New shows with the stature of that one usually did well on try-out periods due to advance sales, so business was pretty good and we did at least get audiences to play to.

C. B. had bolstered up things by adding a cabaret scene to the last act. This brought in specialties by the Six Brown Brothers and Grace Hayes, which helped.

It seemed that we had rounded up all that was possible with the material at hand so the decision was made to go right into New York and not waste any more time on the road experimenting.

Tuesday, November 28, 1922, was the opening night after the usual dress rehearsal. The Globe Theatre was all dolled up with fresh paint and the men were still working at it during the final part of the rehearsal. That was on Monday.

It was an orderly session—no bawling out. I guess Mr. Latham figured we had all taken a beating as it was. As a matter of fact they were more inclined to bawl you out in a successful show than in a questionable one.

We were through early and had a good rest before opening night. The acid test was at hand and we were wondering.

It was the usual Dillingham ritzy crowd and the opera went all right. There was no great acclaim for anything in particular although several high spots showed up. I thought the Dooleys scored a bit heavier than Adele and I, which was fine, even though the original idea was for it to be our show. That didn't bother us. I've always felt that as long as somebody scores and the thing is a hit—that's what counts.

This, however, was no hit.

The visitors backstage after the show were embarrassed and wished they could escape, I'm sure: "Congratulations!" "Swell show!" "Going to be swell!" "*I* like it!"

All very kind and patronizing. There's nothing worse than visiting a flop backstage. What can people say? "It was lousy"?

Some didn't say anything. Just squeezed my arm and winked. C. B. disappeared.

My father, still not feeling well, braved the adverse advance reports to come out and see what I had been complaining about. He opined, "That bagpipe scene was slow, wasn't it?" I nodded and made a face. He said, "Don't worry—you and Adele were good."

Mother declared she really didn't think it was so bad.

Next morning we could tell quite easily just how we stood by the lack of demand at the ticket agencies. That mysterious message always gets out.

The press notices were suprisingly good. I've often thought that the critics adored Charlie Dillingham so much that they simply wouldn't pan anything of his to any devastating extent.

For instance, Percy Hammond said:

MR. DILLINGHAM'S "THE BUNCH
AND JUDY" IS ONE OF THE BEST

We do not recall anything recent in a musical comedy way quite so entertaining as Mr. Dillingham's "The Bunch and Judy." It seems to have about all the merits possible to exercises of its type, including a comparatively innocent libretto, not devoid of sparkle. The dress, of course, is as costly as purse can buy. . . . The Dooleys and the Astaires are active and Mr. Kern's music affords its customary sweet compulsions.

Is "The Bunch and Judy" then a perfect thing, you may enquire, containing no causes for disapproval? Well, we suppose that something or other must be wrong with it, since it is a show.

And Kenneth MacGowan said: "The Bunch and Judy luxuriates. There will be no other Globe show this year!"

We ran exactly three and one half weeks in New York.

Chapter 11 *London*

Alex Aarons came to me one day toward the end of the short run and said, "You know this thing is going to fold any week now. I've got a hunch that you two would be a great bet for England. How'd you like to do *For Goodness Sake* in London?"

We liked the idea, being pretty sunk at the outcome of *Judy*, and said we would talk about it as soon as we were at liberty to do so. That there had been some talk of a road tour with *Judy*.

Alex said he knew the English situation pretty well, was acquainted with several producers over there, one in particular who was already interested. He felt very strongly that the show was more suited to English audiences than to American ones.

He then went back to Europe to promote the deal.

In the meantime, we went along with the business at hand, salvaging the bits and pieces of our defunct venture, and did our best to make a go of it on the road. There was no chance. This was a major flop. Our first attempt at stardom turned out to be a conspicuous failure.

Flops are bad enough when they are not too prominent, but this one stood away out. We closed after a few weeks on tour.

I had one satisfaction the last performance of the show. When

Adele and I finished the white wig number and I was about to make my change of costume for the next scene, I yanked that wig off my head and scaled it across the entire length of the stage.

C. B. was always friendly through it all but his joking and easygoing way were noticeably absent. We didn't get any Christmas presents. There was general talk along Broadway: Can the Astaires carry stardom?

The stars get blamed, of course, and we were naturally in line for plenty of doubts.

In that show our joint salary was one thousand dollars a week. C. B. had an option on us for the following season at twelve hundred and fifty, and the season after that at fifteen hundred a week. He did not pick up his option on the first year, automatically releasing us from our contract. He was not inspired to go on trying with us.

We understood the situation and went up to call on him when we returned from the road tour. It was a pleasant visit and we all managed to be jovial.

C. B. said, "We'll get together a little later on, I've got to carry out some other plans for the present. Now, don't go and get too tied up."

We told him we had no immediate plans. We hadn't.

Several other propositions had been made to us for work abroad. One of these came while we were away on the short road tour. It was from Albert DeCourville, of London. He was producing a revue and inquired as to whether or not we would be available.

The answer was that we were under contract to Dillingham and would discuss it a bit later.

There was an offer for us to dance at the Knickerbocker Grill, which was a rather prominent spot in New York just then. This we declined too since we were not interested in any sort of cabaret or restaurant jobs. We also refused a temporary return to vaudeville and a big engagement at the Palace.

Adele and I decided to have some fun and take time to think things over. We were, of course, upset by this failure. Thrown off balance a bit, we decided not to worry about it until later, and just do nothing for a while.

That little idea didn't last long because Alex Aarons' efforts were beginning to materialize.

He cabled us:

CAN ARRANGE ENGLISH PRODUCTION FOR GOODNESS SAKE AS WE DISCUSSED IT. UNDERSTAND YOU'RE CONSIDERING DECOURVILLE REVUE. NO GOOD FOR YOU. DON'T DO ANYTHING UNTIL I SEE YOU NEXT WEEK.

We were longing to go to Europe and anxiously awaited Alex's return to hear more about it.

Father was enthusiastic about such a prospect and remarked that he would be over as soon as he felt a little better. Mother, concerned about his health, did not wholeheartedly agree that she could go with us. He insisted that he would be all right and that we should go, by all means, and take advantage of this opportunity.

When Aarons returned the following week we had several huddles about the project and agreed to do what he planned. He said he had already laid the groundwork and it would be necessary for him to go right back to London and finalize the deal.

This he did, with Sir Alfred Butt, prominent London theatre man and producer. Sir Alfred was also a Member of Parliament.

Alex came back to America with all the contracts and had tickets for us to sail on the *Aquitania* March 23. Passage was arranged for Mother to accompany us. This latter point brought about a rather amusing incident as related by Alex.

When he discussed the deal with Sir Alfred all terms were finally agreed upon, including steamship fares over and return. Alex had said, "Then in addition to Fred and Adele, their mother will travel with them and her transportation must be paid." This caused a vehement query from Sir Alfred. "The mother? What can the mother do? I don't want the mother!"

Alex conquered the hurdle with "She must travel with her daughter on a trip like this."

Sir Alfred came to hand. He said, "Very well—very well! I'll bring the mother over too. Anything else?"

This was our favorite story for years.

The time soon came to sail.

It was an engrossing venture and we were filled with curiosity. We knew very few British people and were somewhat frightened, along with the excitement of the new experiment.

I must add that we were ripe for such a departure and needed inspiration after *The Bust and Judy*, as we referred to it.

The trip over on the *Aquitania* was in itself full of excitement. This was our first ocean crossing and that was a fine ship. We had grand times with Alex and his wife, who sailed with us. One outstanding incident on the trip took place the night of the ship's concert, a usual procedure on all big ocean liners whereby the ship's passenger list is combed for candidates to appear in the charity affair given for the Seaman's Fund. Of course, we were drafted for this and accepted, although we didn't like appearing at affairs where we felt we could not do our best work. Slippery floor, music from strange orchestra, things like that. To dance under those conditions was difficult for us and here we were faced with having to appear on a slippery ballroom floor and also cope with the slight motion of a ship at sea. What would happen, we wondered, if it turned up a bit choppy that night?

It not only turned up choppy but definitely rough—a "following sea," or something, which causes those rock-and-roll movements.

With the ship tossing around violently, I didn't see how we could tackle it. But we did—and were all over that floor.

We made our entrance and aimed for wherever we meant to go in the dance but we promptly found ourselves headed for the opposite side of the room. There was absolutely nothing we could do about it. The laws of gravity took over.

At one point we fell and slid about fifteen feet. The attempts at recoveries were spontaneously hilarious. Naturally, my comic sister was loving the whole thing by now and we threw in a few embellishments of our own, being the hams that we were.

The audience entered into the spirit of it all with amusement and our act came off very well. I must say I wouldn't have missed that for anything. An English gentleman came up to us after the performance and said, "I say, you two should make a jolly good hit in London. I shall be there with a party the first night!" We were delighted. Years later I used this whole idea in a picture called *Royal Wedding* with Jane Powell at M-G-M and it was one of my favorite numbers. We had to construct a ship's lounge on a special rocking device.

Next morning many passengers complimented us for what they called a "perilous dance." We convinced them that it was more extemporaneous than perilous.

A steward told me that, on one of these occasions, a sudden roll came up which sent a divan with three people shooting across the room, causing considerable consternation. Although that didn't happen on our night, I remembered it and used the idea in our movie number.

We were pleased with the experience and the fact that the audience, comprised mostly of English people, approved of our work. It gave us encouragement as to what we might hope for in London.

The rest of the trip was calm and pleasant and we enjoyed the deck games, hot bouillon, tea, deck chairs and everything about the voyage.

The first sight of land, the coast of Ireland, was a big moment. A few years later Adele would be living happily in one of the most beautiful landmarks on that island, Lismore Castle.

Landing at Southampton was exciting. The customs officials were polite. So were the baggage men. We liked the place at once.

Alex arranged a compartment for us all to ride together on the train to London. The whistles amused us. The scenery, everything, was different.

After several hours, we finally pulled into Waterloo Station—and in style:

The train stopped dead with a definite jolt, dumping a few of us on the floor, accompanied by a handbag or two from the shelf above.

The engine had slammed into the "buffers," going about ten miles an hour. The air brakes jammed, or something. It was quite a bump and Alex came up with a timely remark: "Well, you can always say that you came into London with a bang."

We hoped the incident was significant.

After some confusion rounding up our bags and finding a porter, we walked toward the terminal building on our way to a taxi.

It was interesting, all this. We were really in London—too good to be true. We even liked the hazy, somewhat smoky atmosphere.

Adele and I went taking in everything intensely. As a brewery truck, drawn by a team of big grays, went past, Adele handed me a laugh with "I wonder if those horses have English accents?"

Pretty soon we were unloading at the Savoy and Alex led us into the lobby. He knew all the ropes, so we followed him like ducks. We liked the hotel, which was furnished in rather exotic modern style, settled down, had dinner in our rooms and finally got to bed in sort of a daze.

Next morning Alex suggested that we go with him to meet our new sponsor, Sir Alfred Butt, and that night we would see our first British show, Jack Buchanan in *Battling Butler*, at the Adelphi Theatre.

We walked along the Strand, and made our way to Leicester Square, peering in shop windows and acting like a couple of yokels, I'm sure, finally arriving at Sir Alfred's offices, where we were warmly greeted.

It was all working out well. The ice was broken. We began to feel rather at home.

That night at the Adelphi, Jack Buchanan was great in *Battling Butler*. His manner and comedy methods were all his own and I was tremendously impressed.

Next night we went to the old Empire for an opening. It was a revue and the audience didn't care for the show at all. The galleryites booed, talked out loud to the actors, and at the final curtain there was a bedlam of noises. It took on the aspect of a rather menacing hassle between stage and auditorium. A tense atmosphere.

Adele and I turned slowly to look at each other and she said, "How've you been?"

We immediately began to visualize the razzing we would get if the gallery didn't like us. It was something to think about.

On the way home, Alex reassured us as best he could. "Remember this. You are going to be good and so is the show. That thing tonight was lousy."

We still didn't like the penalty of the razz hanging over our heads—if we didn't happen to click.

In a few days our rehearsals were under way. The all-British cast was delightful to work with and did everything possible to make us feel welcome.

One thing we had difficulty getting used to was the cold, inside and outdoors. It was so raw compared with home, and the lack of central heating was noticeable. However, we came around and were soon used to everything.

A few changes were made in the show. A number of dialogue variations were necessary for local purposes, some phrases Anglicized to suit the cast, and the title was changed to *Stop Flirting*. Fred Thompson did the rewriting.

Jack Melford played the Jack Hazzard part, Marjorie Gordon the Helen Ford role. Henry Kendall and Mimi Crawford were also with us. Felix Edwardes was the stage director. We added a George Gershwin tune for an ensemble number in the first act, "I'll Build a Stairway to Paradise." This pepped up our show and we were quite encouraged as we prepared to leave for Liverpool after about five weeks of rehearsals.

We were scheduled to open at the Royal Court Theatre there and the nerves and jitters started to move in.

The old Court Theatre presented us with a jolly fine slanting stage. The kind that throws dancers into the footlights until they get accustomed to it. Although we were used to that sort of thing, having rehearsed on one most of the time in London, this one seemed more vicious than most of them.

Funny how you get used to dancing under those conditions. It becomes second nature after a while. Then when you suddenly move to a theatre with a flat stage again, you find yourself heading up toward the back wall all of the time. On tour at home there were a few vaudeville theatres, old opera houses, where we first had our experiences with slanting stages.

We had to rehearse a lot to be sure we could handle ourselves perfectly for the all-important opening. That moment was soon on top of us.

It was an excellent performance as I remember it. We were nervous but the audience was responsive. They laughed in the right places and for the songs and dances applauded and shouted what we thought sounded like "More—more—more." It was that, intermingled with " 'Core—'Core," an abbreviation of "Encore." I hadn't realized we might get this sort of enthusiasm, although we had heard some at Jack Buchanan's show.

We had never heard noises like this at home except in the college towns.

Our numbers went fine and the old run-around came through again. They called for so many encores of that one that we ran dry and had to repeat some. Adele had them laughing both in her dialogue and comedy dancing.

We had to make curtain speeches at the end of the show. Incidentally, this occurred at every evening performance of the Liverpool week.

Needless to say, we were overjoyed—stunned—by this successful start. But we couldn't help but think that maybe the Gallery First Nighters (as they were known in London) might take a different viewpoint. Maybe they didn't like Americans in London. Somebody was always bringing that up, too.

However, for the moment things were fine.

It was a well-dressed audience—some white ties and tails and all that, even in Liverpool. Many friends of Sir Alfred's and the cast came backstage after the show. Noel Coward was visiting in the country nearby and came to tell us that he was glad to see his prediction come true.

I said, "Thanks, Noel, but this is only Liverpool. In London they might give us the bird."

He said, "Don't worry, they won't," and hustled us off to a supper party at the Midland Adelphi Hotel given by Lord Lathom.

Next morning the local press treated us very well and we were thankful for everything.

Glasgow was the next stop, at the King's Theatre. That too was successful. It was a different sort of enthusiasm (less boisterous) but they liked the show and the Scotch newspapers went whole-heartedly for it. I had an opportunity to play golf almost every day, since there were no matinees except Saturday. One of the boys in the show, Dickie Dolman, was a good golfer and we played all the courses that we could get to: Bogside, Gailes, Western Gailes, Troon, Prestwick, all in a line out of Glasgow by train. We started at the nearest one and then would pick up the next farther out each day. They were fine courses. Plenty cold and windy, too.

Next stop was the beautiful city of Edinburgh, the Queen's Theatre there, and it was a perfect engagement. We were to open in London the following Wednesday night.

The show was in good shape. We had nothing to do now but bring it in. I began to worry that too much might be expected of us. I always managed to dig up something to worry about.

Adele said, "Oh dear, Moaning Minnie's at it again."

We boarded a Scotch sleeper express train on the Saturday night and were in London Sunday morning. Those trains could really move. We left a call to be awakened with tea and a biscuit one hour before arrival.

It was cold, cloudy and clammy arriving in London early Sunday morning. Anything but cheerful. We went straight to the Savoy and took it easy. The Savoy was an interesting hotel, a sort of meeting ground for all nationalities. Various Indian maharajas made it their headquarters while visiting London. They would take a whole floor or two for themselves and retinue.

We spent Monday and Tuesday rehearsing and being generally nervous. The dress rehearsal was smooth enough. We liked the Shaftesbury Theatre; it was a good size, comfortable to work in.

There was talk about the show from reports on the road, and no doubt about it, a lot was expected of us.

I spent the entire afternoon, Wednesday, in the theatre trying to stay with the atmosphere, too nervous to go out of the building.

Just before curtain time Alex Aarons stopped by to wish us luck on his way to his usual opening-night retreat, the men's room.

As the zero hour approached I began to feel a little easier, and when the curtain went up, all nervousness vanished.

It was a memorable sight, that beautifully dressed audience in the stalls. They were friendly, but not demonstrative through the first act. They seemed to be waiting for something. Although the laughs were coming fairly well, I was getting concerned as to whether or not we were quite making it. The gallery crowd was well-behaved but not too encouraging.

Between the acts I asked, "Is this thing getting over? I don't hear much from them." Aarons said there were favorable comments out in the lobby, but nevertheless he was going back to the men's room for the rest of the show.

The first reassurance we had was in the middle of the second act with a number that Adele and I did. It was called "Oh Gee, Oh Gosh, Oh Golly, I Love You," a song and dance, and when we made our exit the roof came down and the " 'Cores" and "Mores" started.

We knew then that we were in. Most of our best numbers were still to come, including "Whichness of the Whatness" with run-around.

They weren't giving too much away, that audience, but "Oh Gee, Oh Gosh," got the job done. Things felt better and Alex came backstage to tell us that the noise he heard in response to that number brought him out of the men's room.

The comedy and everything picked up from there on, and the old run-around accomplished what we hoped for.

English theatre audiences are vociferous when they want to be. They let loose with everything and it is a performer's dream to experience it.

The "Oompah Trot" was perfect for their sense of humor and there seemed to be no limit to the encores. After a while they were singing "Oompah-Oompah-Oompah-Oompah" with the music as we dropped into the run-around. Adele absolutely panicked 'em. She made one of the greatest personal hits of any girl ever to appear in England.

The final curtain of the show brought calls for speeches and left no doubt as to the success of the show. All of the principals said a few words. I stood there while Adele spoke. "My brother and I thank you from the bottom of our hearts and—and we want you all to come and have tea with us tomorrow." They laughed at that and then wanted a few words from me. I couldn't think of a thing to follow it so I stepped forward and muttered, "She said it."

It was a great night and we couldn't have hoped for anything more. The evening was over and there were no boos. What a relief!

Backstage was a busy place for about an hour after the show. The many visitors were emphatic in their enthusiasm. Adele and I were dazed. The whole cast congratulated us warmly.

Alex Aarons was gloating over his accomplishments and we thanked him. Sir Alfred and Lady Butt were there, highly pleased.

When we left the stage door, the Gallery First Nighters were

en masse, some standing on top of our car, some on the hood—
all over the place. It was a grand sight. A spokesman said they
would see the show every night for the rest of the week and then
regularly a few times a week from then on.

One night after about six months I asked one young fellow:
"Harry, how many times have you seen this show now?" He
replied, "One hundred fourteen times." I asked whether he had
seen any other shows lately and he replied that he had not. I
asked him why.

"Well, I don't know whether I'd like them or not, and I know
I like this one," he said.

There was Sophie too, a famous first nighter, and many others
we knew by name.

We would often have conversations back and forth with these
loyal devotees over the footlights during the curtain speeches as
the play ran on and on, much to the amusement of the rest of
the audience.

When we finally said good night to the stage-door crowd after
the opening, we headed for Claridge's Hotel, where a large party
had been arranged with many theatrical and other celebrities
present, including Gertrude Lawrence, Noel Coward, Somerset
Maugham, Tallulah Bankhead, Alex and Ella Aarons, Sir Alfred
and Lady Butt.

We went home that night the happiest. I sent a cable to Father
with the details.

We were enormously grateful for the generous British criticism,
which turned out to be a good deal more sprightly than we had
thought it would be. The reviewers not only liked the show (one
headline went so far as to call us "Dancers of Genius"), but
positively got into the act themselves. They greeted us with all
sorts of swift and funny lines. The *Evening Star,* for instance,
noted that "two American dancers were shown how wildly enthusiastic a London audience could be," called the show "an
extraordinary success," and wound up with this bouquet for
Adele: "She could dance the depression out of an undertaker."

Sidney W. Carrol in the London *Times* said that "they typify the primal spirit of animal delight that could not restrain itself —the vitality that bursts its bonds in the Garden of Eden. . . . They are as lithe as blades of grass, as light as gossamer, and as odd as gollywogs."

The *Pall Mall Gazette* discovered that "they neither look nor behave like ordinary dancers. Mr. Fred Astaire has both the air and figure of a highbrow. He has a bulging forehead and no display of chest or calf or anything of that sort, and wears a commonplace dress jacket all the time. Miss Adele Astaire is equally careless about appearances—just a romping anyhow with a happy-go-lucky manner, all temperament and intelligence. . . . Their final shoulder-to-shoulder gallop not only brings down the house but is one of the funniest things of its kind I can remember."

St. John Ervine went overboard for Adele. He called her "that singular person, an exceedingly agile and original dancer and a real comedienne. Miss Astaire has a tiny little American voice which first of all vaguely irritates you and then becomes irresistible. I could willingly have watched Miss Astaire dancing for the whole evening and so, judging from the applause, could the rest of the audience."

So there it was, the reviews all great. There was no longer any question about *Stop Flirting*. It was in.

Now the only thing to be sure of was to keep it that way. We settled down in London for a long run. There was a big ticket brokers' deal or, as they put it over there, "The libraries bought out a large section of the stalls each night and well into the future."

Now came the job of enjoying life, meeting people, hundreds of people. Spending weekends in the country, going to parties, seeing the night clubs on which London thrived. There were the Kit Kat Club, Café de Paris, Ciro's and the old Embassy Club, when it was in its prime with Luigi in full swing.

We often had supper after the show in the Savoy Grill. It was a rendezvous for theatre people and we saw numerous American friends from time to time. They were colorful days.

Many English stars and theatrical luminaries entertained us. We were so kindly treated by members of our profession. This stands out in my mind.

I went on a clothes-buying binge in Savile Row, mostly at Anderson & Sheppard's. It was difficult not to order one of every cloth that was shown me, especially the vicuñas. They never wore out. I outgrew most of them. It was Hawes and Curtis and Beale and Inman for shirts and such.

I'd get lost for days in the Burlington Arcade.

There were many beaus hanging around Adele but she was never serious. We were carefree.

My interest in racing led me to investigate how it was done in England. Sir Alfred Butt was a serious racing enthusiast and maintained a stable of useful horses. He invited me to several of the more important race meetings and my appetite for the sport was being whetted.

My valet, George, whom I found over there, was also an avid race fan. George was a great fellow, about twenty-five, and a more faithful helper would be hard to imagine. George had the most utter disregard for h's of anybody I ever knew. He not only omitted them in his speech but also in his writing.

One night I noticed the following strange code written on the upper right hand corner of the large mirror on my make-up shelf:

AT ERE

I said, "George, now will you please tell me what the hell that means?"

"It's your 'at, sir," he replied.

I said, "Well, go ahead, I'm listening—what about my 'at?"

George quite calmly explained, "I didn't want to forget to take it with me for your entrance, sir. I wanted to remind myself that the 'at was 'ere in the room, sir."

George often casually mentioned a horse that would come up a winner of one of the big handicaps, although he himself seldom cared to bet. I asked him how he picked these winners so nonchalantly. He said:

"I count up from the bottom, sir. I take the number of letters in the name of the bottom 'orse in the entries—say it 'as ten letters in it, and I count up from there including the bottom 'orse. The tenth 'orse from the bottom is the one I play.

"It only works in the big 'andicaps though, sir."

I said, "Oh, I see," Which, of course, I didn't. Funny thing about it was that it worked quite often.

Racing in England gave me much pleasure. And, while I still didn't think of entering into it as an owner, I did have accounts with about ten bookmaking firms, including Ladbroke, Heathorn, Joe Lee, Dougie Stewart. I enjoyed my wagers immensely. And so did they.

Of course betting on the animals away from the race course is legal in England and the bookmaking firms were and still are a legitimate business. Some of England's most famous race horses were owned and bred by the proprietors of bookmaking establishments.

After a few months the show was transferred to the Queen's Theatre, a block or so away and across the street. We liked this better than the Shaftesbury. It was more intimate. Both of these theatres were bombed out during World War II.

The nobility patronized the show, not with just a single visit, but quite often, and we met many of them.

There was never a black tie in view those days either in stalls or boxes, for many months. That sea of white ties and stiff-bosomed shirts, along with the bejeweled ladies, an occasional diamond tiara here and there, was an imposing sight.

One night a few weeks after the transfer to the Queen's, the word went around backstage that the Prince of Wales was out front. He arrived with his party just after the curtain had gone up and was seated in about the eighth row. When Adele heard this she said, "Well, good. What delayed him?"

I peeked through a hole in one of the wings and sure enough, there he was. There were four in the party.

It was an exciting and memorable moment. Not only for us— everyone was always excited when they knew the Prince was anywhere nearby. He was unquestionably the most vibrant personality of the times.

The whole company was very much concerned with his presence and they were all taking a peek at various intervals to watch his reactions to the show. I thought he seemed to like it all right. He would look at the stage for several minutes and then turn his head a bit and talk to the lady at his left.

That was good enough for me—at least he was looking, and what was more, he had not yet walked out. In fact, he` and his party stayed for the final curtain.

Several nights later, the Prince of Wales again appeared at our theatre. This time he sent his equerry, Major Metcalf, around between the acts to say that H.R.H. would like us to join him and his party for supper after the show at the Riviera Club. We were knocked cold, of course, and accepted, but it made us both mighty nervous for the rest of the performance.

Major Metcalf said they would be back after the show to see us.

It was a rather frightening thing for a couple of hoofers like us and we were not too sure we were going to enjoy the experience, even though, like everyone else in the world, we were thrilled and eager to meet the Prince.

Adele said to me, "Can't we just meet him and go home?" Then we both agreed that it was not quite proper to refuse the royal request. Anyway, we would have to go home and change to evening clothes after the show and meet the party at the Riviera Club as soon as we could get there. That would give us a chance to gather up our equilibrium after being presented in the theatre.

It all worked out well. The Prince, Mrs. Dudley Coates, Major Metcalf, and Lady Alexandra ("Baba") Curzon all came backstage to our dressing rooms and they made it easy for us. The Prince was most gracious and kind and said to me, "We loved the show. You must be very fit to get around like that."

I thanked him and told him how pleased all of us in the company were that he had come to see us a second time.

He said, "Oh, I'll be back some more. I was away on a tour when you opened and everybody told me I must be sure to see it." He then said to the Major, "Fruity, you did ask the Astaires to join us for supper at the Riviera?"

I replied, "Yes, thank you sir, we'd be delighted but we'll have to go home and change—it won't take long."

He said, "Oh, don't bother to do that."

We said we'd rather and he replied, "Just as you wish. The Riviera is a new place—the band is pretty good. 'Fruity' will come to pick you up when you say."

We told him that would be fine, and after about five minutes of very pleasant conversation they left by the stage door.

We didn't mind it so much now. He, as is usual with royalty, knew how to put one at ease.

All this time I was taking special notice of how he was dressed —impeccably in tails. H.R.H. was unquestionably the best-dressed young man in the world, and I was missing none of it. I noticed particularly the white waistcoat lapels—his own special type. This waistcoat did not show below the dress coat front. I liked that.

I heard that Hawes and Curtis made the Prince's dress shirts and waistcoats. Next morning I was there and asked if I could get a waistcoat like H.R.H.'s. I was apologetically told that it could not be done. So I went somewhere else and had one made like it.

We made a rush for it and got out of the theatre fast. The galleryites at the stage door were thrilled at seeing H.R.H., too, so everybody had a good time.

In about an hour we were picked up at the hotel and brought

to the Riviera. It was an attractive place—not too crowded that night—midweek. After we had settled awhile, the Prince asked Adele, "Are you too tired to dance with me?"

She said: "Sir, I'm exhausted," and with that she jumped up and rushed at him.

Everybody laughed. We all danced and laughed the whole time. It was a good party, lasting until about 2 A.M., and they dropped us at home.

The Prince saw the show ten times and often came backstage to chat awhile, bringing his party, or he would send word asking us to come up to his box between the acts. In this way we met other members of the Royal Family, the Duke and Duchess of York and Prince George, the youngest brother. Prince George became a close friend.

After about two months at the Queen's Theatre, for some reason or other we had to move to the Strand Theatre. This worked out well. The Strand was much like the Queen's. Our friends the galleryites took great pleasure in inaugurating each change of residence.

Business was capacity wherever we went and we began to wonder how long we might have to stay in England. We didn't want to go home, but also didn't want to be away too long for professional reasons.

Father's health was not improving so Mother decided to go back to be with him.

Our London activities went on and we did about everything there was to be done.

A few weeks before Christmas we were obliged to vacate the Strand owing to a previous commitment for the theatre. The pantomime season always caused a theatre shortage and we had to go to Birmingham for five weeks, after which the show would return to London for its indefinite run.

The Birmingham engagement turned out well although we were rather gloomy about having had to leave London for the holiday season. Prince George, then a student at the Naval Academy nearby, came over with his roommate and spent a week-end with us at the Midland Hotel. We managed to find some amusement.

Birmingham, while a very nice city, was no London around Christmastime. We were due back in London at the Strand about February to resume where we left off.

However, we had a three-week interim and took the opportunity to go to Paris for our first visit, staying at the Hotel Crillon. We saw as many sights and shows as we could, including Chevalier, the Dolly Sisters, Mistinguett and others. Sir Alfred happened to be over for a few days and took us around the town. It was a nice vacation.

We loved Paris but there was the unfinished business in London, so we were eager to get back there.

This time we lived at the Carlton Hotel, corner of Pall Mall and Haymarket. Our friend Eddie Tatham, a partner in the renowned firm of Justerini and Brooks, liquor merchants, had offices in the hotel building. Eddie kept things gay—he knew just about everybody in London.

Douglas Fairbanks and Mary Pickford, on one of their trips, stayed at the Carlton. The front of the place was constantly blocked by crowds of people eagerly waiting to get a glimpse of them. It was difficult to get in and out of the hotel.

Lord and Lady Mountbatten brought Doug and Mary to see *Stop Flirting* one evening. They were seated in the upper right-hand box and sent word requesting us to come up to the box between the acts, which we did. Doug had some kind words to say to us about the show but I'm sure he never remembered seeing us before.

The show ran on and on. We were seeing our friends and having a time. Among the most enjoyable parties we went to were those given by Esmond Harmsworth, the present Lord Rothermere.

Noel Coward induced me to go to the Guildhall School of Music with him to take a course in harmony. We both took it quite seriously, but Noel gained much more out of it than I did, judging from his compositions and musical accomplishments ever since.

I recall an amusing incident that happened when Noel was having a slight discussion with our teacher, Orlando Morgan.

One of our homework chores was to create a short composition, write it down, and bring it in next day.

When Noel handed his in, Mr. Morgan played it on the piano and said, "But you can't have two consecutive fifths." Noel said, "But I have." Morgan went on, "But you can't," and Noel insisted, "But I have."

It went on:

"But you can't."

"But I have."

"But you can't."

"But I have," until Noel pointed out that Debussy had done it, after which our teacher let him have his way.

All during this period Adele and I, while we were very ambitious about our work, never did any practicing to speak of.

Every now and then I would try to get her interested in a workout session, a dancing shakedown. There were things that seemed to need brushing up in our work as we were in the throes of a long run. I knew I needed a going-over, and would try to induce Delly to join me. I'd say:

"Delly, how about a little practice tomorrow for a couple of hours. I want to try something. Let's rehearse."

She'd let me know fast. "Rehearse? Who wants to rehearse? I know this show backwards." I'd reply, "Yes, and that's the way you're doing some of the steps, too."

She'd say, "Very funny. Now, listen, you know I hate to rehearse. I'll go stale if I do any more than I'm doing with this show. If you're worrying about that one spot near the finish of 'Oh Gee, Oh Gosh,' I know the place you're thinking about. I'll go over it with you between the acts tomorrow, but I couldn't possibly come in and put practice clothes on and rehearse. Ugh! That word gives me the creeps."

Whatever it was, we straightened it out that way and I would do my practicing alone. But I needed it.

We made no effort at developing new ideas for the future. We didn't have time. We were so busy running around having fun. We adored London and all that was happening to us.

Sir Alfred Butt was attentive, visiting backstage now and then, and occasionally he would ask us to supper after the show. We always enjoyed these visits and would discuss the possibilities of our next trip to London, hoping that the next vehicle, whatever it was, would be a good one to bring over after the New York run.

One night Sir Alfred came around in somewhat of a different mood than usual. He approached me as I arrived in the theatre at about seven o'clock.

He said, "Fred, you know that your father has been quite ill, don't you?" I told him I did know, and that Mother had gone back to America some time before on account of it. He went on, "You wouldn't be surprised to hear that he has been getting a bit worse, would you?"

It dawned on me that he was breaking some sort of news to me—gently. I looked at him for a moment and he came out with it.

"I've just had a cable from your mother asking me to tell you that your father has passed away."

Somehow I was not prepared at all, even though I knew it was pretty serious about him. In our letters there hadn't been any reason to suspect too much. Mother had been keeping it rather back to alleviate our worry.

I was pretty stunned and Sir Alfred quickly said, "Now, I'll do whatever you and your sister want to do. I'll close the show for a week or two—or just for tonight if you wish. But if I may, I would advise you to go right on."

After a moment or so I agreed that we must go right on with

the work and thanked Sir Alfred for his consideration and kindness in conveying Mother's message.

It was a tough night but that was the only way to cope with the tragic news.

Shortly after that we had a letter from Mother with the details. She had taken Father to Wernersville hoping for his recuperation. Father spent his last days in Wernersville.

A good many weeks went by before we could snap out of the effects of this. It was the first really bad news we had ever experienced in our lives.

Mother joined us in about six weeks and was quite ill on her arrival. She went to Sir Douglas Shields' nursing home in rather serious condition. However, she recovered in a few weeks. Sir James Barrie was also a patient there at that time. He sent word asking us to stop by and visit him. He mentioned that he wished Adele would play Peter Pan sometime.

Stop Flirting kept on running and there was no sign of a letup. Adele and I started to get a little concerned about being away from New York for such a long time. It was now about a year and a half and we decided to ask Alex Aarons to bring us back home—even though business was still big. He agreed that it should be done and arranged with Sir Alfred for a closing date a few months later at the peak of our run.

Sir Alfred was a good sport about it and said, "It's a great pity to do this, you know. I'm sure this show could run several more years if you wanted to stay. But I'm counting on the next one. I think you are absolutely right not to spend such a long time away from America."

As the last weeks closed in on us we began to feel sad. The galleryites called, "Come back soon," and it was turning into quite a thing. Many of the regular stalls patrons came back to get a last look at the little old show. When the last night arrived it was a sentimental occasion. The audience sang the songs with us, and we all joined together in "Auld Lang Syne" before the final curtain.

The shouts from the gallery were heart-warming. They yelled: "Give My Regards to Broadway"—"Don't Forget to Write"— "Hurry Back"—

Well—that was it. We were soon on our way home, intent upon making amends for the failure of our last show in New York. We had a verbal agreement with Alex Aarons for our next one and were confident that the vehicle he had in preparation would be something suitable. His advance description of it and the fact that George Gershwin was writing the music with lyrics by brother Ira gave us a feeling of security.

Alex told us of his intended association with Vinton Freedley. He planned that the new firm of Aarons and Freedley would produce our coming show in New York. This was surprising news. It pleased and amused us a lot that our friend Vinton would now be one of our bosses.

It was exciting looking forward to the homecoming after our splendid time in England.

Chapter 12   *Lady, Be Good!*

Before we realized it we were on the S.S. *Homeric*. I don't think either of us knew how tired we were mentally and physically. We had been on the go for nearly two years and this voyage gave us time to collect our thoughts.

We agreed to avoid dancing at the ship's concert and another possible battle with the waves. Adele said, "I'm not in the mood. I'm staying in my room until this yacht reaches Ambrose Lightship."

However, I got out a bit and participated in the concert by announcing a few singers. The next day I auctioned off the ship's pool, but there was no hoofing. It proved to be a smooth and restful trip.

The thought kept running through my mind: "What an extraordinary show *For Goodness Sake* turned out to be!" Here was a decidedly unpretentious vehicle that could hardly compare with some of the major musical comedies, but still it meant so much—both in New York and in London. It really put us on the map.

The Statue of Liberty was a welcome sight and that New York City skyline, too.

The ship's reporters, as customary, got aboard from a launch well down the bay, several hours before docking time.

We were pleased to find that we had not been forgotten during our long stay abroad. They knew all about what we had been doing over there and were eager to get some statements from Adele about her experiences dancing with the Prince of Wales—which was only natural from their standpoint, I suppose.

However, Adele closed the book on them and said, "Now listen, you boys, if you think you're going to get some of those dopey headlines from me, you're crazy. The Prince of Wales and other members of the Royal Family were very kind to my brother and me and I'm not talking about it for publicity purposes."

It was great to be back in New York and we stood on the deck waving to Alex and Vinton and other friends who were there to meet us. Everybody in the entire area was waving at someone. I spotted my old friend Walter Williams, and that touched off some comedy sequences. He was, of course, on salary again with me from that moment on.

Setting a foot on the home soil was the next event. We were taking in all of these homecoming clichés and appreciating them up to the hilt.

Alex Aarons didn't waste much time in getting down to business. While we were going through customs he was telling us the plot for our new show.

"At the moment it's called *Black-Eyed Susan*," he said. "But that title is horrible and we're not going to use it—we're working on several other ideas. Incidentally, you know we only have a verbal agreement on this. You've got to sign some contracts. Will you trust me to ruin your lives for the next few years?"

We assured Alex that we'd like to be ruined by him and asked if he had the contracts in his pocket, at which point he pulled out a whole bunch.

We signed the contracts on a trunk lid while the customs men were going through our baggage. Alex needed them for a meeting with his backers that night.

Our new joint salary was to be $1,750 a week in New York and $2,000 on the road.

Rehearsals for *Black-Eyed Susan* were to start about a month from then, but there was a little delay and we were able to get a fairly decent holiday and rest.

New York had changed considerably, we thought. That old "tempo" was as predominant as ever but it seemed to have become busier and more hectic. Maybe it was just our imagination —anyway, we started finding out what was going on theatrically. It was important to know what we had to follow and what the competition might be.

George Gershwin took us out to several shows and we saw everything of importance.

We covered the night clubs also and were intrigued by the new type of entertainment originated by Texas Guinan. The Texas Guinan Club was a long, narrow, dimly-lit room, one flight up, with a small dance floor at the far end where the entertainers worked. Often frequented by underworld characters, it was an interesting and enormously successful spot.

"Give this little girl a nice big hand," Texas said as Ruby Keeler came out for her dance.

That we all did, and after the dance, too. Ruby was terrific with her military tap. She went on to become the wife of Al Jolson and soon afterward a top star in Hollywood.

It was at Texas' place that I saw what I considered the neatest, fastest Charleston dancer ever. George Raft. He practically floored me with his footwork.

George gives me credit for furthering his career, but I'm sure I had very little to do with it. He claims that because I mentioned his name to Poulsen of Café de Paris in London I was instrumental in his getting a job there which led to more important things.

I did tell Poulsen when I went to London the following season that I had seen a lightning hoofer and that he'd be a great attraction for the Café, which was the hottest night club in London at that time.

It was shortly afterward that George's individuality, aside from his dancing ability, brought him his tremendous success in films.

The shows playing in New York looked mighty good to us and we started to worry about what we would do in ours. We liked *Wildflower* with Edith Day, W. C. Fields in *Poppy*, *Stepping Stones* with Fred Stone and daughter Dorothy, and *Kid Boots* with Eddie Cantor and Mary Eaton.

Alex broke the news that our show was to be called *Lady, Be Good!* instead of *Black-Eyed Susan*. It didn't strike either of us very favorably when we first heard it; in fact, I didn't like it at all. But when I heard the song "Oh Lady, Be Good!," I changed my opinion.

George played the whole score for us next day and we were crazy about it, inspired. He told us that the two-piano team, Ohman and Arden, were to be a special feature in the pit orchestra, and we were eager for rehearsals to start the following week. I told Walter to dig out my practice clothes and dancing shoes.

From the very beginning, it seemed, *Lady, Be Good!* was one of those naturals that jelled. Rehearsals were pleasant and there were no temperamental outbursts that I can remember.

Felix Edwardes was brought over from England to stage the production and Sammy Lee handled the dance ensembles. Norman Bel Geddes designed the sets.

Walter Catlett was our co-star. We had enjoyed him so much in *Sally* with Marilyn Miller and Leon Errol and were elated that he was with us.

Cliff Edwards, "Ukulele Ike," had several important specialties and the whole thing shaped up well. Adele and I had one number called "Fascinating Rhythm" with Cliff that promised to be a show stopper, and we also had the old trade-mark run-around in a new Gershwin setup called "Swiss Miss."

What the plot of *Lady, Be Good!* was I really can't remember, but I do know that it was pretty stupid. Adele and I were cast as brother and sister.

Kathlene Martyn, renowned former *Ziegfeld Follies* beauty, played opposite me in the secondary romantic interest plot. I sang a number to Kathlene called "The Half of It Dearie Blues," which George and Ira wrote for me. It was one of their most ingenious special material contributions.

We were off for Philadelphia after four weeks' rehearsals and opened at the Forrest Theatre on schedule. There were the usual pep talks and the dress rehearsal wasn't too bad.

Opening night went perfectly. The audience laughed and applauded everything we had counted on. It didn't matter, that weak plot. Somehow there was an indefinable magic about the show.

Alex came around between the acts to say, "This thing is a cinch. I just made a deal for six months with the ticket brokers in New York. We're sold out already." I asked him if they had come down to the men's room to find him.

He said, "No—when I heard those yaks Catlett and Adele were getting I came out. Anyway, I'm cured now. I'll never be bothered with that sick feeling any more. I've outgrown that stuff."

Next morning the notices were excellent. We had a big hit on our hands. There was very little rehearsing to do and we were able to get out to "the Dump" to stay with Jim and Liz a few times, as well as go to a few parties. We were in a sort of hit groove and it was pleasant to feel that the London success was about to be safely followed up in New York.

Although Philadelphia was pretty much of a cosmopolitan audience and a good criterion, there was always the chance that one might get unduly overconfident and we were aware of that fact.

At any rate, we were a joyous company coming into New York for the opening at the Liberty Theatre on West Forty-second Street.

This was to be no minor event. We had gained a reputation abroad, and *Lady, Be Good!* had opened in Philadelphia in flawless fashion, so what was expected was a hit of smash proportions. Delly came to me and said, "Do you think they'll stand for this tacky book?" I told her that I thought this was one instance where it might not matter because the whole thing had a new look to it, a flow, and also a new sound with Phil Ohman and Vic Arden playing their two specialty pianos in the pit orchestra with Gershwin's best score to date.

This was no hackneyed ordinary musical comedy. It was slick and tongue-in-cheek, a definite departure in concept and design, and we hoped it would be recognized as such in New York.

We had a fine opening night. Everything scored. Catlett killed 'em. Ukulele Ike stopped the show with his specialty and Adele and I apparently delivered what was expected of us.

After numerous finale curtain calls, the rest of the cast pushed Adele forward to say a few words. She said, rather nervously I thought: "We all thank you so much. Fred and I are very happy to be back home, and—and—a—and—please come and see the show again. Good night."

We hadn't thought about the possibility of a speech. It was our first experience at that sort of thing in a Broadway show at home.

The festivities back stage afterward were gratifying. It seemed that everybody turned out for that opening.

Next morning the *New York Times* said:

ADELE ASTAIRE FASCINATES IN TUNEFUL "LADY, BE GOOD!"

. . . As recently as November 1922, Miss Astaire was seen in the unlamented "Bunch and Judy" to set sail soon thereafter for London. And ever since then the penny posts have been full of the details of her two-year triumph abroad in, of all things, "For Goodness Sake" with the title changed to "Stop Flirting" for no known reason.

But it is a different Adele Astaire whom last night's audience was privileged to see. When she left she was a graceful dancer—and she has returned not only with all her glorious grace but as a first rate comedienne in her own right. Miss Astaire in the new piece is as charming and entertaining a musical comedy actress as the town has seen on display in many a moon.

Fred Astaire too gives a good account of himself.

Herald Tribune:

. . . Fred and Adele we salute you! Last night at the Liberty Theatre this young couple appeared about 8:30 o'clock and from an audience sophisticated and over-theatred received a cordial greeting. At 8:45 they were applauded enthusiastically and when, at 9:15 they sang and danced "Fascinating Rhythm" the callous Broadwayites cheered them as if their favorite halfback had planted the ball behind the goal posts after an 80-yard run. Seldom has it been our pleasure to witness so heartfelt, spontaneous and so deserved a tribute.

The show always went well. Even after the final curtain many of the audience would linger around the orchestra pit to hear Ohman and Arden playing the exit music with the orchestra. Often too, when the exit music was completed, Phil and Vic would put on an impromptu concert for the fans who refused to go home. This happened many times and I was convinced that the new sound of Ohman and Arden's two pianos in the pit had a lot to do with the over-all success of *Lady, Be Good!*

We were again blessed with a long run in a hit show. The on-stage and off-stage activities were always something to look forward to.

I had a dressing room with Walter Catlett and that alone was hilarious. I also had Walter, my valet, and his natural contributions were not exactly on the gloomy side. We had more visitors than you could count. Catlett would invite all sorts of characters in just for laughs and that's what we had.

Walter was a high-salaried man and he loved spending money. Consequently, he'd be a bit short at the end of a week, having already tackled the company manager, Jimmy Whittendale, for a touch on his coming pay day.

Several times after collecting Adele's and my salary, $1,750 in cash, I'd be counting it in the dressing room before the show.

"Uncle Walter," as I called him, would arrive in a whirl and on seeing this beautiful sight would come to me, grab ten one-hundred-dollar bills and say, "Freddie, my boy, Uncle Walter just happens to need a grand tonight—very badly. Oh, yes, Freddie, my boy, it's a long story—my wife needs the rent—I'll give it back to you Monday."

I'd try to explain, "But, Walter, half of this is Adele's and . . ." He'd interrupt, "That's all right—tonight when I sing, 'Oh sweet and lovely lady be good,' to her, she'll understand—that's a good boy." Of course he always paid me back.

Walt is a generous guy. What he often really wanted the money for was to lend it to somebody who was putting the bee on him. One time he came in with a big roll of bills.

"Freddie, my boy, here, take some. Don't you want any? What's the matter with you?"

Alex Aarons came in shortly after the opening to say that he had arranged for the show to be done in England after its American run.

He didn't know the dates but Sir Alfred was already making plans for a theatre so that we could count on an uninterrupted run this time. They thought *Lady, Be Good!* was made to order for London audiences.

We were hoping to return to England with a vehicle of somewhat more size than *Stop Flirting,* and this seemed to be it. We made a new contract with Alex and Vint for the London engagement: a guarantee with percentage of the gross.

So we were riding high, doing the town when we felt so inclined, and then we ran into an offer to appear in a night club.

Leland Hayward, who was in the agency business then, first approached us about it. The Trocadero wanted an attraction to buck the Mirador, which was starring Moss and Fontana, the foremost ballroom dancers of that time.

Adele and I were not ballroom dancers particularly, but the idea struck us that it might be fun—in fact inspiring—to pick up a big chunk of money in a hurry. We might even extend ourselves at staging a special set of dances if the price was right. Adele said:

"Let's do this thing and get a Rolls-Royce out of it. What can we ask?" I said, "Well, let's say we want five thousand dollars a week for six weeks, and if they say no we simply drop it."

That was the plan, and when we told Leland about it, he said, "Oh, that's a cinch, they don't care what they pay."

Mal Hayward (no relation to Leland) and Frank Garlasco were the proprietors of the Trocadero.

We were stuck with it and had to go to work. It was not easy doing that kind of a thing along with the show but we went through with it and knocked ourselves out putting on routines suitable to a night-club floor. That five thousand a week caused talk around town. I believe it was a record figure.

Our friends Billy Reardon and Dorothy Clark were working up above us in the Lido Club and we had some fun with them, visiting back and forth in our spare moments.

We enjoyed getting ready for the new job and working with Emil Coleman's music.

Anyway, before we knew it, opening night was on us. All the swells were there. A night club was an atmosphere we had never worked in before and we didn't like it—except for the thought of the five thousand a week.

Our dances went over fine. It was okay but we were really out of our element and the general feeling was that we were doing it for a lark and that it wouldn't last.

Things went along well. Business had to be big to pay us that figure. It was. Jammed the first two weeks. The third week, a drop took place, and I began to sense that we might be asked to take a cut, so I suggested to Adele that I might buy the bosses a present which would possibly defer the idea of them asking us to cut. I bought a cigarette case for Mal and a flask for Frank, which we inscribed in engraved facsimile handwriting.

It did the trick, but business for the next week was still not so good and I suggested to Adele that we voluntarily cut to three thousand a week for the last two weeks. They had been good sports about the whole thing from the start.

My suggestion was appreciated by the boys.

I told them at the conclusion of our engagement that the reason we had given the presents was not only because we liked them, but that we wanted to knock out any idea they may have had about asking us to cut our five thousand a week. Frank said:

"You caught me just in time. I was all ready to do it, but when that lovely flask came I didn't have the heart."

He also told us that we had done well and that they were entirely satisfied with the venture.

"After all," he said, "we accomplished our purpose. The Mirador closed three weeks ago."

It was fun, that experience, but Adele and I never would work in another café. We decided to wait until we got back to London to get the Rolls.

Several odd things occurred during that café escapade.

There was a prohibition raid one night. After our performance, Adele and I were sitting with some friends at their table when suddenly I noticed a scurrying of waiters. The word had been passed around that the Federal boys had arrived. A waiter flew by us with a tray of glasses filled with champagne. He had changed his mind about delivering the order and switched around headed for the kitchen "on the double."

Just as he was about to make it, he tripped on the leg of a chair and fell flat on his face with glasses flying every which way.

It was a beautiful crash, completely destroying all the evidence as it soaked into the thick red carpeting, much to the misery of the pursuing Federal agent.

My first meeting with Adolphe Menjou came about at the club one night. He said, "Where did you get that suit? I like it." He was referring to my tails, and I was pleased because Adophe was noted as a dresser. I had not worn full dress much at that stage. My rash of tails started in the movies—years later.

It was pleasant to settle down to a normal existence again after the rather strenuous night-club stint. The show was going merrily on. Kathlene Martyn retired from the cast and was succeeded by Gladys Lloyd. (Gladys became the wife of Edward G. Robinson shortly thereafter.)

Jimmy Altemus came over from Philadelphia on one of his frequent visits and we went around the town together on a little night-club tour. He introduced me to Jock Whitney, down from Yale for the weekend, and we all joined up and spent the evening passing judgment on the Charleston and any other kind of hot music we could find. The Charleston had just come in and Whitney was all for it. He was an expert at it except that, in contrast to George Raft's fastest, Jock's was the slowest. He also became an expert at the Black Bottom when that one hit us.

Adele was being pursued by several young men whom I didn't care for and this suddenly loomed up as a menace. It worried me and I went to her about it.

She laughed, "Don't be silly—I'm not serious about anybody."

Well, that wasn't quite true, but nothing really developed.

A long series of buzzers-around set in. This went on for several years, both in New York and abroad.

She admitted that she didn't know how to get rid of them. I said I'd be glad to help and that I could make myself very objectionable if she would let me. She said no, she'd rather work it out herself. That's the way that went.

I saw a lot of Jimmy, Jock and Sandy Hamilton. Did a bit of racing around New York. Jock's mother, Mrs. Payne Whitney, owned the Greentree Stable and my interest in racing was again being nourished. Jimmy uncorked some hidden talents as a gentleman jockey and I watched him at several point-to-point meetings.

What a seat on a horse—magnificent!

I never saw him win a race, but what a seat!

Sandy and I spent many an hour in his office phoning in bets and waiting for results at tracks in various parts of the country. We also cabled Ladbroke's in London for the English tracks. I told Sandy I was sorry I didn't have a Japanese bookmaker or we could go on all night. We'd bet all the Greentree horses. We'd pick 'em ourselves, we'd buy tips—anything to have a bet. Did we win? No.

Up to then I had not done any real solo dancing in any of our shows. All dances were with Adele. I don't know why—possibly it was because we were so closely knit as a team.

Many people asked me why I never danced alone and they suggested that I should. "The Half of It Dearie Blues" number in *Lady, Be Good!* wasn't much of a dance. It was mostly song, and an excellent spot to experiment with, so I went to work preparing a tap routine to try and embellish that number.

Gershwin was pleased about this and often came in to play the piano for my rehearsals. George liked to watch me when I worked on a dance. He would often jump up from the piano to demonstrate an idea for a step, or an extra twist to something I was already experimenting with.

I should have mentioned before that during final rehearsals of the "Fascinating Rhythm" number, just before we were ready to leave for the opening in Philadelphia, Adele and I were stuck for an exit step. We had the routine set but needed a climax wow step to get us off. For days I couldn't find one. Neither could dance director Sammy Lee.

George happened to drop by and I asked him to look at the routine. He went to the piano. Ukulele Ike was doing his stuff with the "Lamb Chop," as he called it.

We went all through the thing, reaching the last step before the proposed exit and George said, "Now travel—travel with that one."

I stopped to ask what he meant and he jumped up from the piano and demonstrated what he visualized. He wanted us to continue doing the last step, which started center stage, and sustain it as we traveled to the side, continuing until we were out of sight off stage.

The step was a complicated precision rhythm thing in which we kicked out simultaneously as we crossed back and forth in front of each other with arm pulls and heads back. There was a lot going on, and when George suggested traveling, we didn't think it was possible.

It was the perfect answer to our problem, however, this suggestion by hoofer Gershwin, and it turned out to be a knockout applause puller. Or, as they'd say way back in 1958, "a gasser."

George threw me a couple for my solo routine, too. I liked to watch him dance. It made me laugh.

It was at these rehearsals that we decided to get a Charleston number in the show for London. George went to work on it with Ira and we had the number lined up to try out in New York before leaving for the short road tour.

I also dropped the solo in one matinee, and felt like kicking myself for not having thought of it long before. The show was considerably strengthened by the addition of these two numbers. "I'd Rather Charleston" was one of Ira's best comic ideas suited to Adele.

We were glad to have this material ready for the London opening. The time was closing in on us; we'd actually be on our way back over there in a few months.

Having weathered the hot New York summer at the Liberty without any real cooling system in the theatre, we ran on into the fall season, which added up to almost a year. Oh, they had some sort of thing, a few cakes of ice in a bucket with a fan blowing over them or something hidden off in a corner, but as I recall it, it didn't do much good, and the heat was almost unbearable. Our run under those conditions was commendable.

We checked out of New York the middle of September, 1925, and headed for the short road tour Alex and Vinton had arranged covering about ten major cities.

That tour was a good one. It's always fun moving around with a hit show.

Among other incidents, we had a distinguished visitor along

with us for quite a while. We didn't know how distinguished he was, however, at the time. He traveled with the company for several weeks through Cleveland, Detroit, and thereabouts, seemingly interested in one of the girls in the show.

Adele said to me, "Who is that guy anyway? I can't figure him out."

Next day she came to me. "They say he's a royal Russian prince. Is he kidding?"

We all liked him for his personality and sense of humor. For the few weeks he was around we rather counted him in as one of the company and nobody discussed his royal heritage, authentic or otherwise.

When he left he gave some of us presents. I was one of the lucky ones—mine was a Dunhill pipe.

A few weeks later, Adele brought me a newspaper headline. She said, "Look—they're giving Mike a rough time."

I read the headline, which said all kinds of things about "Prince Romanoff" and his run-ins with the immigration authorities. This went on for years it seemed, but Mike has emerged as one of the most popular men in America today, with one of the best-known restaurants in the world, in Beverly Hills. Mike and I enjoy reminiscing about his days touring with *Lady, Be Good!* One of his favorite remarks:

"And to think they had the audacity to doubt my authenticity."

Mr. and Mrs. Fred Astaire in 1933

Phyllis with Freddie, Jr., in 1939

Ava at the age of three

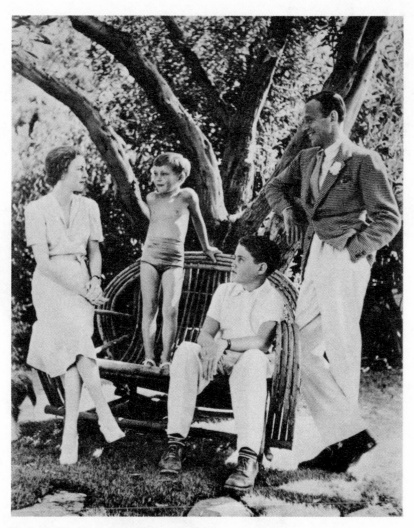

Fred, Phyllis, Fred, Jr., and Peter in 1940

Astaire and George Gershwin
in 1937

With Ginger Rogers and Irving
Berlin in 1935

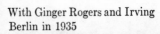

Fred Astaire and Ginger Rogers in *Flying Down to Rio* in 1933

In *Swing Time* in 1936

"Top Hat" sequence from *Blue Skies*

Dancing for U.S. soldiers at Versailles in 1944

In *The Story of Vernon and Irene Castle*, 1939

Fred Astaire and Joan Crawford in *Dancing Lady*, 1933

With Rita Hayworth in *You'll Never Get Rich*, 1941

Chapter 13 Horses

We sailed on the *Majestic*, January 16, 1926, for a short holiday in Paris. It was exhilarating seeing the many shows and cabarets there, including Chevalier and the Dolly Sisters again in a big bright new revue, before going to London where we were due March 1 for the next phase of *Lady, Be Good!* Adele spent much time at Jenny the dressmaker's who supplied all of her clothes for the show.

We were of course keyed up about this return to London. Billy Kent was taking over the Catlett role, Buddy Lee doing Ukulele Ike's part. Jacques Fray and Mario Braggiotti on the two pianos replaced Ohman and Arden, who were unable to make the trip.

On arriving in London we settled down at the Carlton Hotel. The press was kind and hospitable, for which we were grateful.

Being assigned to the old Empire Theatre in Leicester Square pleased us. It was a landmark of much tradition. In size and importance, it would be an asset to our show, which had proved to be of larger scope than the last one, *Stop Flirting*. Sir Alfred had it freshly renovated for this occasion.

We were booked at the new Empire in Liverpool for the tryout, to open March 29. That was an enormous theatre, a modern

137

movie palace. We wondered how our show would play in such a place. It seemed to us more like the Roxy in New York than a setting for musical comedy. At any rate, we opened to a warm reception. Billy Kent registered solidly. *Lady, Be Good!* looked okay for England.

We moved in to London after two weeks in Liverpool, hopeful but anxious. Much fuss was being made about the show's success out of town.

The final dress rehearsal in London went all right in its way as we ran straight through for size and routine. No laughs—no applause, nothing. The theatre auditorium was black and empty —without an audience except for Aarons and Freedley, Sir Alfred and those connected with the show—possibly a few ushers. It was a relief to get it over with. Dress rehearsals were always torture.

I often think of what Mother said to me after that one. She had been watching from a box, and came backstage, where I bumped into her.

"Hello, Ma—how was it?" I said, and started to go. She looked glum.

"Sonny—I wish I could say that I thought it was good but I can't. It was awful."

I did a double back-flip triple take and asked her, "What— what do you mean—what was the matter with it?" She said, "I don't know but it was just awful, that's all—and you looked so cross and your forehead was wrinkled and—"

I interrupted: "Now listen, Mother—this was only a dress rehearsal, you know, so we could get our bearings. I've got an awful lot to think about at these things." She insisted that it was awful and I tried again to ease her mind as well as my own.

"Ma—look—remember we've been doing this show over a year now—it's been good every place we've tried it—didn't you like it in New York?" Oh, yes, of course she liked it in New York. "Didn't you like it in Liverpool last week?" Oh, yes, she loved it in Liverpool last week, but it was awful tonight. Period.

There was nothing I could do about it except to say, "Mother, tomorrow night I promise I won't be cross and I won't wrinkle my forehead—will that do it?"

She stuck to her guns: "That would help."

There was the dear old pep talk by none other than Vinton Freedley, who was an expert at it, and we were allowed to go home early, about ten-thirty.

The Gallery First Nighters sent their representative around to see us before the show. He said, "We hear the show is good and we hope we'll like it."

I replied, "Yes, sir—believe me—*we too* hope *you* will like it."

Among the telegrams and cables received, one addressed to Adele read:

LOVE TO YOU AND FREDDY

C. B. D.

The opening night seemed too good to be true—our fondest hopes realized.

The Gallery First Nighters were at the stage door afterward and we had a happy reunion with Sophie and Harry, et al.

All through that period from 1923 to 1926 we were blessed with a winning way, so to speak. Good things happened fluidly.

Hubert Griffith, *Evening Standard:*

It is good from time to time there should be musical comedies like "Lady Be Good" at the Empire last night with one artist in them like Miss Adele Astaire (and these are very rare indeed) if only to remind us once again how intelligence and vitality are qualities in the world before which all other qualities burn—the Astaires would save any musical comedy—Miss Adele Astaire is, I think the most attractive thing on any stage—she dances with an intelligence, with a gaiety, with a grace and delight—she is a comedienne in her toes and in her fingertips and in every line of a vivid and lovely little body—

Daily Sketch:

I prophesy a year's run for "Lady Be Good" at the Empire in spite of the fact that the book is one of the weakest, even for a musical comedy, that I can remember. Fred and Adele Astaire have only to appear and everybody is blissfully happy. . . . Their dancing was uproarious. Fred's Half of It Dearie Blues solo dance was one of the biggest things of the night. . . . I hope they will stay a long time. I extend the heartiest welcome to William Kent.

That was that, and we were now able to settle again into a swingin' London season. The first step was suggested by Adele: "Say, how about getting that Rolls-Royce we won at the Trocadero last year—remember that?"

I told her I was all for it and suggested rather than the big Phantom model we should try the small one called the "Twenty" (Baby Rolls). I found one, and a beauty it was, too. Black, limousine type, requiring a chauffeur, really, so we got him, too. From then on all sorts of things happened. Some exhilarating, some not so pleasant.

Business was tremendous and, as I forgot to mention, "The libraries had bought a large block of stalls far into the future." Actually, they had bought out the whole orchestra floor for six months, so it was jolly all around.

After a few weeks of smooth going with the show, cheers, white ties and diamonds, our clever comedian, Billy Kent, who scored an unmistakable hit, failed to show up one night. An unprepared understudy was hurried into the role. This was a horrible blow. It was even worse than that because dear Billy didn't show up for three days. Nobody knew where he was.

We carried on all right but it was difficult. Billy showed up finally, most apologetic, explaining that he got loaded and just found himself out in the country someplace. He confided to us that he was so happy about his success and loved London so much that he went off the wagon.

One day we had a phone call from Liz. She had arrived in London and was staying with Edwina Mountbatten, doing some hunting or horse jazz of some kind. Jimmy was to arrive soon. Things were going to start jumping, I thought.

One night, after the show, I took Liz to the Kit Kat Club. Afterward, I dropped her off where she was staying and on my way home told the chauffeur I'd like to drive. It was that little Twenty Rolls.

As we entered Grosvenor Square, a small sports car zoomed in and went around to the left as I took the right. He was flying, and went all around the square. Suddenly he loomed up headed straight for me. I didn't know what to do to avoid him, became confused driving on the left-hand side of the street, veered over to the right and before I knew it we had collided. He ripped the entire left side of my car. I felt a little sick.

A young, bejeweled lady in evening gown got out of his car and fled.

The next thing I knew I was standing face to face with the young man in full evening dress. He said: "I'm frightfully sorry, we seem to have bashed into each other."

I agreed with him. He apologized and I apologized. All during this my eyes were glued to his ruby-and-diamond studs and waistcoat buttons. They were the best-looking ones I had ever seen. We decided that the crash was all rather minor. Said cheerios and pip pips and that sort of thing and went on our respective ways.

As I got into my poor little sideswiped Rolls, I asked my man to take the wheel and we limped under our own power to the garage. All this time I was haunted by those ruby and diamond waistcoat buttons.

Next morning I was up early to break the news to Delly that we had no Rolls for a few days. After which I was on my way to Cartier's to blow myself to some ruby-and-diamond studs and waistcoat buttons.

We had many visitors backstage at the Empire. One evening I met Jack Leach, a well-known jockey. He was a nice guy, I thought, and he said to me, having just seen the show, "You're a good mover," which in turf jargon is a compliment. If a horse is a "good mover," he has a good chance of being able to run. That amused me. We became good friends. His father, Felix Leach, was one of the best known of Newmarket's famed horsemen. Jack had two brothers—Chubb, also a jock, and Felix, Jr., a trainer.

When he found that I was interested in racing, he asked me to go to some race meetings with him. That I did frequently, and before long I knew nearly every jock and trainer in England.

All the "racing swine," as Jack referred to us, used to meet in the bar at the Piccadilly Hotel before taking off for the tracks near London. Steve Donoghue, Freddy Fox, Gordon Richards, Brownie Carslake, Bobby Jones, George Duller, George Archibald, Harry Wragg, Georgie Jellis, Joe Childs, Freddie Winter and Charlie Smirke were some of the lads riding then. We had a million laughs and I won a few bets. Very few.

I soon got to the point with Jack about my buying a horse and found out what expense it would incur. Without getting in too deep, I wanted to own a fairly decent one. He knew a fellow who wanted to sell one. Well, now, wasn't that odd?

Sidney Beer, prominent owner of Diomedes, the outstanding sprinter of his time, had an animal named Dolomite that wasn't good enough for the better-class races but would win in cheaper company, he thought. I bought a half interest in the horse for £500. Liz went with me to Brighton to see the animal run—my first runner. I was now an owner. It didn't do so well. Dolomite never won for me but I sold him for double what he cost to a foreign buyer.

I also had a half interest with Sidney in another horse, Social Evening, that did win several races, unimportant ones. Now, I really went for the game. There's nothing like a winner of your own to give you that certain feeling. I then bought a few more and bred one by acquiring a half interest in a mare with Jack.

I won my share of races—but was never present to see a horse of mine win. It always happened on a matinee day when I had to work. Jack's brother Felix trained for me, Jack rode for me, and so did little brother Chubb. I also had Harry Wragg on a few. My racing education was being well handled. I found it fascinating. And it was always a source of much delight to my man George Griffin.

Among the less enjoyable occurrences during this run was the general strike. It was a serious situation for some weeks—no transportation in or out of town except by privately owned vehicles. Fortunately we had such a big advance sale at our theatre through ticket brokers that we were able to weather the storm, and the people did get there. Many were transients from hotels.

The Prince of Wales saw the show a number of times and usually brought a party with him.

About the fourth visit, word went around that a royal party was in front again and the usual excitement prevailed. This time it was the Prince of Wales, the Duke of York and Prince George.

Between the acts I was in my dressing room relaxing, cooling out in a dressing gown, when my valet, who had been standing guard outside the door, suddenly poked his head in.

"They're 'ere, sir," said George.

" 'oo's 'ere?" I replied, rather absent-mindedly.

"The princes, sir—the 'ole lot of 'em, sir."

I somehow hadn't realized that they might come back, and it took me by surprise. I didn't want to be in too casual a get-up for this visit and said, "I'd better get dressed, George." Just then he pushed the door open, and in walked the three brothers. This was the first time the Duke of York had come backstage and I'll admit I was a little nervous.

I quickly jumped out of my chair and apologized for my

appearance. The Duke remarked that ours was a good show, and as he glanced around the room he noticed about a dozen pairs of my dancing shoes I had on the wall, on hooks. He asked me why I hung them up like that, and I explained that I didn't want to pick one of them up off the floor one day and have a mouse jump out on me. I said I couldn't trust some of the older theatres, such as the Empire.

This brought a laugh and he remarked, "I can't say I blame you."

Another thing that drew his attention was the fact that all my trousers had their own separate suspenders attached ready to use. There were five or six pairs in view, laid out by my George. The Duke remarked:

"I say, that's a damn good idea. I must have my man do that instead of changing the blasted things from one pair to another."

The other two brothers had a good laugh at this and so did I.

We talked about ten minutes, covering various subjects, mostly concerning dancing and the theatre, and how I kept fit. The Duke told me of the forthcoming trip to Australia and New Zealand planned for himself and the Duchess.

They heard the call boy shouting, "Second act, please," and left, asking, "I wonder if we could stop by Adele's room for a moment?"

I said, "Please do," and thanked them for coming back.

Prince George often stopped in for an hour or so to pass an evening. One night he turned up with a package of indoor fireworks he had picked up someplace and started setting them off in my dressing room between acts. They were supposed to be harmless but one must have gotten in by mistake. It made a hell of a noise and filled my dressing room with smoke. This brought the fireman, on permanent duty at the theatre, rushing in.

When he saw P. G. standing there, his jaw fell and he muttered, "I say—I say—sir—what happened?"

P. G. answered: "Oh—nothing—nothing at all—Mr. Astaire has been smoking too much."

One of my favorite memories of Prince George was when he casually mentioned one day, "I'm fed up with things going on at Buck House [Buckingham Palace]. Any time they don't know what to do with an old piece of furniture they wish it on me. My mother puts all the ugly old chairs and tables in my room. My place looks like an old lumber yard."

The Royal Family was extremely kind to us. Adele received this note from the Duchess of York, referring to an invitation to come and "see the baby" (Elizabeth, the present Queen).

Some months afterward the Duke and Duchess of York embarked on that official visit to Australia. We sent a box of roses to their ship.

Several weeks later the following letter arrived from the Duke:

> H.M.S "Renown"
> *at sea*
>
> *January 10th 1927*
>
> My dear Adele,
>
> Thank you all three so much for the lovely roses we found on board on our arrival. It was so kind of you to have thought of us. The roses are still on our table at the moment.
>
> The band played "Lady be Good" last night which made us think of you all good luck to you & dont forget to come back quick with your new show as London is never the same when you are not there
>
> Yours very sincerely
> Albert

On August 9, 1926, we were honored by the presence of Their Majesties King George V and Queen Mary at the Empire—one of their infrequent appearances at a theatre. Newspapers commented: "The King and Queen watched the performance from the Royal Box, evincing interest and enjoyment."

The audience that night was noticeably less demonstrative than usual. A quaint, respectful awareness of Their Majesties' presence was unquestionably felt. A special souvenir program had been prepared. It was twice the size of the regular one with a handsome cover printed in gold lettering and a large royal crest in the center.

The show went rolling on.

Our previous visit to England had brought us the experience of "Boat Race Night." This time we caught "Rugger Night." Both of these are events never to be forgotten.

The lads from Oxford and Cambridge take over the town and go on a ragging spree.

They pick a show to descend upon with the winning or losing team, or both. In this instance it was our show so honored. The choice is made by this group well in advance, so they have it all to themselves and their girl friends. It is something!

They talk most of the dialogue with you, being familiar with it from previous visits. They sing all the songs and in some instances have been known to come up on the stage and get into the act. But they didn't do that with us. One lad was hanging out of the upper left-hand box dropping those big pennies on the timpani which were directly below. He'd wait for some nice open spot in the dialogue and drop one, at a key moment. It was very amusing and brought roars from the audience.

The show goes out the window that night. The only thing to do is to play along with the boys and they treat you fine. However, it's a nerve-racking thing to go through and leaves you rather groggy when it's over.

We had one more interesting episode with our comedian Billy Kent. His pretty wife saw a lion cub somewhere and just had to have it. So Billy bought it for her. It was a mighty cute little fellow and we all enjoyed petting it at first.

After about two months, I thought it had grown considerably and I remarked to Billy about the possibility of its turning savage. He said, "Oh, there's no chance of that, we have it sleeping on the bed every night; it's quieter than a cat."

Well, one night it wasn't so quiet. The lion got restless and started walking around all over the bed, stepping on the faces of Mr. and Mrs. Kent. This awakened Billy. He pushed the lion off.

Little lion didn't like this effrontery and attacked Billy, but right now. As Billy explained it to me, "I couldn't get rid of him—he kept scratching at my face and nearly tore my pajamas off, so I got mad and picked him up and threw him out the window. Yeah, right through that big bay window of our bedroom, and he landed three floors below in a crash of glass."

The lion was found two days later wandering around Hyde Park. It became a member of the zoo.

Billy was an awful sight. One mass of red claw marks all over his face. He worked, however, considerably covered by bandages for a few days.

After about six months we were told that the Empire Theatre had been sold and arrangements for its demolition had been made. An enormous new cinema theatre was to be put up in its place. A date was set for the closing of the show in London. It was to be Saturday, January 22, 1927. Immediately this news got out there was a scramble to obtain seats for the last night.

We still had several months to run, however, and the whirl continued.

Jock Whitney arrived to become a student at Oxford in a follow-up course after his graduation from Yale. Jimmy Altemus also dropped over on a trip and we got together a lot.

Jock was fresh with news and demonstrations of a new dance, the Black Bottom. He would go into it at the drop of a hat.

The next few months rolled by quickly. The final days of the old Empire were being mourned by the whole country, it seemed. Everybody had to get to that last performance. When the fateful day finally arrived, I received a telephone call about ten o'clock in the morning which took me by surprise. I picked up the receiver and a rather officious voice at the other end spoke:

"Mr. Astaire?"

"Yes."

"Just a moment, sir, the Prince of Wales would like to speak to you."

I was sure it was Jimmy or somebody with a gag on me, because I had never had a phone call from H.R.H. before and I was about to say, "Tell him I'm out," when I heard a sort of click on the other end of the wire followed by, "Hello—Astaire? This is the Prince of Wales speaking."

I answered, "Oh, yes, hello, sir," as I recognized his voice. The

Prince continued, "I wonder if you could do me a favor and get me a box for your show tonight? I have a party and I can't get any tickets."

I replied, "Well, if you can't get them, sir, I don't know who can, but I'll try—there must be some way."

He said, "I hope so. You know, I just got back to London. We do want to see your last night and the farewell to the Empire."

I told him I would let him know as soon as possible.

He said he hoped to see us after the show.

I got Sir Alfred on the phone immediately and told him the situation. He explained that it wasn't easy to ask someone to relinquish seats reserved months in advance for this unique event. However, he would ask Solly Joel to give up his box to the Prince.

That was the way it worked out.

H.R.H. was there with his party as planned. People told me they saw him in the back of the box dancing to some of the familiar tunes as the show was in progress.

Everyone in the theatre was in a gay mood that night.

Adeline Genee, the great Danish ballet star, was in another box. This was the lady who had inspired us as children. The Empire had been the scene of some of her former triumphs. During the speeches at the show's conclusion, I paid tribute to her. She responded with a bow.

All during the performance there were friendly interruptions from habitués of the old theatre. They would shout or sing. Some of the ancient wags got carried away. One very loud voice suddenly bellowed: "Why have we got to stand this American stuff all the while? Surely we can have some English songs and artists on the last night of the Empire."

The poor man was shouted down: "Throw him out—throw him out!"

Another man with a monocle kept begging the ushers to "Chuck me out once more please. I haven't been chucked out of here for twenty years now—please—here's a couple of quid."

But nobody was chucked out that night. It was all in fun.

After the speeches and post-mortems, and after the curtain had dropped for the last time, there was a rush of people backstage, including many strangers in search of souvenirs, such as door knobs and other fixtures.

The Prince of Wales came back and organized an impromptu supper party. He asked Jock and Jimmy and all of our visitors, including Gordon Selfridge, Sir Alfred and Lady Butt, my mother and others, to join him and his friends at St. James's Palace, which was his residence at the time. He quickly engaged a small band and the thing was in progress about an hour later.

The Prince kept asking, "Is this party any good?" We all certainly thought so. I told him that Jock was an expert at the new Black Bottom and that I might be able to induce him to give a little exhibition. The Prince was very much interested in this so I jumped out on the floor to start the action. I ad libbed a few steps—got Jimmy out with me, and the two of us fooled around. I whispered to Jimmy that we had to get J. H. out there with his Black Bottom. This was all Jimmy needed. He stepped forward and announced, "We will now have an exhibition of a new dance, the Black Bottom, by that sensational expert from the U.S.A., Mr. J. H. Whitney."

Cheers—cheers—more of 'em, and before anyone had a chance to ask J. H. a second time, he was out there doing his stuff. That tremendous, well-distributed poundage was rocking the royal joint, so to speak. Each time Jock would jump up in the air and come down with both feet in the key step, his unbounded enthusiasm and unrestrained force bent the palace floor, and in one outstanding burst of terpsichorean inspiration our boy slipped and landed on his face.

After all he was never exactly comparable to a Singer's Midget, so something had to give. Nothing could stop Jock. The beads of perspiration were flying by now, and when he finally stopped, the cheers and applause deafened the sedate atmosphere of St. James's Palace.

The party went on until 4 A.M.

After a few days' rest we left London for a limited tour of the provinces, visiting Wales and Scotland once more, and a few of the larger English cities. Our return to the States was set for some time in June of that year, 1927.

The tour was a pleasant one. We were free of mind and just about ready to turn over the page on *Lady, Be Good!*

Adele said to me, "You know, I've had enough of this show. I love it and all that, but I'm glad we're finishing."

We had already signed with Alex and Vinton for another which was being written.

A few days before ending the tour a letter arrived from Alex with word about the new show, temporarily titled *Smarty*. The Gershwins were doing the score and that was all we had to know—no story ready as yet but we had faith in Alex and Vint. Actually, we were never asked to do anything we didn't approve of.

Adele and I never played opposite each other, romantically, after *Stop Flirting*. We avoided these stories when we became well known as real brother and sister.

Lady, Be Good! was a brother-and-sister tale and we didn't want to follow that up with another one. We had discussed it with Alex and Vint, and finally came around to having an idea written up whereby I would be the legal guardian of three girls, one, of course, being Adele. Her romance would concern another fellow. This seemed to be a good idea, but we had no thought about what would happen from there on. Anyway, we were satisfied with the plans so far and the fact that something was under way to follow *Lady B*. Show business is like that. No matter what the present job is, you're always thinking in the back of your mind about the next one.

Chapter 14 *Funny Face*

After our long run in London and the provinces, the boat trip home was pleasant. It helped us to get unwound. We brought the Baby Rolls with us. For a while it was the only one in New York.

The latest reports concerning the writing and plans for *Smarty* were interesting. We were particularly happy that Bob Benchley was to collaborate with Fred Thompson on the book and that we were to open a brand-new theatre on Fifty-second Street just west of Broadway. This theatre, not quite completed, was to be named the Alvin, suggested by the first syllables of Alex's and Vinton's names.

There was nothing for us to do until about September, when rehearsals were scheduled to begin.

Smarty turned out to be one of those things that wouldn't work—even at rehearsals. Bobby Connolly was our dance director and the numbers were coming along well but the script was a problem.

We took off reluctantly for Philadelphia to open at the Shubert Theatre. The idea of opening anywhere with that mess was not pleasant.

Dress rehearsal was so bad and disjointed (even the scenery changes wouldn't function) that Vinton Freedley called everybody to the footlights at its conclusion and announced: "We don't see how it will be possible to open tomorrow night with the show as ragged as this. Now I know it'll be tough, but I am going to ask you to run through the whole thing again without stopping, otherwise we'll have to postpone the opening."

It was about 1:30 A.M and this meant we'd get out about 4:30. We agreed, of course—there was no choice.

Opening night was still ragged and much too long. The numbers went well but the comedy missed. Things were not good. This was the first time in almost five years that Delly and I had run into such a snag, and we were worried. What could be done?

We didn't see Alex until after the show. When he finally came back he was not in too bad a frame of mind, much to our surprise. He said: "I know what's wrong with this thing. I knew after watching those two dress rehearsals last night. You're going to stay out on the road a few extra weeks while we rewrite about two-thirds of it."

People who came over from New York were not optimistic about our chances. The Philadelphia press agreed that much revamping would be necessary before attempting New York. Ticket brokers would not make a deal until further judgment.

All through that Philadelphia run of two weeks we were awful. No business. It was agony. Bob Benchley resigned his task of rewriting on account of other commitments.

Bob's remark after seeing the show the first night went the rounds: "Gosh, how can I criticize other people's shows from now on?" Paul Gerard Smith came in on the rewrite job.

Ford's Theatre, Washington, was the next stop and things were really confused there. The show was being rewritten. We were playing one version while rehearsing another. The first sign of encouragement came when Victor Moore joined us, but business was bad and we couldn't tell how the changes were working out because there was never enough of an audience to give us a reaction.

We went to Wilmington for three days, the last stop before New York, with a new title, *Funny Face*. Things went all right in Wilmington, the show running smoothly, with no more alterations to make. It seemed better, but we didn't know.

Good News had just opened in New York to smash notices and that made us certain we were doomed by comparison.

I told Adele, "I wish I could get hit by a taxi, or the scenery would burn up or something so we wouldn't have to go into New York."

At one of our little gloom sessions with our helpers, Walter and Louise, I blew my top. This was the last evening in Wilmington just before the final show there. I sounded off.

"I hate flops—and this is one. We might as well face it, this damn turkey hasn't got a prayer. I'm sick of this racket anyway."

Walter chimed in pacifyingly: "Now, Mr. Fred, you mustn't carry on like that—you know Miss Adele and you have been ridin' pretty smooth these past few years. You can't expect everything to be a hit."

"The hell you can't," I said. "We've worked ten times harder on this thing than any hit so far, and what have we got? I tell you, man, I's got de miseries."

Louise interrupted: "Mr. Fred, please now . . ." Adele interrupted Louise: "Oh, let him moan. He loves it. This is the first chance he's had for years. Go ahead, Minnie! You know, sometimes you remind me of William Jennings Bryan."

That one made me snicker against my wishes but I came back with, "All right, all right, but I tell you I'm sick of this stuff and if we run into any more of it, I'm going in the horse business."

That ended the meeting.

Funny Face opened in New York the following Tuesday night and was a smash hit. The over-all something was there. What a pleasant surprise!

Having gone through such a series of mishaps and revisions

on the road, we simply didn't know what we had. Adele sang
" 'S Wonderful" with Allen Kearns; I did "High Hat" with an
all-male chorus, also "My One and Only" with lovely Gertrude
MacDonald. Betty Compton had a good specialty dance. Adele
and I did "The Babbitt and the Bromide" with the old run-
around once more. We discovered we had many high spots both
in Victor Moore's and Billy Kent's comedy.

The show had a long run.

Adele and her beaus were a source of worry to her as well as to
me, one of them in particular. She told me she was afraid of him.
Anyway, she became engaged and the papers carried the announcement. He hung around all through that run but nothing
came of it. Adele got rid of him as she did a good many others.

On the second night after the show's opening, Delly was not in
the theatre at her usual time.

She strolled in casually at eight twenty-five a little woozy,
having been to a cocktail party. I was surprised because she never
drank anything to speak of. We were to go on in twelve minutes
with a tricky song and dance. It usually took her at least forty-
five minutes to get ready. Minnie didn't moan this time. He
blew up.

Out front the audience was buzzing with interest about this
new hit and here we were, one of us decidedly unsteady. I pushed
Adele into her room and said, "Go on now, hurry up; I'll tell 'em
to hold the curtain five minutes."

I put some smelling salts under her nose and she made a
horrible face, but we got out on that stage. The dialogue leading
into the first number, "Funny Face," went along all right. I sang
most of the song, pulling her around in a toy wagon so there was
no serious trouble up to that point. But when we started to dance
—oh, brother; or rather, in this instance, oh, sister!

I faked as best I could, trying to make it look like part of
the routine until the exit step, which was pretty close to the footlights, when I grabbed her once to keep her from going over. After

we finally made the exit there was a rather puzzled audience out front and a rather puzzled Delly backstage. She was dazed and I thought quickly that something had to be done, so I gave her a sharp slap on each cheek and said, "Come on now, take a bow and smile." She did her best.

When we got off stage, she started to cry, "You hit me—you hit me." I grabbed her arm and steered her back to her room. "Yes, I know, I know—tell me about it later—now sober up, will you, we've got a whole show to do yet and there's a hell of a house out there."

Adele's next appearance was about twenty minutes later and I signaled her maid to do something about it as I closed the door and ran to get back on stage.

Next time I saw her she had recovered her equilibrium and in very dignified tones said, "You hit me." I answered, "I know, but you were impossible—something had to be done—forget it— I'll give you twenty bucks tomorrow."

Things went all right from then on and after the show I told her I was sorry I had to be such a "heavy." She said, "Where's my twenty bucks?"

All of us in the company were intrigued by a young lady named "Sugar" Jordan, who had a small part in the show. She was assigned the role of understudy to Adele, but never had an opportunity to play the part.

A few years later she became a movie star, Dorothy Jordan, and the wife of Merian Cooper.

Al Newman was our music director and the orchestra was an exceptionally good one, with Ohman and Arden again predominant. That was before many of the famous names in swing bands had been established. Ours was not a jazz outfit in the pit but Al gathered together quite a group of up-and-coming boys to be sure of capturing the Gershwin touch.

Jimmy Walker came to the show a number of times. The

Mayor was a friend of Alex Aarons. I had a telephone call from him quite late one night which surprised me because I barely knew him at the time.

He said, "I saw Adele at a party last night. She's terrific. Fred, your sister's got a boy friend. You're going to be seeing a lot of me around from now on."

I asked Adele about it next day. She laughed and said, "Hm—that's what he thinks." She told me she had been dancing with him at the party and that they had a lot of fun clowning around, but she couldn't understand why he should call me.

Walter Wanger invited us to make a screen test for him. He was with Paramount at the time.

We made the test and thought we looked awful. Walter felt differently about it, however, and for a time we were on the verge of signing to do *Funny Face* on the screen. The deal never materialized, for some reason or other.

Flo Ziegfeld talked to us about a show for the following season. We toyed with the idea for a while but decided it would be foolish not to go to London with *Funny Face*. Besides, Alex had already sailed to arrange the dates for the fall of 1928. We told Mr. Ziegfeld we would be available, probably in 1929, and hoped he would ask us again.

I didn't tell Alex about this meeting with Ziegfeld. He heard about it when he returned to America and hit the ceiling.

I explained that nothing had been definitely set and that I thought it might enhance our value to do a Ziegfeld show. Then we could come back to our old firm and everybody would benefit by it. He finally cooled down.

Alex said, "You may be right—but I think you're sticking your neck out by going with Ziegfeld. He won't know what to do with you. Anyway this troupe opens in London in October at the Prince's Theatre."

Funny Face closed its New York run in a midsummer heat wave and we were scheduled to sail after a few weeks' holiday at home.

One unfortunate day capped the season's climax. July 8, to be exact, Adele was seriously burned in a motor boat accident.

She had gone to Billy Leeds' country place on Long Island to spend the day. His new speed boat *Fan Tail* caught fire while still tied at the pier. Adele was saved by Billy's quick thinking. He grabbed her and put her ashore, untied the boat and pushed it out into clear water, where it exploded a few seconds later.

At about the same time, I turned over in a car while on my way to East Hampton. "Sis" Atwell was driving and we were on our way to spend the weekend with Sherman Jenney and his family. Neither of us was hurt.

Delly, badly burned, remained in the hospital for many weeks. This accident made it necessary to postpone the opening abroad.

Funny Face went over big in London. We had the wonderful Leslie Henson in the Billy Kent role but, of course, Leslie changed it a lot to suit his individual style. Sid Howard played the Victor Moore part. Rita Page, Renee Gadd and Bernard Clifton were also prominent in the cast. We were very pleased to feel that our slate was clean in England, all three shows having scored. Lee Ephraim was associated with Sir Alfred Butt on this one.

After the first week we ran into a little trouble, however. George called me at the hotel on the Monday morning with this message: "I don't think there's much use you coming to the theatre tonight, sir—the 'ole neighbor'ood's blown up."

Being about half awake, I didn't quite get this strange message and I asked: "George, once more, please—why can't I come to work tonight?"

"It's the city gas pipes, sir. One of the workers was looking for a leak with a lighted match, and all the streets around the theatre blew up."

I said, "Well, what happened to the chap with the lighted match?"

"Oh, 'e nearly did 'imself in, sir," said George.

Here we were, sold out for weeks in advance and the people could not reach the theatre, the streets being impassable in the immediate vicinity.

We were forced to close down for several days while temporary repairs could make it possible for us to continue. When we did reopen, it was still difficult to reach the theatre. People were obliged to get out of their cars a block off and approach on foot the rest of the way. There were makeshift repairs with temporary fences and holes covered over with boards.

It was an extraordinary sight to see many dignified evening-gowned ladies being helped over these obstacles by their top-hatted escorts.

In our curtain speeches during this time we thanked the audiences for being with us under such unprecedented and inconvenient conditions. As Leslie Henson put it, "Coming to see *Funny Face* right now is tougher than riding in the Grand National."

George and Julie Murphy were appearing in the London company of *Good News*. We spent many evenings together.

The usual gaiety prevailed throughout this London season but our coming association with Flo Ziegfeld held a predominant place in our minds. Anticipation was heightened upon receipt of this cable:

DEAR FRED AND ADELE: I HAVE WONDERFUL IDEA FOR YOU CO-STAR-RING WITH MARILYN MILLER—

FLO ZIEGFELD

This seemed like the big one we were looking for.

Adele's fiancé was still in evidence but she kept postponing her marriage so I finally asked her for the lowdown on the situation. She assured me that she was not going to marry the fellow.

Closing night of *Funny Face* called for a celebration and many visitors crowded into Adele's dressing room suite. Among them Lord Charles Cavendish, who was with Prince Aly Khan. This was Cavendish's first introduction to Adele.

I stayed around London for a few weeks after that. Adele went to Paris and we arranged to meet on the S.S. *Homeric*.

I sailed for home, Ziegfeld-bound, and Delly joined the ship at Cherbourg as planned. She told me that Charlie Cavendish spent the weekend in Paris and that she had seen him a lot. She said, "He's awfully nice and he's coming to New York this winter on business."

We arrived in New York to find there was already a good deal of interest about the coming Ziegfeld show for Marilyn Miller and the Astaires. Marilyn was in Hollywood making a picture at the time.

This wire awaited us:

DEAR FRED AND ADELE: FLO IS ON HIS WAY TO NEW YORK. I AM LEAVING NEXT WEEK. THINK WE HAVE A GREAT BOOK. LOVE.

MARILYN

We had a talk with Alex and Vinton. It was all understood and on completely friendly terms, ending our business relationship for the time being.

Ziegfeld arrived a few days later aglow with plans and hopes for the show tentatively titled *Tom, Dick and Harry*. He said that he didn't see how it could miss. An original idea which he had bought from Noel Coward was written out by Louis Bromfield as a special favor. William Anthony McGuire was doing the script now and it would be ready very soon. Ziggy talked about many names in connection with the show. Sammy Lee was mentioned for the choreography, also Seymour Felix, and finally our old friend Ned Wayburn. There was much indecision.

Without going into too many details about this experience, I must say that it was a devastating one for everybody concerned. Nothing seemed right from the start, although Vincent Youmans' song, "Time on My Hands," stood out. Mr. Z. wanted some outside songs interpolated. The title of the show was changed to *Smiles*.

We staggered to Boston for the tryout, and opened at the Colonial on the evening of October 28, 1930. It was a shambles.

The following headline from the Boston *Evening Transcript* explains best the result of that opening:

FOR SMILES

MORE QUALITY

LESS QUANTITY

We stayed an extra week in Boston to work on the show. There were revisions of all sorts. Ring Lardner was called upon to rewrite some of the lyrics. A song by Walter Donaldson, "You're Driving Me Crazy," was added. Adele and Eddie Foy, Jr., did that one. I was given an extra number with Marilyn Miller. There were some high spots for entertainment values but it seemed nothing could be done about the complicated story involving a Salvation Army girl in love with a playboy. Rather a throwback to *The Belle of New York*, a big success of the early 1900's.

Flo stayed in Boston with us most of the time, trying his best to save everyone from disaster.

We had been confined indoors so much on account of rehearsals as well as by nightly appearances and occasional matinees that the strain was beginning to get us all down. Marilyn said to me one night: "Let's take a ride someplace. Mecca, you, Adele and I, just the four of us, after the show tonight. Let's escape and get some fresh air." Mecca Graham, one of the boys in the cast, was Marilyn's close and devoted friend.

It was a fine idea and we all set out after the performance.

We had been singing, joking and gagging as best we could for about half an hour when we reached the bridge crossing over the Charles River toward Cambridge. I asked the driver to stop in the middle: I wanted to look over the side down into the water. So Marilyn and I got out while Adele and Mecca decided they were too tired to be bothered moving. Marilyn and I were leaning on the railing talking some kind of nonsense for a few minutes

when a car drove up and the next thing I knew a hand grabbed me
from behind by my coat collar. I looked around and there were
two enormous policemen. I tried to break loose but my cop shook
me like a dice box. He said, "You're not going to do it, buddy."
The other cop took hold of Marilyn. We tried to say who we were
but they wouldn't listen. We had a hard time convincing those
cops that we weren't about to commit suicide!

It seems that particular bridge was a spot for suicides in the
past and the police department had decided to grab anybody who
stood there.

The officer explained they had succeeded in stopping several
dual jumps after a struggle. We all became friends finally, and
we invited the boys to come and see *Smiles* at the Colonial, which
they did. We got even with 'em.

The New York opening was an unprecedented flashbulb flop.
I mentioned earlier in this book how unpleasant a conspicuous
failure can be. This one was not only conspicuous—it was celebrated.

A front-page fiasco. It was the kind of flop that even made
the audience look bad.

That first-night crowd deserved sympathy, in my opinion.
They were subjected to more nonsense by the press photographers,
let alone the actors, than ever before. There were five thousand
spectators standing outside the theatre, trying to make like a
Hollywood première.

The photogs followed their prey into the theatre, tracking them
right down to their seats like dogs. The list of social and other
celebrities filled the papers next morning. A typical Ziegfeld class
opening, outdoing itself.

But it was all mighty painful. Mr. Z. was home quite ill for a
few weeks after it. I wrote him a note saying Adele and I were
sorry he had not been well and that we were worried about not
seeing him at the theatre. He answered:

Dear Fred:
Don't worry—I'm feeling better—I'll fix the show!
I could have fixed it in the first place, only there were too many cooks.
                                                Affectionately, Flo

He hardly got around to seeing us after that—much less to fixing the show.

I had not heard from Alex Aarons except for an opening-night wire until about a month after the première. He phoned me about staging a song-and-dance number called "Embraceable You" for Ginger Rogers and Allen Kearns in the show, *Girl Crazy,* which he and Vint Freedley were about to open. He said they were in a spot, and asked me to help out.

I went over to the Alvin next day and met Ginger for the first time. We worked on the number in the foyer of the theatre, all other space being occupied.

Ginger had been heralded as the latest discovery. I enjoyed my work with this very attractive and talented new little Texan from Kansas City. She was the talk of the town when she opened in *Girl Crazy.*

Ginger and I went out occasionally after that, to a night club, or a movie. Our favorite spot was the Casino in Central Park, which had been converted into a flashy night spot featuring Eddie Duchin and his orchestra. We danced now and then for fun, with no plans whatsoever of working together.

Smiles went on, using up the brokers' eight-week ticket buy, and then the bottom fell out of the box office. The run hung on for a few more weeks and we folded in glorious and glamorous disrepute. That was shortly after New Year's, 1931.

I repeat, there's something about a flop show that is hard to describe. You feel a mixture of embarrassment and inadequacy. You want to hide. You imagine as you walk around on the street or any place that everyone is pointing and sneering at you and if they're not, they should be.

Marilyn came to our apartment the day after the closing and practically collapsed in tears.

Smiles was a shattering disappointment. We were fond of Flo and felt bad for him—as well as for ourselves.

He tried very hard on that one, and I'm afraid I was no help at all. In fact, I was ashamed of my inadequate performance.

This failure presented us with the problem of what our next step would be. We had no plans for the future. There were offers to dance in night clubs, both at home and abroad. Also, another chance to play the Palace now that we didn't want it.

In summing up all the energy, sweat and tears seemingly wasted on failures one experiences, I have found that there is usually something good to come out of it all.

For instance, I got one very good thing out of *Smiles*. It was a number called "Young Man of Manhattan," for which I did the choreography.

The idea came to me one morning about 4 A.M. as I lay in bed awake.

My mother, Adele and I had an apartment at 875 Park Avenue. Adele's room was just down the hall from mine.

I visualized a long line of boys in top hats and imagined myself using a cane like a gun, shooting the boys one at a time and having them drop simultaneously with the sound of a loud tap from my foot, leaving a sight somewhat like a comb with a tooth out here and there. Then I behaved like a machine gun mowing down the whole lot of 'em.

I jumped out of bed, grabbed an umbrella which was standing in the corner, and went through some motions while humming the tune so that I wouldn't forget it when I woke up in the morning.

Pretty soon I heard Adele's voice from her room: "Hey, Minnie, what the hell are you doing?"

I said, "I just got an idea for the 'Manhattan' number."

She answered, "Well, hang on to it, baby—you're going to need it in this turkey."

The number was lost in the show but it became a very important part of my early movie career a few years later. Spotted as the opening number in *Smiles* it was hardly remembered. Eventually, I explained the idea to Irving Berlin and he wrote the song "Top Hat" for it and also named the picture *Top Hat*.

Incidentally, I have had many dance ideas come to me as I lay awake at 4 A.M. This is a habit I've had for many years.

Chapter 15   The Band Wagon

We were tired mentally and physically and I suggested to Adele that we sail for Europe and some fun. Never having tried the big German liners, I booked passage over on the *Bremen* and return on the *Europa*.

Two days before sailing, Max Gordon got in touch with me about a venture he was planning. He wanted us for his new revue, *The Band Wagon*. Material was to be written by Howard Dietz and Arthur Schwartz, with George S. Kaufman directing. It was definitely set for the New Amsterdam Theatre some six months later. We had always wanted to work at the New Amsterdam and, after being told that Frank Morgan, Tilly Losch and Helen Broderick had already accepted, we hurried to sign before sailing. That was a worth-while trip, to "get away from it all." Memories of the unfortunate *Smiles* soon faded. We divided our time between London and Paris.

Returning to New York fresh and full of ambition, we immediately went into huddles with Howard Dietz and Arthur Schwartz to hear and discuss the material which they had written for *The Band Wagon*.

The design of the entire show was new and original. We were anxious to drop the run-around trademark and here was a good opportunity to do so. Even in *Smiles* we had used it to advantage as a last resort but, in *Band Wagon*, with numbers like "I Love Louisa," "New Sun in the Sky," "Hoops," "Sweet Music," "Dancing in the Dark," and "The Beggar Waltz," we didn't need it. Also particularly attractive to us was the fact that there was no story to worry about. There were many comedy sketches instead. We liked a revue again for a much-needed change.

Band Wagon was put together in expert fashion. It was a gem of a show, carrying all of us on and ahead. Another flop in succession could have seriously impeded our progress. In this instance I'll agree that luck had a hand. The timing was good.

It turned out now that Adele was seriously interested in Charles Cavendish, who had come to America to work for J. P. Morgan & Co. The romance had been developing for some six months past. She was anxious to retire from active professional life and to do so at the top of her career. *Band Wagon* fitted into this over-all plan.

There were no rehearsal problems. Things happened the right way. A revolving stage was used for most scene changes—an important part of the setup. Max Gordon remarked to me as we were on our way to Philadelphia for the tryout, "You know, I'm not concerned about the actors or the material in this show—but if the revolving stage gets fouled up on opening night, we're dead!"

We were definitely subjected to the mechanics of the revolving stage and a rather complicated piece of machinery it was, too, requiring expert handling and timing by a special crew.

The opening at the Chestnut Street Opera House took place on schedule and the revolving stage worked without a flaw. The show was a positive hit from the first note of the overture. It had a new look, that one, and was quickly recognized by the critics.

The usual trainload of first nighters from New York was on hand and the ticket brokers bought plenty. Everyone agreed that this was a knockout of a revue. There was not much rehearsing or rewriting necessary during the stay in Philadelphia and we concentrated mainly on perfecting what we had.

The show gave me my best opportunities so far for characterization and acting bits. I was in numerous skits and blackouts in addition to dancing numbers. There were so many quick costume changes that I had to engage an assistant for Walter, giving me two valets on the job.

The New York opening was everything we had hoped for. This time the viewpoint was different. It was a classy affair but without the "knobs on"; nothing went amiss. The revolving stage revolved at the right times and the sophisticated comedy registered.

The press next morning: Brooks Atkinson, the *Times*:

BEGINNING A NEW ERA

After the appearance of "The Band Wagon" which was staged at the New Amsterdam last night, it will be difficult for the old-time musical show to hold up its head.

Burns Mantle, *Evening News*: THE BAND WAGON STARTS SOMETHING. New York *Graphic*: NEW REVUE IS WITHOUT A FLAW.

We settled into a summer run at the now air-conditioned New Amsterdam Theatre, and it was a grand feeling. My sister was a happy girl. Her fiancé and I became close friends. Adele told me that she wanted to finish out the run in New York with the show and possibly a few weeks on the road but that she and Charlie were definitely going to be married in England the following summer (1932). She would have to leave the cast in time to prepare for the wedding. Charlie was the second son of the Duke of Devonshire. The wedding was to be a big one.

I had never felt upset about the prospect of Adele's retirement because I knew I'd have to face it sooner or later. I was, of course, concerned about whom she would marry and in this case my worries were over because I was truly fond of Cavendish and I was convinced that they adored each other.

The show ran on beautifully, attracting major attention on Broadway.

I saw Ginger again a number of times. *Girl Crazy* was nearing the finish of its long run. She had made a movie at Paramount's Long Island studio on her spare days and said she liked picture work. I told her it probably wouldn't be long before she would be a movie queen out in California. She was on her way to the coast in a few weeks.

Frank Morgan, Helen Broderick and Tilly Losch were wonderful to work with. We especially enjoyed the "I Love Louisa" number, performed on a fancy merry-go-round for the first act finale.

The lovely ballet star, Tilly Losch, and I had the dance production called "The Beggar Waltz." I was the beggar on the steps of the Viennese opera house. As the star ballerina enters the stage door, she drops a few coins into my outstretched hand. The beggar then falls asleep and the revolving stage moves around to disclose his dream.

He is now on stage of the beautiful opera house performing with the ballet star and chorus. My costume was an impressionistic affair—a combination of rags and riches. Choreography for this sequence was done by Albertina Rasch.

At the conclusion of our specialty ballet number, the lights dim out as the stage revolves back to where I am just awakening from my dream as the ballerina is coming out of the stage door.

I am looking up at her. She notices me again and tosses me her small purse as she walks away. The beggar then sinks back dejectedly as the curtains close.

This thing usually went very well and we would come before the curtain for calls.

I enjoyed teasing Tilly, and during one of her very dignified bows I placed my finger under my chin and made a silly curtsy to the audience, which got a laugh. Tilly fixed me with her Austrian accent: "You Palace ham, you," she whispered under her breath without moving her lips or cracking a smile, as she maintained her ballet dignity.

One night Greta Garbo was in the house. During one of the lifts in our dance, I mumbled to Tilly as I held her up in the air, "Garbo is out front—she just sent word back that she wants me for her next picture." Tilly could hardly keep from breaking up. She chased me all over backstage when we finished with, "You ham, you."

I spent quite a bit of time at Belmont Park furthering my interest in the furtherance of the thoroughbred, and was getting to the point of wanting to race in America. Spending a good bit of time around the Greentree barn with Jock Whitney as I did, I became well acquainted with and attached to their trainer, Clyde Phillips. Clyde was a top horseman. Jimmy, Sandy Hamilton and I had a fine time with him. Since our first meeting at Saratoga a few years back, we had always hit it off well together. I mentioned to him one day that I would probably wire him sometime a few years later to buy some horses for me. That, when I started to race in this country, I wanted him to train for me. He agreed that was okay with him. This time he reminded me, "Say, when are you going to send me that wire?" I told him I wasn't ready yet. He said, "Well, don't forget."

Chapter 16 Phyllis

There were a lot of parties down on "the island" as usual that summer. One, a "golf luncheon," given by Mrs. Graham Fair Vanderbilt at her place one Sunday afternoon, was destined to become the outstanding event of my life. It was there that I met Phyllis.

Mrs. Vanderbilt had a private golf course on her estate and this was a party designed for luncheon with golf to follow. A tournament with prizes.

Charlie Payson and I were assigned to a table with Phyllis Potter and Dorothy Fell. These two lovely girls made the day unforgettable. Dorothy was delightful and amusing.

I was fascinated by Phyllis. Her exceptional, fragile beauty and gentle charm held me rather spellbound. I loved the way she could not pronounce her r's. Another thing that captivated me was the fact that she did not mention ever having seen me on the stage. I knew she had not been to *Band Wagon,* but she couldn't remember anything I had done before that either.

I had seen Phyllis at Belmont Park before but was never introduced to her. When she told me that her uncle was Henry W. Bull, I no longer felt like a stranger, having known Mr. Bull for several years as president of the Turf and Field Club, which was one of his many interests.

Well—there wasn't any golf for me that day.

When the party ended, I asked Phyllis if I could call her. She said I could. She was going out of town, would return in a few days, and I could call her then.

Five days passed before I managed to talk to her again. We arranged to meet after the theatre with some friends.

I was more than ever convinced that this was the loveliest girl in the world, twenty-three, about five feet three, graceful and completely unaware of herself. Whether or not she liked me I couldn't tell for sure, but I made up my mind to find out. She asked me to come and see Peter, her child of a former marriage, next day at teatime. Anything and everything about Phyllis was first and foremost with me. I was gone.

She had been brought up by her aunt and uncle, Mr. and Mrs. Henry Bull, and I was soon asked to meet "Auntie" Maud. We got along beautifully at once. Uncle Henry and Auntie Maud were very kind to me. What a wonderful memory I have of their kindness and consideration!

Phyllis had so many beaus and I had to mow them down, one at a time. How I suffered!

For some time I urged her to see *The Band Wagon*. I said, "After all, you may hate me after you see me on the stage. It's a risk, but I've got to take it. Please come and see the show."

She finally did, and came backstage afterward with her friends. I waited and waited for some comment and, while she mentioned liking the show, she never said a word about me. So I came out with it: "Well, all right. How was I?"

"Oh, you were very good," said Phyllis (rolling the r in "very").

To me that was the most valued praise of all time.

One night soon after that she came to the show again with some young wag who seemed slightly inebriated. They sat in the fourth row center and I could see him talking to her and being somewhat annoying, I thought.

I was having a fit and it was all I could do to keep from jumping over the footlights.

They came back to see me after the show. I took her aside for a moment and asked her, "Where did you dig up this little snail?" She said, "Oh, he's a very nice boy—I've known him for years. He's just a bit tight."

I replied, "Well, do you have to spend the rest of the evening with him?" She laughed and said, "No."

I unloaded him. He wasn't a bad kid, it was just that any beau of hers became a horror in my eyes. Phyllis enjoyed all of this, as she told me later.

It was a tough struggle for two years. I was a jealous suitor. And how!

The Band Wagon rounded out its New York run and took to the road intact—a "natural" wherever we played.

Adele kept her promise to stay with us until the spring. She retired from theatrical life on the evening of March 5, 1932, at the Illinois Theatre, Chicago.

It was not a sad affair. There were a few tears but we soon laughed our way out of it.

I continued with the show, Vera Marsh replacing Adele for the remainder of the tour. The season ended in May and I was not able to attend Adele's wedding in England. I had planned, however, to visit the bride and groom as soon as I could get away.

All through these past months, while on tour, many hours were spent on the long-distance telephone with Phyllis. I insisted that we get married as soon as possible. Phyllis told me she wanted a little more time to think out the situation, not being sure that our lives could coincide. She was getting ready to sail for Europe with her aunt.

My career had come to a halt, mostly because I did nothing about it. I was far more concerned whether or not I was going to lose Phyllis.

Flo Ziegfeld offered me a part in a new show. Guthrie McClintic asked me to do a straight dramatic play. I was afraid to attempt that.

There was one offer from Dwight Wiman and Tom Weatherly for an intimate-type musical called *The Gay Divorce,* by Dwight Taylor. This one I liked but felt it needed some revision for me and if that could be arranged I would consider it.

With Phyllis away, my existence was a lonely one—I missed her so much. So I did the next best thing; I called her attractive sister, Kathleen, and we went out dancing at the Central Park Casino. Uncle Henry joined us to enjoy Eddie Duchin's music.

I sailed for Europe wondering what the outcome of all my quandaries would be. Gene Sarazen was aboard, on his way to compete in the British Open Golf Championship. Gene was sympathetic with me in my lovesick plight and he counteracted the pain.

Before London, I stopped off in Ireland to stay a few days with Adele and Charlie, who were now happily in residence at beautiful Lismore Castle.

Phyllis was in London. We spent as much time together as we could but, after a few days, I received a cable from New York asking me to come back to discuss the new show, *Gay Divorce.* Plans had to be made at once if I was interested in doing it.

I told Phyllis I didn't care whether I worked or not. I simply couldn't leave her right now with all those beaus hanging around and the heck with *Gay Divorce.*

Phyllis knocked me off my feet with "I think you should go back and investigate your future career. After all, if we are going to be married you'll have to work—won't you?"

Next day I was on the S. S. *Berengaria* bound for New York and discussions of *Gay Divorce.* I hoped I would like it well enough to do it. I had to make my solo before too long, or else run the risk of not being in a position to marry Phyllis. It was also rather important that I should make some prominent theatrical step quickly to counteract the problem of whether I could carry on with my work alone or fade into oblivion without my illustrious sister. I was a crazy, mixed-up hoofer. (Only that phrase wasn't coined then.)

On the boat trip back I found my old friend Gene Sarazen. He was the happiest guy I ever saw, having just won the British Open. I said, "Well, Gene, are you satisfied?" He just looked at me. "I'm the champion."

We had a few quick drinks on that and he mentioned that he might just win another American Open that year, too. He did.

He asked me how things were going with my romantic problems. I told him I was encouraged but it was going to be a struggle, what with my career and everything hanging in the balance, but at least I had reason to believe that Phyllis really loved me. He came back with the simplest, most logical tranquilizer:

"What more do you want? You could always hoof—the rest is easy."

Back in New York, the meetings on *Gay Divorce* were satisfactory, and when I learned that Cole Porter had agreed to do the score, I signed a contract.

Rehearsals were to start in September. I was on the transatlantic phone almost at once with all the news for Phyllis. This went on several more days and I decided it made no sense to spend a fortune on telephone calls, so off I went on the S.S. *Paris*.

I was a frantic character those days, enjoying the kind of misery you wallow in. Phyllis had gone off to Le Touquet with her family. I joined them there. It was a worth-while trip, although I could only stay a few weeks. I would have been miserable at home.

Phyllis always had a way of easing my worries. Just a few words from her were all I needed. I became anxious about my coming work and whether I could make the grade alone. She'd merely say, "You'll be very good," and I'd know that I would.

It was like that through later years, too, pertaining to my picture work and its problems. She never failed.

Just before I left this time, I brought up the point of our proposed marriage and wanted to set some sort of date to go by. Phyl suggested that we discuss it as soon as the worries of my new show were past.

I was off for New York once more, happy but miserable—if you know what I mean. Phyl would not be returning home for another month.

Rehearsals for *Gay Divorce* started the day after my arrival. The script was in good shape, I thought. We had a top-notch man in Howard Lindsay to direct us and I was enthusiastic about the possibilities.

I worked a lot with dance director Carl Randall and we came up with some useful tricks for both Claire Luce and me.

Claire was a beautiful dancer and it was her style that suggested to me the whole pattern of the "Night and Day" dance. This was something entirely different from anything Adele and I had done together. That was what I wanted, an entirely new dancing approach. Randall gave us a swell trick in one of the other numbers. It was a spectacular thing on the hazardous side, in which the climax of the number was reached as we waltzed around the room at top speed going over chairs and table as if they were part of the floor. We took many a fall rehearsing this and occasionally we fell during the show, too, much to the dismay of the audience. When that happened, we would just get up and do it over properly, like the juggler who misses a trick the first time. Then, when it finally worked, the audience would give us twice as much applause.

I felt that the show was coming along well and was pretty sure I would get away with my first solo attempt, with the help of our excellent cast, which included Luella Gear, Eric Blore, Erik Rhodes and G. P. Huntley, Jr.

Phyllis arrived from Europe and I met her at the boat. She said she could arrange to go to Boston and stay with friends if I wanted her there for the opening. I told her of our difficulties with the show and advised her not to come—that I anticipated a lot of work.

We opened at the Wilbur Theatre in Boston. It was a shaky debut. There was book trouble.

I've always felt that my presence in a story makes it tough on a writer. I think I tend to ruin a book because everybody expects me to hop into a dance every minute.

The press notices were not exactly conducive to the sale of tickets.

"No EVENING OF UNALLOYED SATISFACTIONS," said the Boston *Transcript*. It went on: "An Astaire must dance and still does very well—but not for the general good is he now sisterless."

The Boston *Post:* ". . . stars Fred as a lone star, his popular sister, Adele, now being a member of the British aristocracy and is probably sending cablegrams of hope and congratulations—'Gay Divorce' is what might be termed light-waisted."

We worked, rehashed, rewrote during the entire two weeks in Boston and then stopped off in New Haven for three days on the way to New York, where we were booked to open at the Ethel Barrymore Theatre the following week.

There were signs of life in New Haven and the show was well received. It had gained some sort of pace to go along with the musical numbers which always held us above water. The students gave out with some enthusiasm and we were encouraged. W. J. Schuler Watts liked the show and in his review for the *Yale Daily News* said, " 'Gay Divorce' will unquestionably be a standing room success in New York." This little assist helped us to face the music there. We were grateful to Mr. Watts.

I was, of course, on the phone to Phyllis every night or day with details of our problems. Her advice was, "Don't worry—don't worry," and I found that I didn't.

That New York first night was another opening to end all openings. It was a fashionable audience—late in arriving, disorderly, impatient and skeptical. Obviously they had heard that the show was not so good out of town.

Once in the theatre they listened occasionally to what was going on but seldom did they laugh. There were audible noises and applause for the numbers. Phyllis was in front with a party of friends. I wasn't nervous. There was nothing to do but face it. A cable from Lismore, Ireland, gave me the necessary humor tonic I needed. It read:

NOW MINNIE DON'T FORGET TO MOAN, LOVE

ADELE AND CHARLIE

It had to end sometime, that miserable night. Phyllis came backstage afterward to pick up me with her party and she merely said, "What a *dwedful* audience!"

I said, "So is the show." She answered, "I liked some of it."

The Gay Divorce took it on the chin next morning:

John Mason Brown decided: "Not since 'Here Goes the Bride' collapsed with a thud on the stage of a local playhouse about a year ago has a musical show that seemed promising in advance turned out to be as dull a disappointment as did 'Gay Divorce.'"

One critic said, "Fred Astaire stops every now and then to look off-stage towards the wings as if he were hoping his titled sister, Adele, would come out and rescue him."

"One thing is certain," quoth another, "after viewing last night's performance we have come to the conclusion that two Astaires are better than one."

Some national weekly magazine came forward with: "'The Gay Divorce' received a tremendous reception on opening night due to the brandied roarings of Cole Porter's friends."

Harold Lockridge, New York *Sun:* "Fred Astaire, when his miraculous feet are quiet, gives a curious impression of unemployment."

Burns Mantle, New York *Mirror:* "—Of course, you never would pick Fred Astaire out of any line-up to play a romantic hero, with or without music. He hasn't the hair for one thing. It is only when he dances that the crowd is prepared to whoop and rattle its fins."

Mark Barron (syndicated columnist): ". . . But as an actor and as a singer, Astaire does not approach the perfection he achieves with his feet. In 'The Gay Divorce,' it must be recorded he has perhaps taken on too much of a task."

Walter Winchell gave me encouragement which I welcomed no end. He said, "The personable and talented brother of Lady Cavendish never before seemed so refreshing and entertaining—but 'Gay Divorce' has a tendency to go flat—for more than two minutes at a time—too often."

I was not upset because they missed my sister. I'd have been disappointed if they hadn't, but at any rate my job was cut out for me and the show had to be put over. We worked on it for the next month and threw the upstairs portions of the theatre into LeBlangs Cut Rates. That gave us nearly full houses to work to and the show picked up. The song "Night and Day" helped a great deal as it became an outstanding hit. In fact, the show became known as the "Night and Day" show.

We moved to the larger Shubert Theatre on West Forty-fourth Street and actually enjoyed what seemed to be a successful run. There were any number of repeaters noticeable in the audience and that is a fair sign that you've caught on. Claire Luce left the cast after about six months and was succeeded by Fred Stone's lovely daughter, Dorothy. It was a joy working with her.

All through this period I was living in my mother's apartment at 875 Park Avenue. I led the typical New York theatrical life, appearing at various affairs when called upon, and had a rather conspicuous radio introduction on Rudy Vallee's show. Rudy was the rage of the country at that time.

There were several indications that the movies were interested in me.

One day I ran into Mervyn LeRoy on the street and he mentioned that he liked the show and thought I should do it in pictures. I told him I would like to. He was with Warner Bros. at the time and said he would take it up on his return to the coast.

I never heard any more about it from Mervyn until I brought it up one day, many years later, after I had done the picture for RKO.

I asked Mervyn, "How did it happen that I never heard any more about doing *Gay Divorce* with you after our meeting in New York?"

He laughed. "When I suggested *Gay Divorce* to Jack Warner that time, Jack replied, 'Who am I going to put in it—Cagney?'"

Phyllis and I saw each other as much as we could. She went away for several months during the winter to Aiken, South Carolina, with her family. She liked me a lot, I could tell, but I wasn't at all sure that she would marry me and it was driving me crazy.

I decided to make a stab at Hollywood and the movies. Having had so many years on the stage, I was looking for a change and a chance to prove something brand-new for myself professionally. Frankly, I didn't think I had too much of a chance, but I would try.

I ran into an old friend of mine, Eddie McIlvaine, who was associated with Leland Hayward at the time. I told Eddie to tell Leland that I was fed up with the stage and wanted to try my hand in Hollywood.

Leland came to see me at the theatre that night and said, "You're a cinch. I was talking to David Selznick on the long-distance phone today. He's head of RKO. They want you for a big musical, *Flying Down to Rio*, when you're through here." I explained that I was definitely interested but had to fulfill my obligation to go to London with *Gay Divorce*.

We figured that I could go to Hollywood at the conclusion of the New York run, do the picture, and then go to London in the fall for the presentation of *Gay Divorce* at the Palace Theatre.

Contracts were signed accordingly and I was very much pleased with this busy and interesting outlook for my career. I rushed to Phyllis with the news and asked her to marry me at once. She was hesitant, a bit frightened at the thought of Hollywood, I guess, and again said she didn't think we should get married yet. I said:

"All right, I'll go out there and get the first picture out of the way, come straight back here afterward and *then* we'll be married."

She said, "No—that's not good—if you go away from me to Hollywood, you'll start running around with some of those girls out there, and whether you do or not I'd always think you did, so we'd better get married right now, as soon as possible."

We were married July 12, 1933, and spent our one-day honeymoon on Mrs. Payne Whitney's yacht, the *Captiva* (which she loaned us), cruising up the Hudson River. That was July 13. On the fourteenth we boarded a Ford tri-motor plane for California. It took us twenty-six hours, I think, with a lot of stops. I loved the trip. It was my first experience on a commercial flight, and anyway I was "in the clouds."

We arrived at the airport in Burbank and were met by an official from M-G-M where I was to make a quick guest appearance in a Joan Crawford and Clark Gable picture before starting my RKO contract. This last assignment had come up suddenly and I was now plunging into some confusion in this new career.

Chapter 17 Hollywood

I had thought I might have a few weeks of easing into things and getting acquainted. Nothing like that—it was pitch in right now. All this with my beautiful, untheatrical bride stashed away in a hotel room at the Beverly Wilshire most of the time waiting for me to come home. She didn't think it wise to bring her youngster, Peter, with us on this trip. We planned to rent a house the next time out after the London run of *Gay Divorce*. I didn't have much money—the stock-market crash of '29 had messed Adele and me up a bit; but I was making a little now and it was possible that I'd make a lot if I hit in pictures—a thing that I was not at all sure about. In fact, I was ready to leave after I saw some of my first film.

Joan Crawford was kind to us. We were impressed by her thoughtfulness and warm welcome. She had the sitting room of our hotel suite covered with flowers of various kinds—all white. She also entertained us at her house quite often.

I finished that picture, *Dancing Lady*, after a few weeks of rehearsals and two or three weeks of shooting. I didn't have much to do, but it was indeed a wonderful way to make an auspicious but not too ostentatious bow in the movies. I was cast as myself in the story, a backstage yarn in which the dance director says to the leading lady, "I've got Fred Astaire here from New York to dance with you—Oh, Fred, would you come here please?" and out I came into the scene. Clark Gable played the dance director.

To have Clark Gable call me out by my own name and to play a scene with him and Joan Crawford was, I thought, a great way to be presented to the vast movie public—to many who had never seen or heard of me in spite of all my years on the stage.

When I first saw myself on the screen in that picture—I came on from the side, at an odd photographic angle—it shook me. I said to Phyllis, "My gosh, I look like a knife!"

Dancing Lady was one of the big Crawford-Gable grossers and served as a very useful steppingstone for me. I've always been grateful for it. Bob Benchley, Nelson Eddy and Ted Healy were also in the cast.

A few years after I had established myself, so to speak, at RKO there was a saying going the rounds that Metro had had me under contract originally and let me go. That was not so. As I mentioned before, I was loaned to Metro by RKO just for *Dancing Lady.*

I was supposed to have come up with the smart remark, "I can think of nothing more wonderful than being buried in a Joan Crawford picture."

That rumor was not true, but I thought it was a good crack and went on letting them give me credit for it.

My first days of working on a movie lot were interesting and exciting even though I didn't know which way to turn or where to go. It was all so big, so much more important than being cooped up in a theatre, I thought. Jerry Asher, from the publicity department at M-G-M, sensed very quickly the difficulties of a greenhorn, fresh from the New York stage, and he came to the rescue.

For many weeks Phyllis and I depended largely upon Jerry. His kindness in seeing us safely through the launching pains in strange territory was deeply appreciated by us both. Walter arrived by train a few days after we did and he was welcome as an old friend from home. Walter was a good cook when he wanted to be. He often cooked dinner for us in the kitchenette of our suite at the Beverly Wilshire Hotel and we three would sit talking. We found much to laugh about.

Once I got into the swing of working at the studio, I loved the movie business. Bob Leonard was my first director, patient and helpful, always. I wanted to be successful in this big, new field but somehow couldn't picture myself making it.

Little as I had to do in that first picture, the dances with Joan Crawford required a lot of rehearsing, and I did mostly as I was told. My old friend Sammy Lee was the dance director. Knowing absolutely nothing about photographing a dance for the screen, I did a a great deal of listening and studying. I was pleased with lots of things but kept thinking of what I would like to try if I ever got in a position to make my own decisions.

My work in that picture was finished in a few weeks and I began to feel like an old-timer. The purpose of that job, as far as I was concerned, was to sneak into the movies and, at the same time, gain some experience before tackling the RKO picture *Flying Down to Rio,* in which I would have a lot to do.

It worked out well. When I reported at RKO I had a pretty fair idea of movie procedure. It was a great relief to get that "first day in school" feeling out of my system.

Phyllis and I were pleased with the simplicity of Hollywood home life, if you chose to have it that way. I enjoyed going to bed early and getting up early. It was pleasant to drive to work before all the hustle and traffic had really started. In California we were seldom up after midnight. The weather was beautiful, and I never failed to appreciate those nice mornings. The feeling has never changed. I am always glad to get back.

I found working before the camera much more interesting than theatre appearances.

Many people told me, "Oh, you will miss the audience's reaction. You'll miss the applause."

It was not so. I didn't miss those things. My numbers were built for applause reactions, and as I found out later when the numbers were right they would get applause in the movie theatres.

The first day at RKO was a pleasant one. Lou Brock, the producer, greeted me and promptly took me to Merian Cooper, who had just taken over as head of the studio. I had known "Coop" in New York. His encouragement about my screen possibilities helped me a lot. I then went about meeting the heads of various departments and soon found out that RKO's routine operation was different from M-G-M's. In fact, I've found that each studio in Hollywood has its idiosyncrasies: individual ways of conducting rehearsals, methods of recording music, spending money for equipment, everything. There's always that "This-is-the-way-we-do-it-here" approach.

The cast for *Flying Down to Rio* had not been entirely decided upon when I arrived at RKO. Thornton Freeland was the director. Dolores Del Rio, Gene Raymond and the new South American singer, Raoul Roulien, were set but I had no idea for two days with whom I would be dancing, if anybody. I didn't look at a script or question anything. All I wanted was to stay in pictures.

The third day I was told that Ginger Rogers might be in the cast. This was great news of course, although I wondered whether or not she really wanted to work with me. She had been in Hollywood for over a year doing mostly straight nonmusical pictures and I wasn't sure if she cared to dance.

Being old friends, we both had a good laugh when we met that first day of rehearsals. Gin had just returned from location on a film with Joel McCrea. We soon got down to business. I was anxious to know how she felt about our current venture and I asked her:

"Do you like this picture?"

She answered, "I don't know—do you?"

I said, "I'm a stranger—I don't know anything, but I like it here."

Ginger then explained, "Well, to tell you the truth, I didn't want to do any musicals. I was satisfied to keep on with the straight ones. But I guess it'll turn out all right. Anyway, we'll have some fun." Then we reminisced about the Casino in Central Park and the New York stage and the fun started right there.

Dave Gould was assigned as dance director but I did most of my work with his assistant, Hermes Pan.

We fooled around a lot that first day, experimenting with a few steps, trying to see how we could dance together for money. The music was played to us for the first time.

Vincent Youmans' score for the picture was excellent, we thought, with such songs as "Orchids in the Moonlight" and "The Carioca," "Flying Down to Rio," and others. We had hopes.

Phyllis was getting more accustomed to California and beginning to like it. Being a real Easterner, she did not find it easy. I always asked her to come down to the studio to visit me on the set. She did for a while, but didn't like staying very long. She was intensely interested in my work, however, and I often asked her advice about it.

She would say, "Please don't ask me. I don't know anything about show business." But she did know. Her snap judgment was most valuable to me. I wanted her first reaction to many things and particularly in this new career. If she said, "Mmm, I like it," I knew that it was all right.

The mechanics of picture making became increasingly fascinating to me. One thing I found difficult was seeing myself in the "rushes" (showing of film shot the previous day). That difficulty has remained with me evermore.

I often asked to have the day's rushes run through again and again, finding that I didn't mind it so much after a few times. It was that first look that threw me.

My getting married and going into the movies at about the same time gave the press a chance to have a little fun at my expense—or at least that's the way it looked to me.

One instance that stood out: a national weekly magazine was quite new then and their policy was considerably different from what it is today. In my case, they referred to the actor marrying the nonprofessional New York beauty. And then ran two photographs: the first a single one of me, and the second, one of Phyllis and me taken informally at our wedding, with the following captions:

"Here is Fred with his wig, but without his wife—and here is Fred with his wife, but without his wig."

The fact that I had to wear a hair embellishment in the films never bothered me. It merely came under the heading of make-up and of being a nuisance. I was only one of many actors who were blessed with "high foreheads" and thinning temples. The camera accentuates these lofty intellectual characteristics!

Phyllis found a house on North Cañon Drive which we took on a six months' lease. It was an old English manor house with palm trees in front of it and bananas in the back yard. The plumbing was not so good—but it was home. She started in at once looking for the next house.

One day Phyllis went to answer the front doorbell. I was in the back yard fooling around with the banana trees or something. Phyl suddenly returned in a rather frightened state. She said, "There's a dwedful man at the front door without a shirt on who says he knows your sister and that he's just been playing tennis at Don and Bee Stewart's house. He wants to see you."

When I came face-to-face with this individual I detected immediately a rather military-looking Britisher of unquestionably fascinating personality.

We had a drink or two and heard all about his stint in the Cuban army since getting out of the Scots Guards, his racing mules in Florida and I don't know what all, and that he was thinking about going in the movies but so far he had had no chance to do anything but think about it. To us he certainly seemed to qualify with that personality. He had us in stitches the entire time. His name was Niven. Oh yes—*the* Niven, David, it was. I need say no more. How glad we were that he stopped by that day. We gained one of the closest of lifetime friends.

Eddie Rubin, then with the RKO publicity department, took charge of many responsibilities for me and was a big help in the intricate phases of handling meetings with fan-magazine writers and other obligations. Eddie got himself in many a jam trying to protect me from interviewers who wanted to see me while I was creating or rehearsing dance routines. I could never rehearse without privacy and it wasn't easy to convince these writers of that. Some took it out on me, too. I explained that I would like to be able to oblige them, but it slowed me up too much. I couldn't concentrate on my work and get it done when time was limited. They learned to understand.

Ginger's mother and I were good friends. Back in New York I had often visited with Ginger and Lela at their apartment. We would sit around chatting, discussing careers, theatre business and so on. But we never mentioned anything about doing pictures together. I guess it never occurred to any of us.

Ginger and I hadn't any idea at all that we were destined to start something in this first movie together. She had already proved herself, but I was just a yokel from the East, an unknown quantity in this medium. We had no thought of being a team.

There were many musical sequences in *Rio* but we actually did only one important dance together, "The Carioca." I was also in a little tango sequence with the lovely Dolores Del Rio. In addition, Gin and I each had quite a bit to do in dialogue and in separate numbers.

I enjoyed the shooting of the picture and felt that I was learning fast. Ginger was sweet and helpful, advising me about techniques in handling dialogue scenes for camera purposes.

When all work on the film was finished, Phyllis and I remained in town only a few days. I was due in London for rehearsals of my stage show *Gay Divorce,* scheduled to open there in October, and there wasn't much time. We had to stop in New York, pick up Peter, and sail for England as soon as possible.

I'll always remember seeing Pandro Berman, then an executive producer at RKO, in the Beverly Wilshire Hotel the day before I left. Although Berman did not produce *Flying Down to Rio,* he had kept his eye on the film. He was, incidentally, one of the youngest executives in Hollywood, still in his twenties.

Pandro was standing on the mezzanine balcony of the hotel lobby looking down at me. I called up to him: "Good-by, Pan, we're leaving tomorrow and I don't think you'll be seeing me here any more." He asked me what I meant. I told him I had just seen some of my film in *Rio,* and I thought I looked pretty awful. He said, "Don't be silly, everybody likes it, you've got a great chance."

I thanked him and said I'd have to wait until the picture was released or at least previewed to the public before I could believe it.

He said they were going to preview it in a few weeks and he would cable me himself because he expected to be coming to London to see *Gay Divorce.* He wanted to produce my next film and thought that should make a good movie vehicle.

With all this encouragement, I still couldn't believe it was possible. Actually, I avoided seeing the whole picture of *Rio* before I left because of my apprehension.

Next day Phyllis and I were off for New York by train. We had lots of time on that trip to rest and talk over our experiences in California.

We agreed that it would be nice to go back, rent a house and stay awhile—providing of course that I had made the grade. We were very happy. Phyllis was excited about the forthcoming trip abroad and the fact that Peter would join us.

Those were perfect days for me. Phyllis was mine, and the outlook for my work was at least promising. My sister was happy in her marriage and expecting the birth of a child within a few weeks. Also, my mother was very well. No one could ask for more.

We had a wonderful ten days in New York. Phyllis saw many of her old friends. Dorothy Fell and her sister-in-law Fifi, Mrs. John R. Fell, were with us much of the time. Fifi, Dorothy and Phyllis had been devoted friends since childhood, and they took great delight in putting me on the ribbing block. To be more explicit—those three beautiful girls teased hell out of me about being a potential movie star. I was helpless in the hands of that trio.

We stayed at Mr. and Mrs. Bull's residence at 121 East Sixty-second Street through this interlude between movies in Hollywood and the London stage.

The boat trip abroad was perfect, and young Peter, who was then about four years old, showed signs of liking me. We got along extremely well, except once when I made him pick up something which he had thrown on the floor. In retaliation he squelched me with, "You old damn man." This delighted his mother no end. Peter had a few, shall we say, destructive traits all his own.

Arriving in London, we went to the Carlton Hotel to stay until Phyllis could find a house that would suit us.

I had cabled George Griffin to be there waiting for me. He was ready on our arrival with all the racing news.

My rehearsals started immediately and the opening was set for Birmingham at the Royal Theatre, five weeks later.

Things took shape at once. Our show was good. We were confident of that, having renovated it thoroughly at the expense of New York.

Lee Ephraim was our impresario this time. Sir Alfred Butt had retired from active producing.

About the second week after our arrival, my brother-in-law

telephoned me from Ireland the sad news that Adele had lost a baby girl in premature birth. She was quite ill and would not be able to get to London for some time. The tragedy was a bitter disappointment to them and to all of us. Adele had longed for this baby. Mother received the news while on the ocean, bound for Ireland.

Chapter 18 *Last Stage Show*

The tryout of *Gay Divorce* in Birmingham was good. "The libraries bought large blocks of stalls well into the future" for the London engagement and there were no complications. Mr. Ephraim imported Eric Blore and Erik Rhodes from the New York company, and Olive Blakney, Claud Allister, Clifford Heatherly, Joan Gardner and Fred Hearne rounded out our excellent cast.

Opening night at the Palace in London brought out the inevitable jitters before the starting gun. I met my Gallery First Nighter friends and they were encouraging. There seemed to be no doubt in their minds about the show from the reports they had heard. They also spoke of how they would miss my sister and were sorry to read in the papers that she had lost her first baby.

The show went very well that first night with one exception. I "blew" one of my best tricks with Claire Luce, the show-stopping over-the-table trick in our last dance near the finale. It was just one of those things. We didn't fall but we bobbled on top of the table as we went over, causing an uncertainty to the finishing step which followed. When the number ended there was a hand but it suddenly stopped dead and we could not do an encore. The audience seemed puzzled. I felt terrible about it because usually there were unlimited encores to that dance. Minnie sure had something to moan about there. Everything else had gone so well with "Cores" and "Mores." I felt sick.

The only way I could appease myself was to mention it during my curtain speech at the end of the show. I thanked the audience for their kindness and added, "I must apologize for tripping up my partner in that last dance and nearly falling off the table." They laughed, but I had the feeling they really didn't know what I was talking about.

After the show I rushed to my dressing room to tell Phyllis. She had been there all evening. She told me the only time she had drummed up courage to watch any part of the show was for that number, her favorite, and she had wandered out on the stage to see it from the side.

"It wasn't as bad as all that . . ." said Phyllis. "Stop worrying." And I did for a few minutes.

The visitors arrived backstage and of course I asked everyone. Nobody noticed anything except Prince George, who said, "I thought one of the legs of the chair gave way a bit as you stepped on it up to the table. I could tell by your face that something was wrong."

They all liked the show, however. We knew we had a hit and would be there for the maximum six months' run I had agreed upon.

Not one critic mentioned the mishap I worried about and no one said anything about my being unable to carry on without Adele. They all agreed that *Gay Divorce* was the ideal vehicle for me to make the solo step since it was totally different from anything that Adele and I had done together. I felt that the difficult obstacle had been surmounted.

Phyllis found an attractive little house, No. 3 John Street in Mayfair, which we leased for several months and settled down in for the season.

Adele and Charlie arrived from Ireland with Mother about

three weeks later and came to the show immediately. I could see them out there in the fourth row of stalls.

It was the first time Adele had ever watched me from out front as a spectator, and she was nervous. I was in good form and threw lots of extra bits in. The show went great. The audience was aware of her presence and she had to acknowledge her applause during the intermission with a little bow and a wave to the gallery.

We all went out on a party afterward. It was a wonderful night —one I had looked forward to for a long time. I asked Mother if I had wrinkled my forehead and looked cross. She said it must have been all right because she didn't remember anything about it. We had a lot of encores on the table trick. I was pleased that there were no mistakes that night—I wanted to do it right for my sister. She liked the "Night and Day" number, too. Adele and Charlie stayed over a few days and then rushed back to their Lismore Castle, which they loved so much.

Being so busy with the activities at hand, I completely forgot about the movie situation for a few weeks and it suddenly occurred to me that I hadn't heard a thing from Hollywood. I told Phyllis, "I'll bet they've had a preview and I flopped. That's probably why we haven't got any word."

Phyllis said, teasingly, "There's no question about it—you'd better take up farming."

Next morning this cable arrived:

YOU WERE A SWELL SUCCESS IN PREVIEW FLYING DOWN TO RIO LAST NIGHT. PANDRO BERMAN.

I also had several other cables which convinced me that everything must be satisfactory. With this tremendous news, Phyllis and I went on the town that night to celebrate.

There were many parties, weekends in the country, charity balls and performances to keep us busy throughout the season. One in particular was called "Performance in Aid of King George's Pension Fund for Actors and Actresses." This one, attended by the King and Queen, was held at Theatre Royal, Drury Lane. It comprised skits and specialties by various performers in town. Claire Luce and I went over to do "Night and Day."

These shows are usually referred to as "Command Performances" by the newspapers but they are really *not* that. Many years have passed since the sovereigns have "commanded" anyone to entertain them.

Lord and Lady Stanley, long-time friends of Phyllis' and mine, asked us to lunch one afternoon to meet their young ones. Portia urged Phyllis to be sure to bring Peter. That visit ended with our Peter throwing a toy locomotive at the younger Stanley and then taking off like a rocket into the street, followed by a frantic footman.

Phyllis called, "Peter, Peter, please somebody, he'll be run over by a taxi!"

The footman snaffled the escapee handily and restored him to safety. The boy who got hit by the airborne locomotive that day is the present Lord Derby.

I was notified by Leland Hayward that my option had been taken up by RKO and that Pandro Berman was on his way to London to see *Gay Divorce*. If he decided so, it would be my next picture and most likely with Ginger Rogers.

The plan seemed very good to me and I awaited Berman's arrival anxiously.

In the meantime, I received a batch of clippings from New York pertaining to *Dancing Lady*, which had recently opened. They surprised me because I was actually noticed, with so little to do.

They said in part:

Rose Pelswick in the *Evening Journal:* ". . . the star's dancing partner in the revue sequences is the nimble Fred Astaire who, while he isn't given much to do, acquits himself elegantly in those moments when he does appear."

Thornton Delahanty: ". . . and the niggardly use made of Fred Astaire is no joke either."

New York *Evening Sun:* ". . . The film winds to a big musical show wherein Miss Crawford leads the male choruses and clogs it around with ease and with—of all people—Fred Astaire, who you may be sure is put in his proper place."

It surprised me to note that I was "put in my proper place" and "used niggardly." Actually there was no such design. The producers and Joan were very particular that I should be satisfied with my assignments.

There was a conviction in those days that New York stage stars were often subjected to incompetent or neglectful treatment by the Hollywood studios. Obviously, the press wasn't aware of my wish to appear inconspicuously at first.

I was flattered and delighted at their apparent interest and concern. The last reaction to my work by most of the New York press had been to the effect that I could not quite make it without my sister.

A few weeks later, *Flying Down to Rio* opened at Radio City Music Hall in New York and shortly after that countrywide. Reports were that the picture was doing fine business. I received another big lot of newspaper clippings. They indicated that I had clicked and had a chance to go on.

I was again amazed that the reaction could be so good because I knew I hadn't yet scratched the surface with any real dancing on the screen. The numbers in *Rio* were put together rather hurriedly, I thought, and I was not at all pleased with my work. I thought Ginger and I looked all right together but I was under the impression that we weren't doing anything particularly outstanding in "The Carioca." I had thrown in a few solos, too, in the limited time given me but I never expected that they would register so well. However, everything clicked, including the dialogue and comedy scenes.

Dancing Lady opened at the Empire and Phyllis insisted that we go to see it. She practically had to drag me there. That was where I saw my knifelike countenance come sliding in for the

first time. It was a successful film—very well received. We were
encouraged.

One night when Phyl and I dropped over to the Savoy Grill for
a bit of supper after the show I ran into Doug Fairbanks, Sr.,
with some mutual friends. Doug greeted me with "What do you
mean by revolutionizing the movie industry? I've just seen
Flying Down to Rio and you've got something absolutely new.
It's terrific."

I was bowled over by such a compliment coming from Doug.

Pan Berman arrived in London on schedule and saw *Gay
Divorce* at once. Phyllis and I met him and his wife after the
performance and we all went out to supper. He told us the show
would be very adaptable for pictures and thought Ginger would be
ideal for that part. He said he wanted Mark Sandrich to direct
and was sure we could get a better picture out of it than the
stage show.

I was delighted with the plans and particularly about working
with Ginger again.

Rio was not released in London while we were there. The
studio wanted to run it privately for us but I preferred to wait
and see it in a theatre with an audience. I knew we would be
closing *Divorce* soon and I could see the film in New York.

At the completion of our London run, Phyl and I left for home
almost immediately. There wasn't much time before I had to be
in California and we were also going to run down to Aiken, South
Carolina, for a week to stay with Phyllis' family, who had a
house there.

It amused us both that I was greeted everywhere as a movie
star on my arrival back in the States. It seemed funny that it
could happen so fast. I couldn't find the picture, *Rio*, playing any
place in New York. By that time it had run itself out in the
area.

Off to Aiken we went to catch the final week of that lovely
winter resort's season. The Palmetto Golf Course was in beautiful

shape. Most of the seasonal residents had gone home. It was a wonderfully restful change from all the show-business talk I had been through in recent months.

Along about the fourth day we were there, Phyllis called to me as she was reading the Augusta newspaper over her breakfast tray: "Fred, it's here. *Flying Down to Rio* is playing in Augusta. I want to see it."

Sure enough, there it was, billed in some little third-run theatre, having already played its other runs.

The old apprehension came over me and I really felt reluctant about seeing myself on the screen again. We drove over to Augusta that night and sneaked in the theatre unnoticed. I must say we enjoyed the film.

On the way out of the theatre, a youngster spotted me. Walking in front of us, staring, he finally shouted, "Hey, Fred! What are you doin' here?" That attracted attention and I was soon surrounded. It's this sort of thing that solidifies the realization that you've possibly caught on in the movies. I needed it. I always need a lot of convincing about the acceptance of my work.

We were on our way back to California, after a few days in New York, on the old Santa Fe Chief. There wasn't even a Super Chief then. In those days, every station stop would be crowded with townspeople out to get a glimpse of their movie favorites who might be passing through. All these things were new and interesting to us.

When we arrived back in California, the RKO publicity department gave us the full treatment. Perry Lieber had Eddie Rubin and all the boys there to meet us.

We went to the Beverly Wilshire Hotel again to stay until Phyl could go on a house-hunting expedition.

There were many meetings scheduled for me at the studio to discuss the screen version of *The Gay Divorce*. Press announcements referred to it as *The Gay Divorcee*. Mark Sandrich explained that they thought it was a more attractive-sounding title, centered around a girl. I agreed with them.

One of the important changes in the rewriting for the screen was to make my role that of a dancer by profession. In the original stage version I was a writer. This change made a lot of difference in the story line and unquestionably improved the vehicle. The musical numbers dropped into place more naturally and we all felt now that we could top *Flying Down to Rio*.

Numerous improvements were made, due to the ingenuity of Pandro Berman and Mark Sandrich. Through the ensuing years of my experience with these two men, I was fully aware of their capabilities and my good fortune in being associated with them.

Ginger was pleased with her part in the picture and that was nice because she was noted for not being too readily pleased with anything in the way of scripts.

There is an amusing story which went around about "Gin" some few years later:

She had been sent the script of a forthcoming picture and returned it with an accompanying note saying in no uncertain terms that she did not want to do it. This, incidentally, was one which she was to do apart from me. In the note she gave all her reasons for turning the story down, and why she thought it would be a failure.

It so happened that Gin was obliged to do the picture, anyway, against her wishes. The ultimate result, *Bachelor Mother*, a smash hit.

She never did agree that she was wrong. All our Ginger said was, "If only I hadn't written that note."

Among the many added values to *Gay Divorcee* was a big new number, "The Continental," written by Herb Magidson and Con Conrad. Hermes Pan was again with us on choreography.

There was a lot of dance planning and rehearsing for us but we were not rushed this time as before. The success of the last show qualified us for the big-time treatment. When I spoke my piece about needing time and said that the result would pay off, I was told we could have what we needed. We rehearsed about six weeks on the dance routines, those tricky ones like "Night and Day" and the table dance I brought from the stage show. I wanted Ginger to have plenty of time on them with me so that we could surely top whatever we had done before. *Divorcee* was a production of some size—much more so than the stage version, with a slick cast featuring Edward Everett Horton and Alice Brady, Eric Blore and Erik Rhodes.

In the middle of the picture the studio notified me that my next would be *Roberta,* again with Ginger, and that we would be with Irene Dunne and Randolph Scott. I was enthusiastic about the outlook with Pandro Berman as producer—more convinced than ever that I liked the movie business.

Walter, who had been with me through the first three pictures, confessed to me one day to my regret that he was homesick for New York and wanted to go back East to stay. He missed his friends and was really not too fond of living in California.

I sent a cable to George Griffin asking if he could come to work for me again, giving my new address in Beverly Hills.

His answer:

YES SIR. I WILL LEAVE AT ONCE STOP DIDN'T KNOW YOU WERE IN BEVERLY ILLS THOUGHT YOU WERE IN OLLYWOOD

GEORGE

The technical side of making a big musical picture presents numerous complications. For instance, in my earlier films I found it difficult working with an orchestra of some fifty musicians on the extreme opposite side of the stage about a block away.

This separation was technically necessary to control the sound properly when picked up "live" on the set. Most of the dance numbers in my first four pictures at RKO were made that way. This system is seldom used now. All music tracks of any real size are done on the regular recording stage. We use the pre-recorded sound tracks played back on loud-speakers for actual photography.

When I first started in films, my problem was to find some feasible way to rehearse, record and shoot the quantity of musical numbers that came my way for each picture. It bothered me to have a lot of unfinished dances hanging over my head as we progressed through the dialogue and story of a film. But for some years now I've had a design for the creating and photographing of dance numbers. That is to prepare and shoot four or five to start with. These are usually the ones we consider the most difficult. If an idea doesn't jell, so to speak, the staging of that one is postponed until the rest of the picture is completed.

I have done many of my most important trick solos after everything else was finished—with plenty of time to concentrate.

Another complication to overcome was that of forgetting a routine after having it set and rehearsed. Often I would complete work on one, put it aside for several months in favor of something else, only to find that, when it was time to return to it for actual shooting, a good portion of it had slipped my mind. Then came the job of recapturing it.

Other technical difficulties which mount up are the dubbing sessions after all production on the picture is finished.

The foot sounds had to be dubbed in, due to the difficulty of picking them up satisfactorily on the set during shooting. If it was a tap dance, all those sounds had to be matched back to the picture. In order to do it, you are also obliged to wear earphones, through which comes the distorted sound of the original pre-recorded track. In recent years the use of a remote unit consisting of ear plugs without overhead wires helps some but it's still a laborious chore. These technicalities are heavy on me because of the number of musical numbers I am always concerned with—in some instances as many as eighteen dances and songs in a picture.

Even though an audience may not notice the less important numbers so much, those too have to be thoroughly and completely presented.

When *Gay Divorcee* was finished, retakes, dubbing, still pictures and all, Phyllis and I remained in southern California for our holiday. We decided to explore the local scene a bit and started out with a short stay at Catalina and some fishing. One night I was refused entrance to the Casino where they dance because I was not wearing a tie. The door attendant didn't recognize me but, even if he had, I would not have been admitted. It was a strict rule then. Several newspaper columnists enjoyed this episode.

We went up and down the coast from Santa Barbara to San Diego and Tijuana, then to Palm Springs for some golf and tennis. Phyllis was a good tennis player but I never could give her any kind of a game. She could beat me six-love anytime she wanted to.

We didn't play much tennis together.

I could take her at golf, although she hit a long ball for her height and ninety-two pounds. The caddies at the Bel-Air Country Club have always referred to her as the longest hitter in the world for her weight.

Phyl was also an excellent dove shot. We often went over the border into Mexico for this sport. Just outside Mexicali was our favorite spot. I never could handle the dove situation but was fair enough with quail and ducks.

Our social activities were few. Neither of us cared to stay up late at night and we were pleased to find that the movie colony was mainly a pretty sleepy town.

We had moved to a house on North Alpine Drive. It was a luxurious Italian Riviera type place, owned by the opera star Tito Schipa, and it had a very fancy swimming pool in the back yard. We enjoyed this house, but Phyllis was looking for some property where we could build our own as soon as possible.

George, my valet, arrived from England as he promised and soon became an inveterate movie studio worker. He loved the place. His only regret was that I didn't have any horses in training any more. I assured him I was hoping to resume my racing operations later on.

Gay Divorcee had a sneak preview one night at some outlying theatre and, although I was notified about it, I didn't want to go. One of my main reasons for liking the movies so much was that I did not have to go to my own opening nights.

I told Eddie Rubin we were going out to dinner at the Trocadero and if there was any good news to report about the preview to call me there. He did—and told me he thought the picture was a cinch.

Pan Berman came to the Troc with a party afterward and told me as we passed each other on the dance floor, "I think we have a very big hit. You will be pleased. The picture went great." I gave Phyl a few fancy spins and we went to our table. The boss had just told me we had another hit. I felt that he must be pretty sure about it. Several other enthusiastic phone calls reached me when I got home.

Divorcee opened at the Music Hall in New York shortly after that and registered, as had been predicted. The press went all out in enthusiasm. Whereas the stage play had been panned unmercifully as to story, these reviews were high in praise of it and what they termed "delightful comedy." Regina Crewe in the New York *American* referred to it as "A lithe, blithe little farce." The *Times* said, "Built around a good story—there is real wit instead of gags." The *Evening Telegram* called it "fine farce."

A few weeks later, when the picture opened internationally, the reaction was the same. It was a holdover smash everywhere and there was no longer any question about my being accepted by the movie public. Ginger and I as a team had registered again and the studio was ready to take advantage of it. In those days, teams were more prevalent than they are now.

Mark Sandrich's success with *Divorcee* and Ginger and me inspired him to plan his next with us. Although he was not assigned to *Roberta,* he had already found something he thought would be suitable to follow it.

Pan Berman's judgment, along with Mark's, about composers for the pictures Ginger and I did was astute. In succession we had

Cole Porter's *Gay Divorcee,* Jerome Kern's *Roberta,* Irving Berlin's *Top Hat,* Irving Berlin's *Follow the Fleet,* Jerome Kern and Dorothy Fields' *Swing Time,* George and Ira Gershwin's *Shall We Dance,* the Gershwins' *Damsel in Distress,* and Berlin's *Carefree.* All these scores brought out top-class song hits, standards that are still recorded and played in new styles each year.

It was indeed my good fortune to introduce so many great songs by these top composers.

Fred and Fred, Jr., at Guaymas,
Mexico, May, 1953

A snapshot of Ava taken by her
father in 1958

Phyllis Astaire in 1953

A recent photograph of Fred Astaire's mother

CECIL BEATON

Fred, Jr., and Ava visit their father on location during filming of the TV show, *Man on a Bicycle*, 1958

"A Couple of Swells"—Astaire and Judy Garland—in *Easter Parade*, 1948

With Vera Ellen in *Three Little Words*, 1950

Cyd Charisse and Astaire in *The Bandwagon*, 1953

Daddy Long Legs, 1955, with Leslie Caron

Among his mementos is a photograph of
his winning racehorse, Triplicate

Practicing a golf shot in his workroom

With his mother, who lives with him in Hollywood

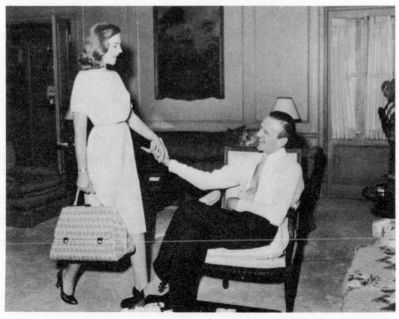

Ava Astaire with her father in their living room

Audrey Hepburn and Fred Astaire in *Funny Face*, 1956

With Barrie Chase in *An Evening with Fred Astaire,* on TV in 1958

Chapter 19 Feathers

I tackled *Roberta* with much enthusiasm and a bit more confidence than usual. It's a help to know that your forthcoming effort will be looked forward to by the public.

I must confess that I hate trying out. There have been many, many times through my career when I have been up for approval. No matter how big a star one might be, there's always that big test when you tackle a different medium. You're trying out again.

Bill Seiter was our director on *Roberta*. I had seen the New York stage version a year or so before and liked it. My part was played by Bob Hope originally. It shaped up as an important musical and the movie script was well adapted. Jerome Kern's music in this show was noted as one of his finest accomplishments. "Smoke Gets in Your Eyes" is a lovely thing. The dance which Ginger and I did to that has always been one of my favorites.

Randy Scott, who had devoted almost his entire time to Westerns, stepped out of character for this one. We became close friends. Scott incidentally is one of the best of the actor-golfers. A low-handicap player and rightly so—between a two and a five regularly. He really has the game licked but he won't admit it.

During the filming of *Roberta,* Mark Sandrich kept me posted on the formation of the next vehicle. Irving Berlin was signed to do the music for it.

I had told Mark about the number which I did for the Ziegfeld show *Smiles*, and that I thought I could elaborate on it for the screen. This is the idea I referred to a few pages back which inspired Irving to write the title song for the picture *Top Hat*.

When Irving arrived from the East to take up his assignment at the studio, he spent quite a lot of time visiting on the set with Ginger and me and would spring his new thoughts and creations on us with impromptu demonstrations at the piano. It was enlightening to know something so good about the next venture.

Musicals are particularly hard to predict in advance because so much depends on how the numbers work out. There has so often been a great deal of last-minute revision necessary on the things I've done.

Pandro Berman organized the choice and development of vehicles for the series I did with Ginger in a masterful way. He was always a jump ahead and we were not usually obliged to worry about what "the next one" would be.

We finished *Roberta* before Christmas in 1934. Phyllis and I went East on our usual holiday to spend some time with her family.

The impact of the success of *Gay Divorcee* was plainly evident. I was beginning to wonder how far it would go and how I could be sure not to get involved with a bad picture. I was confident that *Top Hat* would be a good one, but what about the next one to follow that?

After a few months' rest I was back at RKO, working on *Hat*.

There is so much that I can't remember through this period. Charles Dillingham died in '34 while we were away in Mexico on a hunting trip. The news did not reach me until some weeks later. I found that he had been very ill for some time. It saddened me to think of having lost track of C. B. like that. I had not seen

Adele and her husband for about a year. The latest news from her indicated she was fine and expecting a baby toward the end of the year (1935). We hoped to be over to visit her.

Phyllis and I were supremely happy. She spoke about it many times. Our simple social activities were just what we wanted. We still did not like going to parties and declined as many as we could. With all the success, and the satisfaction and excitement that goes with it, I don't think I ever fully realized the full size of that success.

Roberta opened at the Music Hall in New York—another hit. We were going through the sort of show-business dream sequence when you can't do anything wrong, professionally. I always refer to it as a "winning groove."

At the studio the work was fun. Ginger and I never failed to find plenty to laugh about. Rehearsals with Hermes Pan, now a full-fledged choreographer, brought out many practical jokes. The entire crew on the picture entered into the spirit which prevailed. So much was happening—time flew by.

The dancing dresses of my partners have, for years, been a working problem, and in *Top Hat* I dare say it reached its dizzy peak.

I seldom discuss the style of a dress but I am concerned with how it will dance, or rather, react to the dance. Therefore, my partners are usually willing to let me help in choosing them.

Girls love to wear slacks when learning or rehearsing a dance. They are comfortable and convenient and allow complete freedom of movement. Ginger always wore them for rehearsal. In fact, Hermes and I were so used to seeing Ginger on the rehearsal stage in slacks that one day when she showed up in a dress we didn't know who she was.

What I'm getting at is that when putting on a dance, experimenting over and over with various steps, the slacks work perfectly, but when we finally have to get ready to shoot, it is necessary to try everything with a dress, the actual dress if possible, to see how things will go. That's when the awful awakening takes place, the realization that in some instances it is not possible to do the steps as planned with the dress. If the gown happens to be very full at the hem, for instance, it automatically becomes "our" dress instead of just my partner's, as it wraps around my feet, causing no end of trouble and hindrance to both of us. If it is too tight, the lady cannot negotiate the routined movement, necessitating an alteration of the choreography or a splitting of the skirt. Endless problems can arise out of this situation, and I made it a practice some years back to ask the lady to rehearse in a dress or in some sort of rehearsal prop cloth that behaved like a dress, so that we would not be confronted with impasses on the set at the last minute, holding up production and causing general consternation.

In *Top Hat*, Ginger and I had that wonderful song of Irving Berlin's, "Cheek to Cheek." I arranged a romantic, flowing type of dance to fit the situation in the picture and we took special pains to try for extra-smooth smoothness.

Ginger rehearsed the final few days before shooting in a prop dress. I had seen the drawing of the real one she was to wear—a feathered affair and very nice, too, I thought.

I asked Gin to get the dress on for one rehearsal to make sure about it with all those feathers. Gin tried to get it but was told that the feathers were not yet sewn on, and the dress would not be ready until the day we were to shoot the number. That was that.

The memorable day was soon on us, with nobody anticipating any unusual hazards in connection with a little thing like a dress. Well, Ginger finally arrived on the set after a delay of about an hour while she was getting into this thing. I thought it looked fine but it was somewhat fuller than I expected. We then got ready to rehearse the number right through with the playback for camera and lights. Everything went well through the song, but when we did the first movement of the dance, feathers started to fly as if a chicken had been attacked by a coyote.

I never saw so many feathers in my life. It was like a snowstorm. They were floating around like millions of moths. I had feathers in my eyes, my ears, my mouth, all over the front of my suit, which just happened to be a white-tie-and-tails outfit. (Now, wasn't that odd?)

I shouted out, "I thought these feathers were supposed to be sewn to this dress."

The wardrobe lady answered, "Oh, it's only because it was the first time the dress was moved around a bit. That won't happen again."

I suggested that we'd better start shooting the number pretty quick while there were still some feathers left on it.

Ginger didn't say much. I knew we were in trouble and that the feathers would never stop flying off that dress in dance movement, and we had plenty coming up.

We started by photographing the song, finished that and stopped. So far so good.

We then went for the dance and again the feathers took over. The cameraman stopped us, saying he couldn't photograph the number that way, and also that the floor was covered with feathers. This went on again and again. Ginger's mama rushed on the stage to help—but even Lela couldn't. The feathers kept flying, the wardrobe lady shook the dress and the sweepers swept them up, but they kept flying and we could not get an o.k. take. It got to be funny after a while. The news went all over the lot that there was a blizzard on the *Top Hat* set. The sightseers poured in on us.

Finally, the fallout had run its main course. With just a minimum amount flying, the cameraman decided he would take a chance and photograph the number. We would see how it worked out in the rushes next morning.

When we finished shooting for the day, Hermes Pan and I sang a little parody on "Cheek to Cheek" to Ginger. It went (with apologies to Mr. B.):

> Feathers—I hate feathers—
> And I hate them so that I can hardly speak,
> And I never find the happiness I seek
> With those chicken feathers dancing
> Cheek to Cheek.

Next morning the rushes were good. Very few of the flying feathers picked up on the film and the glossy white floor showed none at all. What a relief!

We laughed about that episode for weeks afterward. It was sort of a running gag with Ginger and me. I used to call her "Feathers"!

There were many amusing and memorable things in connection with the making of *Top Hat*. Irving Berlin was around much of the time.

Jimmy Cagney visited the set one day when I was shooting my "Top Hat" number. Cagney had expressed enthusiasm about my work and had sent me several telegrams to that effect which I prized greatly. But when he turned up on the set, I was nervous. We were shooting the number in which I mowed down the boys with taps using a cane to simulate a machine gun.

Cagney liked what I was doing and told me so. I was pleased that my 4 A.M. inspiration was at last coming into its own. One section of it I could not routine. It was a pantomime bit—no taps—just movement in silhouette and trick lighting. I had to ad lib this section to get the spontaneous effect I wanted. Jimmy watched and whispered to me after about the third take, "Don't shoot it again, kid—you got it on the second take. You'll never top that one." I insisted on one more, but Jimmy was right. Next morning when I saw the rushes, that second take was the one.

Along about this time I had an offer from the Lucky Strike people to do their *Hit Parade* radio show for a series of weeks—a sort of singing M.C. spot. At first I hesitated about accepting because I figured I could not be too valuable without dancing and dancing meant nothing over the radio.

They convinced me that I could do a few tap bits and everybody would be satisfied. I finally accepted the offer to start in about six weeks.

Phyl and I had arranged to take a quick trip abroad on completing *Top Hat*. We planned to stay with Adele and Charlie at Lismore Castle briefly on the way to London. It all had to be done rather hurriedly now with the Lucky Strike radio show thrown in, because I was due back in California within three months to start the next picture, *Follow the Fleet*, again with Ginger.

We were soon off for Europe, and on arriving in Ireland found Adele in good health and high hopes about her forthcoming addition to the family. Beautiful Lismore Castle afforded us much pleasure. Situated in County Waterford, high above the Blackwater River, which is famed for its salmon fishing, Lismore is rich in tradition and historic charm. Charlie took me to the Punchestown races. He was keen about racing too and maintained a small stable of horses in training, mostly jumpers. Phyl and I enjoyed our stay and the beautiful Irish countryside which Adele and Charlie showed us at length.

In London, Phyllis told me that she was expecting a baby and that it would probably arrive about the middle of January (1936). I was elated and we joyously discussed our becoming an aunt and uncle along about the same time. Adele's baby was due in November of 1935.

We ordered a half bottle of champagne, which neither of us cared for too much, but we wanted to celebrate in some way—and as mildly as possible instead of going out to a night club.

I thought it best to curtail our vacation trip because of the news Phyllis had told me, so we headed back to New York, where I was due to start my radio show in two weeks.

I found that I enjoyed the *Lucky Strike Hit Parade* job. Lennie Hayton and his band were fun to work with and the medium of radio was a novel experience for me, although not the best way to exploit my specialties. However, it was pleasant gathering in all that extra money.

Top Hat had just opened at the Music Hall in New York and proved to be the biggest one so far. It broke the house record and the press reception was excellent. My material for the *Hit Parade* came easy, because much of Irving Berlin's score was in great demand and I used the songs plentifully.

We broadcast out of Radio City, New York, the first two weeks and then the whole show moved to California so that I could start rehearsals on *Follow the Fleet*, simultaneously. This arrangement went on for four more weeks and I found it very difficult to rehearse dances for the picture all day and prepare for the weekly *Hit Parade* show at night during most of the week. I was glad to finish the engagement, and vowed I would never try it again, regardless of the monetary attraction.

Follow the Fleet looked like a good show. Ginger and I were enthusiastic about it but we also wondered how long it would be safe to carry on this cycle of team pictures. We didn't want to run it into the ground and we discussed the situation with each other frequently.

Irving Berlin had agreed to write the music for *Fleet*, so we decided it was best to do this one and talk of other plans later.

Along about in here somewhere, I was involved in a contract-revision controversy with RKO. It was timed with the national opening of *Top Hat*, which proved a smash hit everywhere. My agent, a lawyer, and the RKO studios were battling it out. The contract was not satisfactory, according to my recently acquired status, and I was expecting my agent, Leland Hayward, to effect an adjustment. However, in the middle of the negotiations, another lawyer appeared in the proceedings, supposedly on my behalf, and antagonized the studio to the point of their wanting to let me cool my heels indefinitely. When I heard about it I blew up.

All matters were straightened out in a few weeks and I got everything I was supposed to get, but in the meantime I was perturbed and worried.

My original contract with RKO was for a three-week guarantee at fifteen hundred dollars a week, with options for four years at yearly increases of five hundred dollars a week while making a picture. It was the sort of standard document that you sign when you are anxious about the job and somewhat doubtful about making good. Many such contracts are signed for the movies but are usually adjusted if the performer does especially well.

I never gave it a thought at the time, but the only risk the studio took in signing me to the original contract was the total sum of $4,500. If I had failed, I would have been dropped. That was all there was to it. My new deal was one of the best.

In mid-September I received a cable from Ireland that my sister had lost twin boys at birth. This shocking news upset us all, of course, as the similar message had the time before.

It was sad that Delly could not have had the children she wanted so much. She wrote me of her bitter disappointment and near despondency.

Follow the Fleet had its high-point moments, both during re-hearsals and actual shooting with Harriet Hilliard (Mrs. Ozzie Nelson), Tony Martin, Betty Grable and Lucille Ball. Harriet had a prominent role, but Tony, Betty and Lucille were still play-ing minor parts.

The Berlin score for this movie was again one of his best, with "I'm Putting All My Eggs in One Basket," "We Saw the Sea," "I'd Rather Lead a Band" and "Let's Face the Music and Dance." The last mentioned brought out another dress incident which will always remain with me.

In this number, Ginger came up with a beaded gown which was surely designed for anything but dancing. I saw it before shooting of the number started, and I tried a few steps with Ginger. It was a good-looking dress but very heavy, I thought—one solid mass of beads. Ginger said it would work fine, and I, in an absent-minded moment, agreed that it would be all right. The dress had heavy beaded sleeves that hung down from the wrists, which I hadn't bargained for. When Ginger did a quick turn, the sleeves, which must have weighed a few pounds each, would fly—necessitating a quick dodge by me.

If I didn't duck I'd get the sleeve in the face.

After a few rehearsals with this creation, I thought I had mastered the menace. When shooting of the number started, things went smoothly in the first take for about fifteen seconds.

Then Ginger gave out with some special kind of a twist and I got the flying sleeve smack on the jaw and partly in the eye. I kept on dancing, although somewhat maimed.

We had designed the number as a four-minute dance to be shot in one piece with no cuts, and we came to the end of it with me still in a daze.

As usual, at the end of the take the director and everybody asked, "How was it for you?"

Ginger answered, "It was all right for me—Fred, how about you?"

I replied that I didn't remember anything about the take—that I had been knocked groggy in the first round.

I asked for another take, which everybody agreed upon, although Mark Sandrich said he couldn't see anything wrong with the first one. He always liked getting another good one for safety's sake, anyway.

From then on I kept ducking and dodging that sleeve, and we couldn't get one take all through that pleased us, so we went on until about eight o'clock that night, still trying, and finally gave up, prepared to continue the next day on the same number. We were exhausted, Ginger and I. It was a difficult dance and we had done some twenty takes that day.

Next morning we went in to see the rushes of the film and the No. 1 take was perfect. It was the one we all liked best. The hay-maker I got from Ginger's sleeve didn't show a bit. I was astounded. But anyway we had it, so we went on to the next sequence immediately.

In another instance I had a scene with Randy Scott where I was supposed to hit him for some reason or other. Randy played a chief petty officer and I was a gob. I hadn't had much experience with fight scenes and it was explained to me how to hit at Randy, but of course just miss him, and it would come off on the screen as if I had nailed him.

When the time came for me to swing, I got carried away and brought one 'way up from my shoes laces that really clipped Randy on the mouth, bringing blood and almost flooring him.

The "Sheriff" had every reason to be annoyed with me but if he was he never showed it. Always the Southern gentleman.

When I finished shooting *Fleet,* Phyl and I stayed close to home awaiting the arrival of the baby. It was getting mighty close to the time, I thought, and I prevailed upon her to go on to the hospital early—maybe a day or so. Phyl would have none of that idea. She said to me a number of times:

"I wouldn't think of going down there *one second* earlier than I have to. I hate hospitals! Don't worry, I'll know in plenty of time." So I just waited. I didn't want to harp at her by insisting, so I waited.

Suddenly, the morning of January 21, she woke me about four-thirty and said, "Fred—Fred—I think we'd better get down there now." I jumped up and we were quickly on our way.

There wasn't much traffic at that hour as I drove her down in our small coupé. She kept saying as she clung to my arm, "You'd better drive faster—it won't hurt to go through that red light now."

For a few moments I was afraid our first child was going to

have the distinction of being born on Wilshire Boulevard, Los Angeles.

It was about an eighteen-minute run from our house to the Good Samaritan Hospital, and my little Phyllis was in a pretty miserable way as we walked up the steps. She mumbled to me: "I think I'm going to have it right here. We'd better hurry." With that I asked the nurse at the reception desk for some help and we got her upstairs and into bed just as the arrival began.

I went through the old pacing-up-and-down routine. I was scared.

About a half hour later, the nurse came along and calmly said, "You're the pappy of a boy." Just like that.

I looked at her and answered, "Huh?" She said, "Come on with me," and we went to the room where Dr. Vruwink was. He said, as he held the child upside down by one leg, "You see—it's a perfectly good one."

To which I replied with a brilliant, "Is it?"

That was Fred, Jr. Phyllis was delighted. She wanted a boy.

I had an adjoining room at the hospital and we stayed there for about a week. I made a remarkable recovery.

It wasn't too far from Santa Anita races and I went out several afternoons at Phyl's insistence. A couple of nights Irving Berlin came down and played gin rummy with me for hours. Irving is always thinking up new song ideas, and in the middle of our gin games he would often sing and throw lyric ideas and rhymes at me to test them out. At this time Irving was working on the picture and his mind was particularly occupied when he left me at about three. He got into a taxi and told the driver to take him to Joe Schenck's house in Beverly Hills, where he was staying. It happened that he got a driver who didn't know much about Beverly Hills and proceeded to drive Irv around all over the place, out into Malibu or somewhere. Irving told me next day, "I wasn't paying any attention to the driver—my mind was on a tune. When I looked at my watch I found I'd been riding around for two hours."

Mother and son were doing very well. Occasionally I found myself returning home from work surprised and not realizing that something new was going on in the house. Something like a new baby and a nursemaid.

Chapter 20 *Gingerless*

My next obligation to RKO was *Swing Time*, the sixth in a row for Ginger and me, and it was to start within a few months. This one, with George Stevens directing and a fine cast, including Victor Moore, Helen Broderick, Betty Furness and Eric Blore, had a Jerome Kern–Dorothy Fields score. The old cycle kept rolling on.

There seemed to be no sign of a letup in interest for these musicals and it was difficult for any of us to make a decision about breaking up the format.

While we were shooting *Swing Time*, *Follow the Fleet* opened all over the country and was acclaimed as another box-office hit for RKO and the "Ginger-Fred" combination. I had made up my mind to wait for some small clue from the public as to whether or not they had had enough of it—at least temporarily.

So far there were no signs whatsoever. In the 1935 *Motion Picture Herald* list of the ten best moneymakers, we appeared in fourth place just below Shirley Temple, Will Rogers and Clark Gable.

I don't know what these lists prove or how the listers arrive at their choices, but the fact remains, they get a great deal of publicity and seem to impress a lot of people. So there we were, and we decided it was no time to interfere with the studio's plans.

Swing Time had ample values. There were many dance numbers and as usual we did our best to keep things new and fresh. I have always tried to carry out my steadfast rule of not repeating anything in dance that I've done before.

The Jerome Kern melodies were decidedly inspiring. "Swing Waltz," "The Way You Look To-Night," "Bojangles," "A Fine Romance" and "Pick Yourself Up" went on to become standards through the years.

Howard Lindsay and Allan Scott supplied the screenplay. Howard was my director of *Gay Divorce* on the stage and Allan had scripted several of our recent successful vehicles.

Swing Time took a long time to complete, several weeks more than the others, due largely to the trick screen process necessary for the "Bojangles" number, which I did last of all, after the regular shooting schedule was finished.

The next vehicle for Ginger and me was due to start in three months, *Shall We Dance,* scored by George and Ira Gershwin. Again Pan Berman and Mark Sandrich had carefully planned a show with a little different twist for these musical-comedy characters of ours. Sandrich told me of the story line, in which I would be a ballet man versus Ginger's ballroom and jazz dancer. With that background there was plenty of scope for dance ideas we had not done before. The plot was rather complex but it made a good threadwork for our purposes. I was pleased with the outlook and decided it was about time for another quick trip to Europe for Phyllis and me. Young Fred, Jr., was coming along fine and had a head of hair, too. He stayed home with the house crew while Phyl and I set out for our brief vacation abroad.

A few days before leaving I received an attractive offer to appear on the radio for the coming fall season (1936-37).

The advertising firm of Young & Rubicam approached me for Packard Motor Car Company about a thirty-nine-week one-hour variety show, in which I would be master of ceremonies as well as perform four or five songs or dances along with comedy sequences. It would be a big show with Johnny Green and band, also Charles Butterworth and guest stars. I hesitated again, thinking back to my previous experience with radio and movie at the same time.

Phyllis advised me not to do it, saying it would be too much to worry about.

However, I decided to accept the offer and worry about it later. Contracts were signed just before our departure, covering a period of three years—one year with two-year option. All details as to material and staging of the show were to be discussed on my return in July.

We were off as planned, flying to New York, stopping a few days to see a few shows and then on to England by boat.

After a week in London, Phyl and I decided to sneak off to Paris for a few days without letting anyone know. Having been besieged by the usual press coverage accorded most movie stars on our arrival, we wanted to get away from it all. I engaged rooms at the inconspicuous Vendôme Hotel and expressly requested the hotel manager to keep our reservations confidential.

We flew over and were pleased to see that there were no reporters at the airport when the plane landed in France. We were walking toward the main building, joking to ourselves about how successfully our secret trip had worked out, when a little man with a camera approached with his hat in his hand, saying:

"S'il vous plaît, monsieur et madame—une photographie."

I grumbled to Phyl, "Oh, oh—I spoke too soon—we're stuck —I've got to let him take it."

He took his picture and we walked on, thinking we'd probably meet some more before long. After we had gone a few steps, the little man came running, speaking half French and half English, "Attendez, monsieur et madame—zat will be cinq franc—five francs, please."

I quickly gave him his money, he handed me the picture and we were once again free. Phyl teased me plenty about not being such a big shot as I thought I was.

The Vendôme was a delightful little hotel, located in one corner of the Place Vendôme. There was a tiny reception hall and desk with only a concierge and a small page boy in attendance most of the time. It was the ideal place to hide away.

Our suite was on the second floor overlooking a part of the Place Vendôme, and the only entrance to it from the main hallway was through the bathroom. We had a good laugh when we saw this. For some reason or other the rest of the floor was occupied in such a way that our suite of small sitting room, bedroom and bath was accessible only through that bathroom door. Phyl referred to it as our foyer.

We had a delightful time for several days, coming and going as we pleased. Then one evening I was sitting in the living room at the window, watching the passers-by on the Rue de Castiglione below.

I noticed a little man standing on the corner, looking up toward our window. I stepped back and remembered that I had seen this same fellow there two days before. I told Phyl, "There's a sinister-looking man down in the street who keeps peering up here. He seems to be stalking us." I let it go at that.

When we left the hotel a few minutes later, I suggested that we walk past the man, if he was still there. I was curious to find out whether or not he might try to approach me.

He was there all right but made no effort to speak; in fact, he looked the other way as we passed. Then I noticed he seemed to be following us until we jumped into a taxi and escaped.

This sort of thing went on for a few more days. He kept standing on that corner looking up toward our windows. Finally I told Phyl that it was getting my goat and I was going to do something about it.

Downstairs I went and right up to him, standing on the corner. I asked him in my rather mixed-up French if he wanted to see me.

He replied, "Oh, oui, Monsieur!" and then he broke into English, "I do not want to spoil your vacation and I wait here hoping I will get up enough courage to speak to you before you leave town. You see I am reporter for newspaper."

This broke my heart. Such consideration from a newspaperman!

I had found one—a shy reporter.

I invited him to come in and have a drink with us and gave him a story, with apologies for having caused him so much anxiety and delay. I asked him how he discovered that we were in Paris, and he told me his sister worked in a shop where we had bought a leather bag.

When we returned to London next day I had a message from him saying he was so pleased that our interview had worked out the way it did because his was the only story to appear, now that we had left town, and all his contemporaries were very jealous and wanted to know how he had done it.

It was great fun, that trip. Phyllis enjoyed the simple things as I did. We were never bored because we didn't have to be doing anything in particular to find life and enjoyment.

We were on our way back home after another week of London parties and activities. It would soon be time to jump into rehearsals for the next picture and we planned to stop in New York for the usual visit on the way to the coast.

We took the old 20th-Century-Limited-change-in-Chicago-to-the-Santa-Fe-Chief-route as usual. Phyl didn't like to fly. The number of fans at the station stops was diminishing each year as the majority of movie stars had adopted flying from coast to coast. It was interesting to see this change.

Pasadena was our de-training point and we were greeted by dear old Eddie Rubin and the boys from RKO as well as by several members of our house staff, including the nurse and Fred, Jr., who looked very much surprised at the whole thing.

It was becoming nicer and nicer to come home to California with each succeeding trip.

I was back on the job at the studio in a few days.

One evening I was called to the telephone by my agent to re-mind me that I was needed urgently at a meeting to discuss my radio show. Radio show? This came as a distinct shock. I had forgotten about the commitment and for the moment could hardly figure out how I would ever be able to fulfill it. I even asked tim-idly if I could get out of my contract, because I didn't realize what I was doing accepting such a job to run concurrently with the staging and rehearsing of so many dance routines for the coming picture. Old Minnie started to moan—and how.

Leland Hayward told me very plainly that I most certainly could not get out of anything and that I'd better start figuring out right now some way to cope with the situation, even if I had to cut myself in two.

This sort of multiple-job-taking is fine for almost any type of performer but a dancer. When it comes to rehearsing new stuff for hours daily the physical strain is pretty rough. My favorite gag line, "Oh, why did my mother ever give me dancing lessons?" came in handy here.

Of course I know I belly-ache and worry more than is neces-sary, but this situation gave me the greatest opportunity of my life to enjoy my misery to its fullest extent.

Phyllis said, "You know, I don't think you've ever enjoyed anything in your life as much as those two jobs—but please don't do any more of it after this year. I like it better when you are only miserable about one job—pictures."

Swing Time opened at the Music Hall in New York to smash business and a nifty press. Some critics referred to it as the best of all our films. I knew it wasn't, but that's how strong the old machine was—we still could do no wrong. When it opened nation-ally, the reception was as usual, and I could not get any indication of a possible decline or weakening.

We were listed as the number-one box-office attraction in sev-eral national movie box-office polls. The *Hollywood Reporter* had us number one from a certain group of exhibitors. We were number three on the *Motion Picture Herald* list, just after Shirley Temple and Clark Gable.

I labored with my radio show and we got it into pretty fair shape for the opening. After I caught on to the knack of the thing, I rather enjoyed it and was told that the Packard people were satisfied, so it worked out well for a while, until the shooting of *Shall We Dance* started. I was in so much of the film that I had very little time to prepare and approve of material for the other job.

Phyllis had found the property for us to build our dream house on. She was engrossed in plans and blueprints for building operations which were to start almost immediately. The property, acquired from John Boles on Summit Drive in Beverly Hills, was ideally located and not too far from any studio. It was some two hundred feet higher than the city, and the air was better, she thought, without having to go high into the hills. The parcel covered about four acres, a small area on a fairly steep hillside, which provided good protection.

I complimented my bride for her ingenuity in finding this lovely spot but asked why she took such a large piece. Wouldn't about two acres have been enough? She had it all figured out: "Oh, it's a very good investment. You see, we'll build on two acres and I have a plan for the other two in the meantime."

Across the way was the Spalding estate with orange groves separating us from the residence about a quarter of a mile away; just above was Pickfair, Mary Pickford's attractive place, and next door, below, Charlie Chaplin's house. On the other side there were no obstructions at all—we were high above and far away from any other house.

Building started. The plans for the two acres included a swimming pool and tennis court, naturally. When I told Phyllis that I was not dreaming of playing any tennis she said: "Oh, we're not building the court for us, it's only for resale value. You know out here nobody wants a house without a tennis court, and besides, it'll be useful if the children want to learn."

As long as I didn't have to get beaten six-love every time, I was in thorough accord with Phyllis' plans. She always handled business deals and finances. I never knew or wanted to know what I had or was in the process of accumulating. I signed papers, that was all.

Phyl spent hours at the adding machine keeping figures for income-tax purposes. I often asked her not to bother, to let someone else do it, but she insisted that she loved her work and wouldn't think of having anyone else take over.

The building of the house, pool and tennis court was making good progress but I was still curious as to what Phyllis had in mind for those two extra acres.

Shall We Dance seemed to be working well. I had one ballet-type number with the lovely Harriet Hoctor; Ginger and I danced on roller skates for the song "Let's Call the Whole Thing Off." There were various novel approaches to make us feel that we were keeping up with what might be expected of us.

I continued to wonder how long this Ginger-Fred bonanza could go on.

The first clue pointing to the possible saturation point came in a letter I received from my sister. She sent me a clipping from the Cork *Examiner* reviewing *Swing Time*, which had just opened in Ireland. Adele wrote across the top of the page: "Must send you this as it is the only unfavorable one by some sour-puss." The article read:

THE SINGING AND DANCING LIMIT

Ginger and Fred are at it again in "Swing Time," singing and dancing like anything. One begins to wonder how many more of that type of film the public is prepared to enjoy. I know of at least one member of it who has reached the limit. . . .

Well, there it was.

I wrote to Adele telling her I rather sympathized with that chap on the Cork *Examiner* and that I could picture him sitting in his little office, with clay pipe in the mouth and shillelagh on the desk, airing his mind, and that we were probably fortunate to have had him on our side as long as we did. I showed Phyllis the clipping. She tossed it away with:

"What a dwedful man!"

George Gershwin was with me a lot through the making of *Shall We Dance*. We enjoyed reminiscing about our past associations on the stage with Aarons and Freedley. George was very keen about the progress of the entertainment world. He was always impressed by the growing numbers of talented new young people and their ideas.

With the picture finished and out of the way, I was still lashed tightly to my *Packard Hour* radio show for several more months and made overtures to them about releasing me from my coming options—if they had any idea of keeping me on. They told me they were eager to have me continue inasmuch as the first season had been successful from their standpoint. However, they agreed to release me if I insisted. This was done gracefully by them, accompanied by page advertisements in several trade papers announcing their regret at having to terminate my engagement at my request, for personal reasons.

I thought it was a kindly gesture on their part, avoiding any impression that they had fired me out on my ear.

Johnny Green and I had many interesting numbers to do through that thirty-nine weeks and some of our shows were considered tops. Charlie Butterworth was delightful to work with, too. He often told me that performing on the radio made him terribly nervous. He could not understand why, with all his theatrical experiences.

One thing that amused me about radio was the ready-made applause. I mean that which came when one of the assistants signaled the audience to crash through with an ovation.

When I did my dance bits, I was limited to a four-by-four-foot square dance mat and had to stay within the confines of the floor microphones. There wasn't much I could do in the way of steps, especially, because my regular style was to cover ground and also get off the floor and up in the air a lot. Here I found that the only effective steps for radio were those with a lot of taps close together—a string of ricky-ticky-ticky-tacky-ticky-tacky taps. If you got off the floor there was just nothing, but nothing, coming over the air. I didn't have time to routine a new set of ticky-tacky taps each week so I would ad lib each dance and hop into a finish step when I knew I was about twelve bars or so from home.

I had a dozen of these sustaining exhibition tap steps to choose from which were designed to please our live studio audience as well as the multitudes out in space.

One was a spinning tapping affair, another was just a tapping and arm-waving gem, and another might be a half-falling, half-standing-up flash that sounded like a riveting machine—and so on. Any one of these would be bound to kill the customers. I had them numbered in my mind, and at rehearsals, when we came to the part where the man signaled for the applause, I would say, "All right, boys, and here's where I go into studio wow number seven," or some other number.

That show was well worth the effort, and not only just for the money. Working with Johnny Green was a highlight always. It was a whole lot of experience and I've often felt that I did not make the most of my opportunities in that field.

Although *Swing Time* was an all-out hit in its initial runs, as the weeks went on there was a premature falling off in box-office attendance. The signs that the cycle was running out its course were beginning to show.

The slightest decline in a situation like this shows up tremendously, of course, so what we'll call a concernment started. I asked for, and all hands at the studio agreed to, a picture away from Ginger, to keep us from falling into a rut.

Ginger was for it, too, and she was immediately assigned to *Stage Door,* with Katharine Hepburn.

Pan Berman had been planning my picture ahead and he told me that *A Damsel in Distress* was already under way with another Gershwin score and that George Stevens would direct. This P. G. Wodehouse book measured up to being pretty useful, I thought, and I was happy with the outlook. However, I was preparing myself for another siege of attacks because my usual partner would not be with me this time. We had not announced any permanent dissolution; in fact, we had our next meeting all planned to follow this slight intermission.

We were to do *Carefree* with a Berlin score as our assignment in 1938.

There wasn't any room for a holiday or relaxation by the time I finished the radio show. It was close to *A Damsel in Distress* time for me. I began to visualize what the critics might be calling it, such as: *Dancer in Distress,* probably followed by a few fitting remarks about Fred being "Gingerless" this time. It was interesting to try again to work out some dance things that would not be up for comparison. I had no leading lady as yet but I knew George Burns and Gracie Allen would be with me and that, of course, opened up many new avenues of divertissement. We had our fun, George, Gracie and I.

George brought along an idea for a dance in which we three would use whisk brooms for props, whisking in rhythm, brushing each other off. I can't recall how we worked it into the plot but we did.

At first there was a discussion about Ruby Keeler playing *Damsel* but I missed out with her because the part called for a more British type of girl. It was finally settled that Joan Fontaine, the lovely young actress recently signed at RKO, would play the part. Joan was not a dancer but she had studied some and it was assumed that she could do whatever was necessary in that line, should we need it. Her role did not require much dancing. Any girl following Ginger at this point was on the spot anyway, and we hoped to avoid unfair comparisons, if possible, by not asking too much of our leading lady in dance. Joan and I did only one dance together and she handled it beautifully. An outdoor number, it was photographed on a hillside near Malibu.

We had a big cast with George and Gracie, Joan Fontaine, Ray Noble, Constance Collier, Reginald Gardiner and Montague Love.

I noticed, at this point, that George Gershwin had not been around to see us as often as usual during the shooting of the picture.

I called him on the phone, saying we missed him, and asked why we hadn't seen him. He explained that he had been painting at home—that he was getting more and more interested in it—and asked me to come to his house and see some of his work. It was that day I first heard of his being ill. He told me that several times while working on the score of *Damsel,* he had suffered terrific headache attacks and that on one occasion his hands would not function—he could not play the piano. I had never known George to be ill. It seemed incredible. Only a few weeks later he died, shortly after an operation. That was some months before *Damsel* was released.

Shall We Dance opened in New York and did the usual top business at first, but it began to hang a bit sooner than usual, indicating that the tide really was ebbing. The notices were fine but a number of them around the country showed signs of the "Well—here we go again" attitude.

Damsel turned out to be a goodish picture and it accomplished what we tried to do.

The Gershwins' score, with such songs as "Foggy Day in London Town" and "Nice Work If You Can Get It," was one of their best. The press reception was generally favorable and in many instances Ginger and I were given credit for having been smart to foresee the necessity of a change.

I was relieved that the great divide had taken place. This was my second professional separation, of course, and I felt certain about never wanting to get into that sort of predicament again.

Phyllis and I were in Aiken, South Carolina, when the picture opened nationally. First reports were big. After a week or so I had this wire from Pan Berman:

DEAR FRED RESULTS RATHER DISAPPOINTING AROUND COUNTRY AT END OF FIRST WEEK STOP BELIEVE WE WILL FALL A LITTLE SHORT OF GROSS LAST PICTURE.

To me this was not surprising because I did not think *Damsel* was a strong picture, and I knew that without Ginger there was bound to be plenty of letdown from the fans. I realized that I was again going through the de-partnering pains and there was nothing I could do about it at the moment. So Phyl and I enjoyed our winter vacation anyway and I decided to stop worrying about "show biz" until later. I concentrated on my golf game.

Young Fred, Jr., was with us and enjoying himself at Phyllis' Uncle Henry and Auntie Maud's house.

There was so much of interest to do in Aiken. Several of the biggest racing stables maintained winter quarters down there.

I hadn't given much thought to racing these past few years, mostly because there were so many dance routines cluttering up my existence.

Frankly, I was a bit fed up at the thought of fighting my way back to a movie status again. Not that I was considered through or anything of the sort, but it so happens that when you go through a lull like that, the general feeling is you're going to lull yourself right through the cellar floor. I was a bit worried because with a dancing career such as mine, highly specialized as it was, I couldn't figure for sure where I would be able to go. I would have liked to go straight dramatic, but that was not possible. I felt I wasn't qualified to do it.

I told Phyllis I was thinking of retiring and asked for her advice.

She told me just because I had had a good round of golf I was carried away and that if I had a bad round the next day I'd surely have no idea of retiring. She was right. I shot a ninety the next day. That was the last of the retirement talk for several years.

Chapter 21 *Box-Office Poison*

We were due back in California for *Carefree*, Mark Sandrich directing, and a score by Irving Berlin.

"Feathers" Rogers and I liked the script and the idea of resuming our partnership for another film or two, although we knew that a splitting up of the team was imminent and necessary.

Pan Berman had already scheduled *The Story of Vernon and Irene Castle* to follow *Carefree* and that was to be the last of the series. It was an attractive idea, the Castles, and we both were eager to do it.

Ginger had definite nonmusical plans to follow that. She wisely figured on expanding her dramatic ability.

As for my plans, I had none except to finish my commitment at RKO. I felt it advisable to make a change at that stage, and was discussing deals for two years hence with several other studios.

Once again we plunged into rehearsals on the many dance creations needed for *Carefree*. This was a happy chore with those Berlin tunes at our command. I think we had as much fun with "The Yam" as any number we ever did together. It was not exactly a dance for popular ballroom use but it made a good screen gimmick.

"I Used to Be Color Blind" was another one. We dreamed up a dream dance for that, partly in slow motion, which I think turned out well.

There was a legend going the rounds that I was not allowed to kiss my leading lady in pictures because my wife did not approve. This was ridiculous and untrue.

It was my idea to refrain from mushy love scenes, partly because I hated doing them and also because it was somewhat novel not to have sticky clinches in a movie. Mark Sandrich agreed on this idea in our early films, and it proved to be an asset. Anyway, it was different.

Well, that idea ran its course as we progressed from one kissless film to another.

Rumors about my being forbidden to partake of this ecstatic movie privilege appeared in print frequently.

One fan magazine came up with a jolly article headed:

WHY WON'T FRED KISS GINGER *? ? ? ?*

I finally decided to capitalize on this world-shaking interrogation and asked Ginger if she'd mind if I gave her the kiss of the century in this picture so that we might end this international crisis.

She answered, "Oh, all right—but you'll have to speak to my agent."

At the end of the slow-motion part of the "Color Blind" dance, I installed a slow-motion kiss that figured to make up for all the kisses I had not given Ginger for all those years.

When we shot the dance for slow motion it of course was danced in normal fashion. But the special camera for that sort of thing sizzles away at four times faster speed, so that when the film is run normally, the action moves four times slower.

The dance finished with the celebrated kiss and we had to hold that position in repose until the director said "Cut." Mark let it run on for an extra fifteen seconds to allow for a dissolve.

That night I told Phyllis we had finally given them the kiss everybody was hollering about, and I wanted her to come and see the rushes next morning.

"Oooooh, I can hardly wait," said Phyl.

She accompanied me into the projection room, one of her rare visits, I must add, and we watched the rushes with a number of other people, including Mark Sandrich and our technical crew.

The slow-motion dance went through nicely. Phyllis remarked how much she liked it, and when we finally reached the end where Ginger and I settled into the kiss, we settled as only a slow-motion camera can settle you. We were there holding that kiss for about four minutes! All of us started to laugh, especially Phyllis.

It was very funny, and everyone in the room had been waiting for it. Mark Sandrich had purposely kept the camera rolling extra long in order to put on this little show. Phyl took proper advantage of the opportunity to rib me, "Did you say you were going to make up for all the kisses you missed? Well, you certainly did!"

I explained as we walked away from the projection room that I actually only kissed Ginger for a few seconds, and how remarkable it was to see it stretched out such an extraordinarily long time in slow motion, and that naturally the only thing to appear in the finished picture would be about four or five seconds into the dissolve and—

Phyllis jumped in with, "Oh, yes—I know—and I also know that this is the first time you ever really made an effort to win an Academy Award."

For several years I had been planning a golf dance solo but could not find a suitable spot for it until *Carefree* came along. Fooling around at Bel Air one day, I did a few impromptu rhythm steps just before hitting one off the tee and was surprised to find that I could really connect that way. I tried a second one quickly to see whether it was accidental or not. That one moved right out there, too. I stashed the idea away in the back of my head. When I mentioned it to Mark Sandrich for this story, he told me he thought it could be written in, but he wanted me to demonstrate what I had in mind. I took him to the practice tee at Bel Air and ad libbed a few steps, hitting the ball while humming my own accompaniment. He approved.

The next move was to set up a private driving range at the RKO ranch for rehearsals.

I had about three hundred golf balls and five men shagging them, a piano and Hal Borne to play for me, and several buckets of iced beer. It was about ninety-five degrees or more out in the San Fernando Valley sun and that beer came in mighty handy. This went on for two weeks—a most enjoyable job. Berlin came up with a Scotch type of tune for me and the number lingers as one of my favorite solos.

Another favorite number of mine in that picture was "Change Partners." As I played a psychiatrist, it was an opportunity for a hypnotic dance, so we gave it the full treatment. Gin was swell, dancing as if in a trance the whole way through. It was a useful bit.

The show worked out well but not up to our biggest grosses at the box office.

That year the operator of a large chain of independent movie houses caused an upheaval in the newspapers by announcing in several press conferences his views on Hollywood and its stars. He named a group of the most prominent star names as "box-office poison."

The first list, consisting of about half a dozen very top men and women, appeared in a paid ad taken in a Hollywood trade paper. The Eastern press picked it up by arranging an interview with the exhibitor. This time he threw in many more names—including mine.

They printed his quotations verbatim and the whole thing

was then carried world-wide. I was one of his labeled "box-office poison" stars.

Ouch!

Jimmy Fidler's broadcast that week went as follows:

Hollywood is reading this week's issue of Time magazine with astonishment today, and most of the colony is wondering what Fred Astaire is going to do—because in the motion picture department of this current issue there appears an article dealing with the recent trade paper advertisement which named a group of stars who were, according to the ad, poison to the box-office. But Time magazine, in quoting from the advertisement, has included the name and picture of Astaire. In so doing the editors have made an unfortunate mistake, for Astaire's name was not one of those mentioned in the original advertisement. In other words, the editorial staff of Time finds itself in the embarrassing position of having included Astaire as one of the group of box-office poison stars, when in fact records indicate that he is one of the top ten box-office stars.

My studio, incensed by this attack, considered demanding a retraction, but then decided wisely that it would be best left alone. It all fizzled out in a few weeks and every one of the names mentioned continued on and to this day—some still as top attractions.

The incident bothered me, of course. In fact, it burned me up. Phyllis dismissed the whole thing with "Oh, stop worrying about it."

And I did.

We had moved into our new house on Summit Drive, a lovely place and all Phyllis' doing. It was completely simple in design and just right for our needs. It had Phyllis' charm and I was delighted with every bit of it and the fact that it had actually come into being. The landscaping, while not pretentious, was attractive, and the lawns were spacious enough to make you feel well apart from any city limits.

I finally got around to asking Phyl to let me in on the plan she had for the two extra acres of our property which were still undeveloped. She said, "Oh, haven't I told you? I'm going to make it a pheasant run." And she did, too.

It was such a pretty pheasant run.

Since our next house was built on that property some years later, the residence now occupied by me, I figure that I am writing these lines in my room at about the exact spot formerly inhabited by Phyl's pheasants. A nice thought.

It was time for us to pick up young Peter in school and bring him home for summer vacation, so off to Tucson we went on our six hundred-and-somethingth trip. Fred, Jr., came along and spent most of the time climbing back and forth over the front seat. He was nearly two and a half now and very active indeed.

The two boys had no difficulty in keeping the journey home eventful. I asked Phyl if she could please make them sit still for five minutes and suggested that they needed a good bawling-out. She answered, "Why don't you do it? You're the stern father." And then she laughed at me as usual. The boys kept moving around until one or both of them fell asleep. It was a long ride. This sort of trip went on many times. Peter was in that boarding school for seven years.

Announcements of the farewell film for Astaire and Rogers were released in about September of 1938, when we began rehearsals on *The Castles*.

Quite a ruckus was started by this, mostly from fans, although there were also a few newspaper mentions of regret. Nobody said "Hooray," at least not where we could hear it.

I received several threatening letters which looked phony to me; one especially, from an unsigned admirer who threatened, "We will kill your baby if you split up with Ginger." Cute?

This one was obviously somebody's idea of a good joke. I handed the letter to the studio police just through curiosity and that was the last I ever heard of it.

There were some sentimental aspects to this farewell appearance of the dear old team, but they were all in the form of some gag or other, such as a jazzed-up version of "Auld Lang Syne" by our rehearsal pianist or one of us arriving on the set wringing out a soaking wet handkerchief.

Ginger and I never felt that it was any last-time thing. We expected to do another picture or so when the right time came along.

The Castles was not an easy one to get on the screen, owing to the personal obligations necessary when doing a story about someone still living. But we had Irene Castle on hand under contract in an advisory capacity. She naturally was very particular about every detail, including those pertaining to her styles and hair dressings. I was glad I didn't have Ginger's job of living up to such an important matter as Irene's fashion reputation.

I remembered so well the overwhelming influence inspired by almost every move Irene Castle made when she and Vernon swept the world with their fabulous dancing success. The present generation cannot possibly realize the size of the rage created by these two people. They were easily the most potent factor in the development of ballroom dancing as a public pastime and were received with such acclaim both professionally and socially that it seems almost impossible to describe it.

When Irene bobbed her hair, I think every woman, young or old, wanted to, or did bob her hair, too. The Castle bob is legendary. Vernon was a fine eccentric comedian as well as a dancer and together he and Irene starred in several big Broadway musical comedies along with their other activities.

Everything was Castles in their day: Castle Hats, Castle Shoes, Castles by the Sea (a restaurant at Long Beach, Long Island), Castles in the Air in New York, Castle House in New York, where society gathered for tea dances, and numerous other Castle things.

Adele and I went to see them in *The Sunshine Girl* and *Girl from Utah* many times and also *Watch Your Step* when they worked for Charlie Dillingham.

They were a tremendous influence in our careers, not that we copied them completely, but we did appropriate some of their ballroom steps and style for our vaudeville act.

Having been imbued with this idolatrous feeling for so long, I was doubly intent upon pleasing Irene as far as my portrayal of Vernon was concerned. She had told me sometime before that when and if their story should ever be done, I was her choice for the role of Vernon.

On completion of the film, she wrote me expressing her approval and enthusiasm. She agreed that it turned out to be a swell picture in spite of the few personal objections and misgivings she felt she was bound to have.

Producer George Haight and director Hank Potter were largely responsible for the merit and values of the picture.

The press reception proved satisfactory here and abroad and we felt that our concern about finishing with a good one was over.

I liked that movie very much but always regretted that it was not made in color. Never having done any film in color, I was anxious to, and thought this had the ideal scope and subject matter for it.

Edwin Schallert in the Los Angeles *Times* remarked: "A beautifully-told story of the dance, much more significant than any Astaire-Rogers picture. It will be a great pity now if the two stars are separated or should this remain perhaps a climax to their mutual careers?"

Jimmy Starr wrote: "Astaire-Rogers are at their very best. If this is actually their last film together, then they have left us with a lasting, unforgettable impression."

The London *Observer* observed: " 'The Story of Vernon and Irene Castle,' which is, we are told, the last film in which Fred and Ginger will appear together, is a fine swan-song for the pair. . . ."

Well, that was it. We had accomplished what we hoped for— a high-level climax to the series. However, the picture, although it did well, did not measure up in the box office to our top ones of the past.

Ginger went on and on dramatically, and in short order grabbed off an Academy Award for herself. She was wonderful in *Kitty Foyle*. As for me, I kept hoofing away, hitting some medium and some high spots.

I was off the screen a whole year after *The Castles,* although *Broadway Melody of 1940* with Eleanor Powell and George Murphy at M-G-M was made during that period. Since I had no new film released according to my established routine, people were beginning to wonder about it—whether I had pulled a ligament, developed water on the knee, or on account of being Ginger-less had just plain vanished.

What really happened was that I arranged to take a breather, a long trip abroad with Phyllis, another one of those catching-up-with-myself plans. The M-G-M deal was set some months previously and I wanted to get away, far away, in order to return to it with a fresh approach.

This new assignment with the knockout dancer Ellie Powell was something very special, as planned.

Our trip as usual proved helpful in every way. I think I prefer the faraway feeling of a trip abroad in the old days, compared with the present. When it took at least four and a half days to get from New York to London you felt as if you had done something.

We spent a while in Ireland but stayed mostly in France and England.

There was quite a lot of Hitler talk going on at this time as he maneuvered several conquests and delivered a number of disquieting speeches.

London was not quite as gay as usual during that visit as I recall it, but I didn't think any real war was in the immediate offing. Perhaps I was preoccupied with my own career problems but it seemed to me things were quite calm in Paris and London.

Prince George and his lovely wife Marina, by then the Duke and Duchess of Kent, asked us to lunch to see their children. It had been some few years since our last visit.

"P. G." said they had seen *The Castles* picture and thought it was good, but he preferred seeing me do my own new dances rather than "someone else's old ones," as he put it. The Duke was always very observant and definite about his theatrical opinions.

The royal children were exceptionally attractive. The little girl delightfully charming—wide-eyed and friendly; the little boy somewhat bored with the visiting strangers—not that I blamed him a bit.

After our luncheon that day, the Duke had to hurry off to attend some official function. I never saw him again. He was killed in World War II in an airplane accident on an official mission.

When we returned to California and my obligation at M-G-M, I found that studio somewhat apprehensive about the precarious conditions abroad. It was my understanding originally that *Broadway Melody* would be made in color, and now I was informed that owing to the ominous state of world affairs, it would not. This was a disappointment, of course. I was still waiting for my first Technicolor show.

Jack Cummings, the producer, made things very pleasant and I was glad to be at Metro working with him.

Eleanor Powell and I had a busy time beating the floor of her rehearsal bungalow to a pulp, making plenty of noise experimenting with all sorts of tap steps.

We rather specialized in tap dancing for that film. George Murphy and I had a Cole Porter "Broadway" song and dance that was a lot of fun doing. There were many lavish numbers for all of us and the picture developed into an all-out dance festival. It was received as such with enthusiasm by some of the press. That film had its moments but did not develop as any smash hit.

Like all *Broadway Melodys*, it did business, but this was the tail end of that series and there were no more *Melodys* after that.

On my list I counted it as thoroughly worth while if only for the opportunity of working with Eleanor, who certainly rates as one of the all-time great dancing girls. Her tap work was individual. She "put 'em down" like a man, no ricky-ticky-sissy stuff with Ellie. She really knocked out a tap dance in a class by herself.

At this point I decided that one picture a year was all I should make. With so much preparation necessary, it was really all I could do to get even that much done. As I pointed out earlier, it took seven to eight months and sometimes more to complete one of my films. Each one seemed to get increasingly difficult. More dances and musical sequences crept into them as we went along, mainly because the audiences wanted it that way.

Next on the slate for me was *Second Chorus.* Artie Shaw and band had already been signed for this one by Boris Morros, to be produced independently with a Paramount release. No story was yet written but I wanted to do it as a sort of departure, because there was a war going on and it had become necessary to consider doing smaller-budget pictures with so much of the world market gone. Things were in an uncertain state in Hollywood at that time. My main reason for doing this one, however, was that I had an idea for a solo number in which I would dance-conduct Artie Shaw's band. The jazz background of the whole thing interested me—it was the first real swingin' outfit I had hooked up with.

As the show developed it looked promising, with lyrics by Johnny Mercer, music by Bernie Henighen and Artie Shaw and direction by Hank Potter. Hermes Pan on the numbers. Lovely Paulette Goddard, Burgess Meredith, Artie Shaw and I tackled the job with hopes.

There were many headaches "getting the show on the road," but it was enjoyable as usual when we finally got rolling.

Frank Cavett and his associates did a noble job of turning out a hurry-up script from nothing but a thread to start with.

Paulette was a swell sport about the dance we did together. She had not done any dancing to speak of up to that point, except in the chorus some few years previously, as she told me. We worked hard on that little thing called "Dig It" and I thought it turned out fine.

After the number was finished and she had seen it on film, she remarked, "I know one thing—*I* loved it!"

Second Chorus got by all right. Oddly enough, I believe it has been seen by more millions of people in America than any other film of mine owing to its release on television. *Chorus* was one of the first to be let loose, and has appeared innumerable times during the past seven or eight years. Incidentally, it looked better on TV than in a theatre.

During a long career such as mine, there are bound to be ups and downs once you reach the top—if there is such a place. I mean, when you have a succession of hits the law of averages seems to catch up with you and you'll have your "nothing" intervals. I say that because they seem like nothing in comparison with a hot streak.

When I first came to Hollywood and was knocking things over in pretty easy regularity, about eight in a row, I sensed that there would have to be a letdown sometime.

It's a worrisome thing because there seems to be no escape from it. Anyway, I was aware of the dangers. I didn't want to run into any decline even temporarily, and I remember Douglas Fairbanks, Sr., saying to me, "Now you're hitting 'em hard, and it may go on for quite a while yet, but when you run into that slump, just go away, take a breather, get fresh ideas, and you'll get your second wind. Something will inspire you. You'll get new ambitions and find your groove again."

I have had at least five slumps in my working career. It's like horseracing. In that game you have your winning streaks and suddenly you can't win a Tootsie Roll. You have to wait for your racing luck to change. In my work, there is that period every now and then when the proper vehicles don't present themselves. You can dance your head off and perhaps it is one of the best things you've ever done, but if it's smothered in a "nothing" opera, you are dead, that's all. Then the public and the studio heads seem to wonder what's the matter. They say, "Well, I guess he's through," or they don't really know what to think but they do know you are "not hot"; that diminishes the effort on the part of your audiences to rush to see you and the studio heads get a little chickeny about wanting to throw a couple of million or more into your pictures. I suppose you can't blame them. That's why my sister and I used to just take off on holiday trips. We overcame slumps that way.

I have had it in the movies several times, but always managed to crawl out and not lose my place. I have a horror of not delivering—making good, so to speak; and I can't stand the thought of letting everybody down—studio and public as well as myself.

When *Second Chorus* was wrapped up and out of the way, I found myself in the amazing position of having no picture scheduled, not even for the distant future.

One of those musical calms had been on for several years and the big studios were not too interested in risking large budgets in the unrestful atmosphere of the day.

America was about to be called into the war.

Chapter 22 *Musicals Are Back*

Gene Markey, then a producer at Columbia Pictures, asked me to discuss an idea about working with a little girl they had under contract there. She was primarily a dancer, he said, and sure to become a terrific star. She had only done a few B pictures up to that time. Her name was Rita Cansino—recently changed to Hayworth.

I had heard about this beautiful daughter of my old vaudeville-days friend Eduardo Cansino.

Markey and I were to have another meeting about the project as soon as a suitable property could be found.

Shortly after that I went off to Aiken with Phyl to sweat out this blank future of mine on the golf course. It was a wonderful winter and I practiced so much golf that I twisted and strained all sorts of muscles trying to add some distance off the tee.

After getting my game in pretty fair shape my career began to bother me mentally. I was wasting time, it seemed, in spite of the enjoyable vacation. I had received various offers for the New York stage, radio, personal appearances, but I liked the movies and was bound to wait a little longer for the right one to turn up.

The United States had just gone into the war and all sorts of changes were taking place in Hollywood. I read that Gene Markey had been called into the Navy and concluded this was the reason I had heard nothing more about the proposed film with Rita Hayworth.

Several weeks passed and then a long-distance call broke up my vacation. Columbia Studios wanted to discuss the picture for me and Rita, and they also had a second one with her to follow, if I was available. Another call came through from Paramount Studios, paging me for a big one with Bing Crosby. This was Irving Berlin's *Holiday Inn*. I liked all three propositions.

Suddenly, I had so many pictures to do that they were getting in each other's way.

An extensive musical cycle was cooking in Hollywood, inspired, I suppose, by a desire to counteract the gloomy wartime atmosphere.

Phyl and I returned home so that I might try to straighten out the problem of dates on all three pictures, and possibly do them all.

It worked out perfectly. *You'll Never Get Rich,* the first with Rita, was to start in a month. Then, by cutting down on my usual three months' rest period, I could fit the Crosby epic in next, to be closely followed by *You Were Never Lovelier,* again with Rita. I would get them all completed, if plans worked out, within a two-year period. That, and a number of U.S.O. camp tours and War Bond appearances sandwiched in between times, made a heavy schedule for me and my hoofing, but I was certainly pleased to be out of that movie slump.

My first meeting with Rita was in a rehearsal hall at Columbia Studios. It was upstairs in one of the buildings and, as I recall, the stairway led directly into the large rehearsal room.

As I came up the last few steps I gave a hurried glance around, expecting to see Rita, as I had been told she would be there. I didn't see her and asked one of the assistants, "Isn't Miss Hayworth going to be here this morning?" He pointed to a remote corner of the room, "Why, yes—she's been here for some time."

There she was. Oh yes—a beautiful sight.

Bob Alton, choreographer on the picture, brought her over and introduced us. I said, "I'm an old friend of your father's."

"Yes, I know," murmured Rita.

I then asked her how tall she was as I stood alongside of her. This was always an important item to me because if the lady happened to be about five feet seven minus shoes and came up on the set with three-inch heels, she'd be just a bit above my five feet nine and one half.

I think Rita mentioned she was no more than five six. As we stood there, both in flat heels, I was easily three inches taller and I told her I hoped she didn't have to wear very high heels with me. She quickly answered, "Oh, no, I don't have to."

We then danced around the mirrored room in impromptu ballroom fashion, as I wanted to get an idea of how we looked together.

I kept thinking how extraordinary it was to find myself about to play opposite my friend Eduardo Cansino's lovely daughter, and I told her so. She laughed.

Our regular work started next day and Bob Alton helped with the routines. There were many of them.

Rita danced with trained perfection and individuality. She, of course, knew through experience what this dancing business was all about. That was apparent the moment I started working with her.

The usual six or eight weeks of rehearsals over, we were about to start shooting our first sequence. It was a dancing bit and took place on the stage of the Shrine Auditorium in downtown Los Angeles.

This being Rita's first co-starring picture, I was particularly anxious that the kick-off would run smoothly, and frankly I was nervous. A slippery floor and technical complications didn't help matters, but we got along nicely with the help of director Syd

Lanfield. I had hoped for this to be a Technicolor job, there having been some talk about it beforehand, but no luck on account of war conditions and budget restrictions.

The Cole Porter score didn't have a full chance to catch on because of a radio network ASCAP strike during which no ASCAP music was played for quite a long period.

I enjoyed making the picture because of Rita and the fact that it was one of the first films with a World War II service background. I could wear a uniform much of the time instead of having to worry about numerous changes of wardrobe, something that hadn't happened to me since *Follow the Fleet*, when I was a plain gob most of the time. Some people objected to me in these outfits, thinking I should always be decked out in those damned tails, I guess, but I liked it.

Bob Benchley, Big Boy Williams, Frieda Inescort and Marjorie Gateson were prominent in the cast and there was plenty of comedy.

Rita and I landed with our dances and I managed to knock off a couple of useful solos in a guardhouse scene.

It was quite a satisfactory show in its way and we figured to really expand with our next one, to follow my commitment with Bing at Paramount.

Phyllis and I took a short trip to Guaymas, Mexico, for some marlin fishing and dove shooting, followed by a few weeks of War Bond and service camp appearances by me, after which I moved into Paramount Studios.

I was in a fine mood—things were going so well, and Phyl had just given me the wonderful news that we could expect another addition to the family about the following March. I told her I had hopes about it being a girl this time.

She quickly replied, "Oh, no, I don't want a girl." I laughed, knowing she would say that again, and asked her why she set her mind so against having a girl.

"Oh, it would probably be an awful little brat like I was—no—no—I don't want a girl."

I argued that it wouldn't be so bad to have such a "little brat" sister around the house and that I was curious anyway about what she was like then.

"Well—I'll think about it," said Phyl.

Paramount Studios were new to me and I went through the usual business of learning their way of doing things, finding the various departments, such as music, sound, wardrobe, and publicity.

Irving Berlin was very much in evidence. I was, of course, delighted to be working with him and director Mark Sandrich again.

Holiday Inn was one of the biggest musical setups of those times and it proved a top grossing picture. (Well, natch, with the great Crosby in it.) I had a lot of numbers and several interesting dance bits with "Cros." He surprised me. Having heard that he didn't like to rehearse much, I was amazed when he showed up in practice clothes to rehearse our first song and dance, "I'll Capture Her Heart."

Mark Sandrich wanted two comparatively unknown girls to work opposite Cros and me. We were fortunate in getting Marjorie Reynolds and Virginia Dale. I danced with each in separate numbers. Assistant choreographer Babe Pierce was helpful to me.

Berlin's score, including old songs as well as new ones, was an outstanding attraction of *Inn*. This was the picture in which Bing first introduced "White Christmas."

I had a solo dance that paid off for me. The firecracker number, in which I threw torpedoes to explode in a rhythmic conglomeration with my feet, took an awful lot of planning and rehearsing. I also had the stage wired to set off what looked like strings of firecrackers with visible flashes as I stepped in certain spots. It was a great satisfaction, that dance, being able to explode things expressing emphasis on beats here and there. Sometimes you want to bang your feet down so hard in a tap dance that you get shin-bucked or stone-bruised. In this one I had a completely satisfactory outlet with those dynamite noises. All this took place in the Fourth of July sequence to a song called "Say It with Firecrackers," which was sung by Bing to start off with. Again I wished the film had been in color.

Marjorie Reynolds and I did a comedy jitterbug dance in a New Year's Eve night-club sequence which emphasized my inebriated condition. I had to look plenty drunk in that bit and figured there was only one good way to do it.

Yes, you're right. I took two stiff hookers of bourbon before the first take and one before each succeeding take. I had to fall down on my face and be carried out for the finish. It was hot on that stage, too! All in all we did it seven times.

The last one was the best.

"Easy to Dance With" with Virginia Dale, "Be Careful It's My Heart" and a "Washington's Birthday" number, both with Marjorie Reynolds, were others of mine. Bing had humorous high spots in that score. It all added up to quite a show.

I appreciated *Holiday Inn.*

The next one, *You Were Never Lovelier,* with Rita Hayworth, due in about a month, gave me some time to relax and fill in a few more camp appearances. The war was really jumpin'. I tried to figure out when I might make an overseas trip for the U.S.O., although my schedule wouldn't permit it in the near future, another picture having crept into my life. One at RKO was called *The Sky's the Limit,* to follow soon after *Lovelier.*

It was getting close to the expected arrival of the new baby and I was prepared.

I put my foot down and said to Phyl: "Now please, this time we are going to get to the Good Samaritan early enough—at least one whole day."

She replied, "I'm not at all sure of that. I wouldn't think of getting there a whole day ahead." But she did.

She was there in good time and expressing her wish for another boy and not a girl, as usual.

Next morning the baby arrived. A girl. When she was finally brought in for Phyllis to see, she looked her over carefully—

stared at her intently for a full minute. Then a little smile came over her face and she said, softly, "Isn't it sweet."

That was Ava (pronounced Ah-Vah).

How she adored that daughter! Just as she did her two sons.

I thought to myself, "I must be about the happiest fellow in the world."

A wire arrived from Buddy DeSylva, then production head of Paramount Studios. It read:

YOU ARE A LUCKY GUY GETTING A HIT BABY AND A HIT PICTURE ALL AT THE SAME TIME   CONGRATULATIONS.

Time seemed to be passing unusually fast. I noticed in the reviews of *Holiday Inn* a bit of reference to my age. Not derogatory, just the "Life begins at forty for Fred" type of thing. Bing came in for it, too, although I have a bit of a head start on him in years. I suppose he was dragged in on my account. Bing with four boys and me with two boys and a girl—a total of seven between us—gave the reporters some opportunities, such as "The Two Dads Are Doing O.K."

This new approach came as a surprise to me because I've never paid any attention to my birthdays nor was I conscious of any decline or physical change. In fact, if anything, I thought I felt better than when I was twenty-five. Well—so much for that. There it was.

Phyllis and I, accompanied by lovely Ilona Massey and comedian Hugh ("Woo Woo") Herbert, made a War Bond tour of the State of Ohio in September of 1942. This trip, arranged by the Hollywood Victory Committee, covered almost every corner of the state.

Our job was to promote the sale of bonds by appearing at factories, banquets, street rallies and theatrical affairs—every move being scheduled ahead of time to the minute. It amounted to quite a hassle in some instances because of the demands on us in each community, in addition to the pinpoint routine which had been prearranged.

Often we would try to co-operate by squeezing in an extra appearance for someone at the last minute, thereby making us late for the one originally planned. This would make the first sponsors angry. If we declined the additional pitch then that group would be upset. We couldn't avoid annoying somebody.

However, the tour worked out well for its purpose even though it was a strange sort of backbreaker. With all the effort extended toward organization and efficiency, it was surprising to see how disorganized almost everything turned out.

Accompanied by two state troopers everywhere, we went flying through crowds and traffic like Mayor Jimmy Walker in his heyday. Phyl and I found it all pretty good fun.

I made twenty to thirty appearances a day over the two-week period, which amounted to some three hundred and fifty altogether as we covered Columbus, Akron, Canton, Springfield, Mansfield, Zanesville, Cleveland, Toledo, Marion, Dayton, Lima, Cincinnati, Middletown and Delaware. . . .

In Cleveland, at a Statler Hotel War Bond luncheon, a pair of my old tap shoes sold for $100,000 in bonds, and the laces went for $16,000.

We were entertained by Louis Bromfield in Dayton and appeared with Governor Bricker several times in Columbus and other cities. The Governor was then considered a possible candidate for President.

Many Hollywood people took on these tours and it was amusing to compare notes afterward, on our return home. We were all exhausted, and everyone, no matter what state was concerned, had been through the same wild experience. It was a wonderful privilege, however, and we were told that these ventures netted many millions in bond sales.

You Were Never Lovelier was on me and rehearsals with Rita about to start at Columbia. Harry Cohn, head of the studio, took more of a personal hand in the preliminaries of this picture than he did on our other one and it all shaped up well.

I looked forward to it mainly because Rita was so delightful to work with and I wanted very much to have a big hit with her. She had gained a lot of experience and was by then one of the top feminine stars on the screen.

The Jerome Kern–Johnny Mercer score was exceptionally fine, with "Dearly Beloved," "I'm Old Fashioned," "Shorty George," "Wedding in the Spring," "You Were Never Lovelier." Adolphe Menjou played Rita's father. He was outstanding, as usual. Xavier Cugat and his band gave us a special kick. Bill Seiter directed.

The Columbia lot was heavily occupied with production at the time and it was difficult to find a place to rehearse. For a while Rita and I had to work out in Hollywood at a civic auditorium. The rest of the time, until the picture started actual shooting, the only available place to suit our convenience near the studio was a room in a funeral parlor of the Hollywood Cemetery on Santa Monica Boulevard. This was a sort of meeting hall—a parlor, to be exact—on the second floor of the building, overlooking the vast sea of tombstones below. We had plenty of jokes about this amazing workshop where we were supposed to be inspired to turn out the gayest, most glamorous entertainment. Tommy Chambers, our brilliant rehearsal pianist, would spread the air with as much jazz and liveliness as possible in an effort to get us into the mood.

Every time a funeral came through the gates we could see it from the windows and naturally we'd have to stop until it moved well on past. One of the men from the office downstairs would come running up half whispering, "Hold it a minute, folks, they're bringing one in."

One day he was particularly excited as he stopped us and looked out the window counting the cars in the procession, "One—two—three—ten—twelve—etc." Afterward, he said, "M-m-m, this is really one of the biggest we've ever had." I must say our little group almost broke up on that one.

Oddly enough, we pulled some good dance material out of those weird surroundings. Rita and I had a romantic type of dance to the song "You Were Never Lovelier," which was concocted in this unique spot. Keeping the laughs going during the intervals was a part of the day's work and I always tried to think up some gag to play on Rita. In one instance I called out, "Well—here we go— I'm beginning to like this place—it doesn't get me down any more, I'm used to it—ready, Rita?"

Up jumped Rita at once and came to me to start our first step together. As I took hold of her two arms she let out one scream and backed away. I had just dipped both my hands and arms in a bucket of ice which we kept for Coca-Cola bottles. That broke up rehearsals for a half hour or so.

The dance turned out well, but it was cut out by the studio powers after the preview. They said it "held up the story."

I also put together one of my best solos in that place. A trick number performed while Adolphe Menjou was supposedly sitting at a desk in his office.

In this scene I was selling myself as a performer for a job in his hotel. The dance had a lot of tricks, including one where I jumped up on his desk and on a certain two beats hit him rhythmically on the head with my cane.

When we got around to shooting the number, Adolphe said to me, "Now, don't be afraid to really hit me on the head. I've got a hard head."

I carried out Dolphe's wishes that first take when the cameras rolled.

He told me afterward, "I wish I had kept my big mouth shut— I didn't know that cane was a baseball bat."

When I told him he should have yelled, "Cut!" or something, he said, "I couldn't. I was unconscious."

Rita and I had a good time with the "Shorty George" number, which, incidentally, did not originate in the funeral parlor. That was devised on Sundays at the studio when we had the place to ourselves.

The whole picture worked out well enough for those times. It played the Music Hall in New York and received a fairly decent press reception. All raved about Rita's beauty and talent. Archer Winsten in the New York *Post* said: "The older Fred Astaire gets the lighter he dances. You can't help looking for the invisible wires enabling him to jig with such youthful featheriness especially since in the region of the eyes, he looks slightly used."

Ah hah! There we have it again—and that was seventeen years ago.

In recent years, *Lovelier* has been fairly steady TV fare.

My sister had become heavily involved in war work in England. Formerly she and Charlie had taken care of convalescing Air Force men at Lismore Castle. The men were invited there to recuperate from battle fatigue. Charlie, having been ill for the past year, could not take an active part in the service, which upset him a great deal. Adele decided to do more work in London and enrolled with the American Red Cross there. Her job consisted of a unique type of service which only Adele could have conceived. She wrote letters to the boys' wives, sweethearts and families for them, assuming the boys would not have much time to do so themselves on a quick visit or leave in London. Her headquarters in a corner of the American Red Cross Rainbow Corner snack bar was the goal of many a GI, and Delly did quite a job indeed according to the many letters I received from families of the boys telling me they had heard from my sister from Rainbow Corner.

I was getting more and more anxious to make that overseas trip for the U.S.O. but my schedule still restricted any such plans. With *The Sky's the Limit* due in the near future, I could continue the local service appearances and that was about all. There were many pitches and campaigns in effect to secure entertainment for our armed forces all over the world. The Hollywood Victory Committee continued to arrange tours of all sorts in every direction and my name was on the list to be sent abroad at the first opportunity.

Life during those war times was so hectic that there wasn't

much chance for vacationing, and the few weeks between *Lovelier* and *The Sky's the Limit* were divided between the usual camp shows and a fishing trip or two.

The talented young actress Joan Leslie was to be my next dancing partner for *Sky*, and the picture, like all those chosen to do, loomed up as a worth-while show under the supervision of producer David Hempstead and director Ed Griffith at my old stamping ground—RKO. I thought the material promised a lot and the score by Johnny Mercer and Harold Arlen particularly, with several outstanding songs, including "My Shining Hour" and "One for My Baby."

Little Joan Leslie, not yet eighteen, was obliged to attend school for a certain number of hours a day on the stages at RKO. We often had to hold up rehearsals and production while my pretty schoolgirl partner finished her lessons. One of the assistants watched the clock carefully and, when the release time arrived, would shout, "It's o.k. now, school's out, we can go ahead."

On would come Joan to start hoofing or whatever there was to do. It was my first experience with this sort of thing and I got a big kick out of it, but couldn't help thinking, "Gosh, the older I get, the younger they get."

Bob Benchley had an important part in the film. We were fortunate to have Bob in that one for his comedy stood out as always in a show which needed him plenty. Robert Ryan and I played Flying Tiger buddies in this story. It was one of Ryan's first movies.

Sky unfortunately did not develop as a strong picture. It wasn't bad but it didn't come off as hoped for, receiving a very mixed press. Some of the notices were bad while on the other hand there were those who went out of their way to praise it. I didn't think it was a poor show and certainly not as poor as Bosley Crowther, critic on the *New York Times*, thought it was. He gave it and particularly me a lousy notice:

"Fred Astaire is a very thin fellow but why emphasize it in a film so thin that daylight shows? Such a film is 'Sky's the Limit' which R.K.O. delivered at the Palace yesterday, and which rattles around like a gourd seed on the single feature program. . . . Mr. Astaire does one solo which is good, but a bit woe-begone and the rest of the time he acts foolish—and rather looks it—in his quick fitting—clothes."

Quick fitting clothes!?

The "woe-begone" solo referred to by Mr. C. was one in a bar-room where I wound up breaking all the glasses in the place in a depressed mood about going back to the wars, a serious plot point. Some liked it very much and I might add it was a tough one to get. I cut my ankles by kicking those glasses around.

I was amused by a letter from a fan, bawling me out plenty for "breaking and wasting all that glass in war time."

I didn't blame Crowther for not liking the picture but I couldn't understand his tirade. He had in the past been receptive to my vehicles.

There were others who made a point of protest, too. However, Lee Mortimer in the New York *Daily Mirror* called the picture "An Astaire-Leslie Gem."

It was just one of those things.

When shooting finished on that one, I found once again that I had run out of pictures. There was none scheduled for me and I tried to pick up my overseas U.S.O. bid. Just then an urgent call from my agent convinced me that this was not the exact time either, because of an offer from M-G-M. Arthur Freed wanted to talk to me about several films and a term contract.

We had our talks and I was soon to be a Metro player and very pleased about it. First assignment, *Ziegfeld Follies*.

The commitment was to start in a few weeks, still not quite enough time for the overseas jaunt, but I made a quick hop to Virginia instead, for a tour of a dozen camps, Navy and Army. The Virginia Beach Hotel, Virginia Beach, was my base for five or six days and all activities branched out of there. It was hot and sultry most of the time but an occasional dip in the ocean helped.

A visit to the Marine base at Quantico was one of my assignments and I have a vivid picture memory of Ty Power standing in the wings of the base theatre watching me as I hoofed for the boys. Ty was then taking his officer's training.

It was very hot, about ninety-five, that night. I was dripping, pouring, soaking wet with perspiration after my act and, as I came off stage into the wings, I grabbed a towel and started to mop myself, still breathing heavily. Four big tough Marines standing by open-mouthed seemed transfixed at this sight. One spoke in a deep voice: "Aw, come on now, it ain't as hard as all that."

I also saw Dick Barthelmess, then a naval officer in the area. Dick was very helpful in getting me through some of the fouled-up plans of my schedule, and at expediting my transportation from here to there when I was expected to be at about seven different places at once.

As before I couldn't understand why things were so confused and unco-ordinated after the plans made at home.

On asking one of the entertainment reception sergeants about this, I received the answer to end all quandaries, "Hey, Fred—ya know somethin'? This is the Army!"

We had a show near the beautiful little city of Williamsburg and stayed at the Inn overnight. Having a couple of hours off during the late afternoon, I suggested to Hap Hazard, one of the boys in the show, that we take a walk to the shopping center to see some sights in this historic town. On the way we passed what was described to me as an asylum or mental institution. This place, surrounded by fences, mostly wooden, over six feet high, covered a vast area. Being curious about what was going on inside the grounds, I was determined to get a look. At last I found a knothole in the fence and peeked through. I kept trying to see something and suddenly realized that I was eye-to-eye with another eye.

Backing away quickly, I said to Hap, "Come on, let's get out of here, I've seen enough." Just then a head popped up over the fence. It was a lady under thirty years of age, I thought, as I stood looking at her leaning on her arms atop the fence, obviously propped up on a chair on the other side.

"You're Fred Astaire," said my eye-to-eye friend.

"Yes, ma'am," I replied.

She smiled, "You see, I'm not as crazy as you think I am."

I assured her that I didn't think she was crazy at all and we had a nice little talk about the movies.

Among other things she said, "I won't dare tell them back at the hospital that I've been talking to you."

She mentioned that she was a telephone operator, had suffered a nervous breakdown, and expected to leave there shortly.

I do hope she did.

On my return to California, I was notified by M-G-M of a postponement in the starting of *Ziegfeld Follies*. They said I could participate in the big bond tour then being organized by the Hollywood Victory Committee if I wished. This one, called *Hollywood Bond Cavalcade*, shaped up as the biggest thing since *Ben Hur*, as far as I could gather, and I decided to go along with the following illustrious cast: Jimmy Cagney, Lucille Ball, Greer Garson, Judy Garland, Kathryn Grayson, Paul Henreid, Betty Hutton, José Iturbi, Harpo Marx, Dick Powell, Mickey Rooney, Ruth Brady, Rosemary La Planche, Doris Merrick, Marjorie Stewart, Kay Kyser and his band and a half-dozen or so beautiful starlets.

It was a tremendous show and netted many millions in bond sales.

We traveled by special train for two weeks, covering only the larger cities from coast to coast, starting in Washington, D.C., and working westward after an appearance at Madison Square Garden in New York.

This trip can only be described as one continuous riot. With that bunch of stars fanning out in the daytime for speeches in each city and then the big show at night fully sold out well in advance everywhere, it was a memorable venture.

Admission to the show was only obtainable through the purchase of a war bond for each seat, and we appeared in places such as Soldiers' Field in Chicago, Forbes Field in Pittsburgh as well as convention halls or the largest available auditoriums.

We always slept on our private train, being rushed back and forth with military escort to cope with the crowds. There was a jeep parade as a rule on arrival in each city, and the press conferences, all planned ahead, worked better than on any other tours of that time.

We carried ten of our own public-relations boys and girls drafted from the major studios and that helped. However, there were some of the usual local mix-ups.

Mickey Rooney was at his jumpingest best. The Mick was all over that train shaking dice, imitating everything and everybody present or absent. Cagney, Dick Powell and I, with the Mick and Harpo Marx, had no trouble in cooking up some laughs in our spare moments, which were mighty few on that trip.

The show was a real blockbuster of entertainment and was readily recognized as such. I stood in the wings night after night to hear the roars for Judy and Mickey, as well as for Betty Hutton, who belted them, and how! My bit was a seven-minute song and dance with Kay Kyser's band and I enjoyed it. Everybody scored.

I wrote Phyllis details of the trip each day, describing the bedlam, mobs of people lining the streets as we rode in parades, and how local holidays had been declared in many cities. At the tail end of the tour we were to pass through Los Angeles on our way to San Francisco. The Cavalcade did not perform in Los Angeles.

Phyllis expressed a desire to go to San Francisco with the company to see some of this fabulous excitement I had been describing, so she joined me and took the trip for that closing stand.

As we were arriving in San Francisco next morning, I told her to be prepared for an awful crushing and pushing around as we waited to get off the train for our usual press reception.

To everybody's surprise, nothing happened when we arrived. There were only a few reporters, hardly any fans, and no bedlam at all. Our usual jeep tour finally got under way but there were no crowds as we rolled through the city. A few amazed natives of Chinatown gathered as we passed by and Phyllis laughed as she remarked:

"My, this is terrific! Did you really get this tumultuous a reception every place?"

Somebody forgot to notify San Francisco that we were arriving —that's all. There was little or no publicity about the show that night and it took a major effort on the part of our public-relations boys and girls to arrange some quick exploitation, which they did by radio and newspapers so that the show did get a crowd, but it was the weakest spot of the tour.

Chapter 23 Triplicate

There were a few weeks to relax after that, while waiting for my *Ziegfeld Follies* job to start. Two of those crazy trips in succession can knock you out.

I did some racing and revived interest in my favorite sport, which I felt I had neglected in recent years.

Rather suddenly it occurred to me that a lot of time had passed since telling my old trainer friend, Clyde Phillips, that someday I would send him a wire about buying a couple of horses for me. I thought by now I certainly must be able to afford it, but there was a question in my mind as to how Phyllis would react.

Finances and business bored me. Phyllis did the money managing and investing most of the time without even discussing it with me because I asked her to take it off my hands.

I told her of my idea about picking up a few thoroughbreds to race, and that I thought there was no point in waiting until we were aged and gray to enjoy it.

Of course there was only a remote possibility that we could be lucky enough to get anything worthwhile just like that, but at least I knew Clyde Phillips was the fellow who could try the right way.

Phyl agreed with me entirely and, after a bit of careful consideration, general summing up and balancing of the budget, we decided to buy two animals of racing age, preferably two- or three-year-olds.

I sent a telegram:

DEAR CLYDE HERE'S THAT WIRE I TALKED ABOUT FIFTEEN YEARS AGO. BUY ME TWO YOUNG ONES POSSIBLY AS HIGH AS TEN THOUSAND APIECE IF NECESSARY AND I HOPE YOU ARE AVAILABLE TO TRAIN FOR ME.

He called me back on the phone saying he was training for himself now and would take my animals on as soon as he could locate something worthwhile.

After a few days he phoned me again saying Colonel Bradley was selling off quite a few and that there were a number of two-year-olds to weed out. Clyde mentioned that he liked a couple of these and had a promise from Bradley's man that we could have first refusal on a certain filly and a colt.

When it came time to take him at his word, Bradley changed his mind and decided not to sell the filly—it seems she was tried impressively and he wanted to keep her. I don't know what happened to the colt but the filly turned out to be Busher. We didn't get her, but it was close. She was not very highly thought of in her early stages and Clyde was told he might be able to get her for about five thousand dollars.

Of course, Busher went on to win a fortune and became one of the most famous of race mares in the colors of L. B. Mayer, who acquired her for a big price, shortly after our close call.

Old Clyde was sure burned up about missing that one after having been promised it.

A few weeks later he wired me:

BOUGHT YOU THREE YEAR OLD COLT BY REIGH COUNT OUT OF FAIRDAY SIX THOUSAND DOLLARS THINK I MIGHT BE ABLE TO DO SOMETHING WITH THIS ONE.

That was Triplicate. Clyde knew his stuff all right.

He bought another one shortly after that with the intriguing name of Fag. On this one he sent me this wire:

JUST BOUGHT THE OTHER ONE FIVE THOUSAND SORE LEGGED OLD DEVIL BUT WE CAN WIN A COUPLE WITH HIM AND THEY'LL CLAIM HIM DON'T THINK WE CAN LOSE NOTHIN.

Clyde called the turn on this one. Fag got third money his first start for me in an allowance race—a little too tough competition with those sore legs. Next time he was dropped into a claimer and, as they say in England, "He doddled it." He won easily and was claimed from me for four thousand. With the purse money on both races I came out a few thousand ahead on that deal. Very satisfactory—and now somebody else could worry about those sore legs.

Triplicate was doing well and I was told by my genius trainer that he should win pretty soon. Trip was above the claiming class type horse and Clyde went along slowly and carefully with him.

Back to Show Biz again—

Work started on *Ziegfeld Follies*. This was planned as a multiple-star revue such as had not been attempted in pictures since the early days of sound, when *Movietone Follies* and others held forth. Arthur Freed designed a show of glamour and size which I looked forward to with great interest and enthusiasm. I liked the idea of a revue for a change, never having done one in films. And this one would be in color too—at last.

Lucille Bremer, newly recruited from New York's Silver Slipper, was my lovely dancing partner in several spectacular production numbers and choreographer Bob Alton helped immeasurably. One, "This Heart of Mine," by Harry Warren and Arthur Freed, with the aid of mechanical devices such as treadmills and revolving stages, turned out well. One of my main reasons for signing the Metro contract was to get an opportunity to put on some kind of number to Phillip Braham's "Limehouse Blues," which had always been a favorite song of mine. When I told Arthur Freed

the thought, he immediately approved and asked Vincente Minnelli and Bob Alton to get busy on a production idea.

This they did, and by the time I threw some dances with Lucille
together, we had a pretty busy and intricate dramatic ballet pantomime combination.

In the midst of rehearsals, I received a cable from my mother
informing me of the death of Adele's husband, Charlie Cavendish.
Lord Charles had been seriously ill for over a year and Mother,
who was living at Lismore permanently then, had been taking
care of him. Charlie adored my mother as she did him, and this
news saddened me a great deal.

Having comparatively little to do in the *Follies,* I thought it
a good time to arrange for my overseas U.S.O. trip. With only
four production numbers and no dialogue to speak of, it appeared
I might be through early enough to get away handily, so I signed
up to ship away in August.

I had just had a wire that Triplicate picked up his first race
at Jamaica, New York, in my colors. These colors, incidentally,
were formerly carried by Phyllis' Uncle Henry Bull, as a gentleman steeplechase jockey some years back. He turned them over
to me, for which I was deeply grateful.

Dark blue, with yellow belt and red cap, they looked extremely
good, those colors, especially under certain circumstances, such as
—winning.

Trip won that allowance race by five open lengths with Don
Meade up. It looked for sure that my trainer was, as I had
thought, an extraordinary judge of horseflesh and how to treat it.

The first time I began to feel that I had a little better than an
ordinary animal here came a few weeks later when Trip beat a
field of older horses. I like it when a three-year-old smothers the
four and five-year-olds in good company, and that's what happened—by four coasting lengths. He beat some fairly useful older
ones in an overnight handicap.

A lot of the boys on the set at the studio won a bet that day.
I missed out myself, however, being heavily involved with a dance

routine which got fouled up and needed some rehearsing. Horse
or no horse, the show must go on.

Gene Kelly and I did a revised version of a Gershwin number
originally introduced by my sister and me in the Broadway show
Funny Face. "The Babbitt and the Bromide" it was, and we had
some fun with it.

There were many high spots in the *Follies,* with such stars as
Fanny Brice, Bill Powell, Lucille Ball, Judy Garland, Virginia
O'Brien, Esther Williams, Keenan Wynn, James Melton,
Victor Moore, Eddie Arnold, Lena Horne, Red Skelton,
Hume Cronyn, Bill Frawley and the Ziegfeld Girls. Cyd Charisse,
then in the preliminary stages of her career, appeared briefly sev-
eral times in the picture, once with me, but we did not dance
together.

The last number I was concerned with—a fantastic bubble affair—hit the cameras a few days before my scheduled departure
for the overseas U.S.O. jaunt. I had just completed my vaccina-
tion shots for the trip, five to be exact, and was feeling miserable,
with a temperature of 102, when Lucille Bremer and I squished
through a sea of bubbles as prescribed in the number.

The setting for this thing was a massive formation of rocklike
scenery and it was our lot to dance through this waist-high bubble
bath in evening clothes. Yes, I'm not kidding.

Beautiful girls were spotted up high on the rocks at different
points like great sea gulls. Several of them fainted from the
chemical fumes used to make the bubbles. All this for an effect
which did not come off, I guess, because most of it was deleted
from the final released picture. Thank goodness everything I did
in that number was cut. It was an awful mess. It was designed
for a colorful finale and the studio went to a lot of trouble and
expense but, as I said, it just didn't come off.

The picture developed as one of the top all-time box-office
grossers in spite of a rather spotty press reception. There were
some objections about its being too gargantuan, massive, gorgeous

and colorful. "The boys" were on an anti-M-G-M kick at the moment.

Well, anyway—we tried!

With my part of the *Follies* shooting completed, I had only a few days to prepare for the overseas U.S.O. trip. There were meetings with various officials at home planning what to do, where to go, etc.

I wanted to be sure that I could perform at any given moment if necessary so asked for an accordion player to accompany me wherever I went. I was fortunate in drawing Mike Olivieri for this assignment. Mike and I stuck together like glue all through the trip. He is a master of the instrument and I always felt that I had my orchestra in my pocket.

Leaving home suddenly hit me like a bomb. I was scared about leaving Phyllis. She said, "Now don't worry about me—please." The youngsters didn't know what it was all about. Young Fred shouted, "So long, Dad—see you in three weeks." I yelled, "Six weeks." Fred answered, "O.K., six weeks."

Chapter 24 *U.S.O.*

I was to fly over from New York by transport plane supplied by the service. On arrival there I went to headquarters for briefing, which was required of all who were going on such missions during the war. My accordion player friend and I were traveling together.

There were about thirty of us being briefed about the emergency exits, use of life preservers, and routine instructions that went along with the flight. At that point none of us knew when we would leave the country. Some of the men were military personnel or diplomatic attachés and we were all in New York on the alert for the call to get down to the airport and take off.

After the briefing session, the lieutenant in charge called me into his office to discuss the actual time and plane I might be assigned to fly out on. He asked me if I had any objection to flying thirteen in a plane over the ocean. I didn't know what he meant and also could not understand such courtesy and consideration from the Army, so I asked him why. He explained that I was being considered for one of three flights and that one of them would carry thirteen passengers if Mike and I went.

He wanted to know if I was superstitious.

I told the officer I was not superstitious and that I hoped to get away as soon as possible.

The lieutenant's name was Shea, and as we chatted a bit he told me he was the son of Mike Shea, of Buffalo—famous theatre owner of my vaudeville days, mentioned earlier in this book.

The coincidence of meeting someone even remotely familiar in a situation like that was gratifying. I was pretty nervous about the whole thing anyway and was grateful to Lieutenant Shea for his consideration.

I went home to my hotel, the Ritz Carlton, to hang around the telephone and wait for the word. There was no call that night.

Next morning I slipped out to Belmont Park to get a look at Triplicate for the first time. Clyde Phillips had him entered in a race that afternoon. I watched the race with Uncle Henry from his box and Trip ran a good race—but ran fourth. I had yet to see a horse of mine win.

Clyde said the animal needed a rest, having had a rather strenuous campaign the past two months. He also thought one ankle needed attention.

I asked him to do what he thought best and bring the horse out to California as soon as possible to run at Santa Anita and Hollywood Park, where I could see him. It was arranged.

That night at the hotel, the big message came for me to be at headquarters the following noon, ready for the flight to England.

Getting caught in a New York traffic jam made me a bit late that next noon, almost too late. Carrying three enormous bags that I could barely manage, I was panicky, strained my back, and almost fell out of the cab, was lame as an old crock from that moment on.

We had all heard plenty about the GI "achin' back," and I had one already just trying to get to the plane. How could I dance for the GI's with that back? I was worried.

At any rate, I found Olivieri and we finally boarded the plane, a stripped bucket-seat C-54. It was loaded full-up with both

Army and Navy men and I wondered again why there had been all that talk about thirteen in a plane.

We took off in a rattle and a roar and almost immediately about six poker games started on the floor. I was soon down there in full participation, forgetting all about my achin' back, but when I tried to get up—oh, brother!

The time passed quickly and very soon, it seemed, we came down at Gander, Newfoundland. Most of our load debarked there to stay, and we picked up some new passengers, including a four-star general who didn't look very happy. I was intrigued by him because he looked at least as miserable as I felt.

At one point I smiled at him and I got nothing back. I suppose you're not supposed to smile at a general, but this was not my racket and I was only trying to be friendly.

There were two plain-clothes gentlemen of some official capacity also and very soon the door was slammed ready for the next rattle and roll. The GI on the door announced in a real good Brooklyn accent, "De next will be a ten-hour hop to Prestwick, Scotland," as we started taxiing out.

I then counted the house and found that our load consisted of thirteen passengers. Finally it dawned on me. I had said I didn't object. Was it possible that some people would refuse through superstition?

It made me laugh in spite of my aching back as I tried to straighten out to fasten the seat belt. I took a sleeping pill soon after we were in the air and almost fell asleep in the crap game which had started.

One of the pilots came and asked me if I wanted to lie down in his bunk up forward just outside the cockpit, which I readily accepted, with thanks. I went in there and got to sleep but couldn't help being aware of the smell of high-octane gas and kept thinking how extraordinary it was that one was allowed to smoke under those conditions. I didn't, however. It was a very strong odor. I woke up about four hours later over mid-ocean and the daylight had just broken through; the sky was clear, the sun was coming up, and all in all it was a fine trip, except for my aching back.

We dropped into Prestwick a few hours later, just missing a thunderstorm by a few minutes—everything was drenched on the ground.

Going through customs we had a friendly inspector who knew me. He asked what sort of a trip it had been and then said, "You must be glad you didn't draw the flight ahead of this one." I told him I didn't understand what he meant.

He replied in his thickest of Scotch accents, "Didn't you hear about it? The bloody plane with twenty-one passengers hit an antenna just before attempting to land, clipping one wing. The ship veered off into town and crashed into a building, killing the whole blooming lot of 'em."

I looked at Mike. "Did you hear what I heard?"

Mike closed his eyes with a wince.

I've always thought that had I not agreed to travel thirteen in the plane we might easily have been assigned to the flight just ahead of us, especially as I mentioned I'd like to get away as soon as possible.

The number thirteen has asserted itself in my direction rather insidiously in various ways ever since that plane episode.

I had not been in Prestwick since my golf trips some years back. It was indeed a changed place, as I had expected.

Mike and I were scheduled to fly down to London next morning to report for our assignments. I was pretty nervous about the whole thing and worried that I could not get a message back to Phyllis that I had arrived safely. My back was miserable and I wondered what was in store for us.

I had a restless night after a pretty awful meal in the hotel restaurant. The breakfast next morning, powdered eggs and sausages with a sort of cottonlike filling, was another shock. Those things are all right when you get used to them, but I wasn't.

We got to London next morning after a few hours' flight in a real jalopy of a transport bucket seater. Everything was so loose and rattly you felt the thing would have to fall apart.

London as ever fascinated me. I could hardly realize I was actually there under these conditions. But it was great to be back again and I went straight to the Ritz to park myself for the few days before going to France. Adele lived there, too, and I soon found her. All in all, it was plenty exciting.

One of the cheeriest moments I can remember was the sight of David Niven when he ran up the staircase in the lobby of the hotel to greet me as I stood on the second floor looking over the balcony railing. David, by then a colonel, made me forget every misery I thought I had.

I was grabbed right away that night to appear at some special show and thrown into the M.C. job. Being so tired I didn't know what I was doing, I must have given a rotten performance. I lost track of Mike, my accordionist, and got hooked for this one on my own, without any rehearsal of music or anything. Anyway, I introduced a lot of stars and also danced myself, in an unconscious sort of way. Jack Buchanan and Brod Crawford appeared, too. There were mostly British stars at this place.

Next day I went to Rainbow Corner with my sister and performed there—some of Glenn Miller's boys were in the band for that appearance. Glenn, himself, had just gone off on the ill-fated flight which took his life. We had a good show and it went great with the boys. I stayed in London a few more days waiting for orders. Bing Crosby, who had just arrived by boat with his group, and I were told we'd be sent to France at any moment. There were a few air-raid alerts but no bombs dropped during the few days I was in London. Adele had been through the full works during her long stretch, however. She caught all the blitzes.

When we got to France, we saw what organized confusion could really amount to. The Red Ball Express of trucks running a continuous supply of gas to the front lines had right-of-way all over the roads. Bing and I went up in jeeps with our respective groups. I was glad we chose this means of transportation because it cured my achin' back—acting as a sort of osteopathic treatment. We passed through the fantastic ruins of St. Lo, Villone, LeMans,

Etampes. Knowing what had occurred at these places, I still could hardly believe what I was seeing. Paris was not yet open— the IFF were still sniping in the streets and it was some few days before we could get through to where we could find any place to entertain. I appeared with Cros at a few places and then his unit went off with the Third Army and I went off with the First. My unit consisted of Mike Olivieri, Willie Shore and four girls— a one-hour show. Incidentally, I always danced in my GI combat boots. The fellows got a kick out of it.

The Army was traveling so fast we couldn't catch up to them at first; we had to wait and were put into a beautiful Rothschild castle to stay a few days. It was occupied by a lot of military personnel, about thirty miles south of Paris. They told me it had been the headquarters of General Stoopnagel just before the recent German retreat. Also that he had left a note: GEN. STOOP-NAGEL WILL BE BACK.

We did several catch-as-catch-can entertainment appearances while based there, one at Versailles, with Dinah Shore, overlooking the gardens. All fountains being turned off, many of our GI audience (about five thousand) were seated and standing in the dry basins.

We also did one show in a mess hall recently bombed out by retreating Germans.

All sorts of unusual things were always happening. On one of our trips—we usually traveled in a convoy of about four motor vehicles, jeeps, command cars, weapons carriers—I noticed that our last car, with five people in it, was no longer with us. We turned around, went back a half mile to find it upside down, having skidded on a muddy turn. Nobody was hurt and all the girls were sitting on the side of the road giggling as usual.

Another time we all stopped to stretch in some Belgian town. It was in the center of the place, no traffic to·speak of and no people around, only a lone M.P. in the middle of the cross streets, directing traffic. It was a small square.

I was standing idly watching when a boy on a bicycle rode by and noticed me. He kept on going around the square and came back to take another look, then went on a few yards, made a quick turn right back to me, got off his bike, and said in a high Belgian voice, "I—know—you!"

I replied, "You do? Who am I?"

The lad thought a moment, kept staring, then sputtered as he pointed at me, "Uh—uhh—oh—Ginger Rogers!"

Paris was a sight when we first rode through. There were over-turned automobiles all over the place and I was particularly in-terested at the sight of about three of them upside down and a large truck blown smack up against the entrance of the Hotel Crillon, where I had stayed at numerous times in the past. The door was blocked completely. We didn't stop in Paris, proceeding on through the country, and into Belgium, still by jeep.

We stopped at La Capelle—ratty quarters—in an old school house, for about five days and entertained a few units of M.P.'s. We gave a show at a large prisoner-of-war camp. This was con-siderably back of the front lines at that time.

Things were pretty slack for a few days so I got hold of a courier with a motorcycle and asked him to go on up ahead and see if they would hurry up and send for us. I wrote a note to whomever it concerned, saying I was only on the tour for six weeks, two of them having already elapsed, and I hoped not to waste any more time, if possible. Would they please let me enter-tain someplace soon?

Everything was disorganized on account of the rapid advance of our armies, and the U.S.O. could not do much about it at that point. Nobody seemed to be "in touch," so to speak. At any rate, my note brought some results and we were soon on our way to-ward Germany. We stopped for a few shows in and around Char-leroix then on into Maastricht, Holland.

We were to give a show but were late in arriving and could not perform out of doors as planned on account of approaching dark-ness and the necessity of maintaining blackouts.

I decided to look for a theatre which we might commandeer for the night. Fortunately, I found one—the Palace. It was not operating but I went up to the door, peered inside and rapped sharply on the glass panels. Soon a man (the manager) came and most graciously agreed to let us have his theatre for the night. He recognized me immediately, much to my surprise, although I was in uniform, and explained that he had played many of my pictures there and hoped to reopen his theatre to the public pretty soon.

We moved in and gave our show that evening to an audience of vociferous engineers. This was an opera-house type of theatre with four tiers. They were hanging out of the boxes. What an evening!

We slept in the theatre that night, on stage—simply lined up our cots and bunked there. It was so black out that we could not venture to find our living quarters, which were in an orchard just outside of town where the company of engineers was billeted. The manager of the theatre said another air raid was anticipated so we'd better stay in.

Anyway, we stayed and the air raid took place, but I slept through it, damn it—I wanted to hear one. I got my fill a few days later, however, when a lone putt-putt German raided our orchard home and dropped a few little numbers just a hundred yards away. He was up above the thick ceiling and couldn't quite locate us.

By this time I was beginning to wish we could get out of there. A very persistent effort on the part of this little German putt-putt bomber to do away with some bridge leading to town made me nervous. We had to cross this bridge a number of times a day getting to and from our various assignments in that area, such as hospitals and camps. Every time we'd get on it I'd expect the stuff to begin to fall on us.

Anyway, after about a week in our orchard headquarters an officer rushed up to me one evening and said, seriously, "I've got some bad news for you—they want you in Paris."

I thought to myself, "This is bad news?" I said to the officer,

"Oh, no—they can't do this—are you sure?" He said, "Oh yes—
I have a special message about it." I looked at Mike. "Isn't that
a shame, Mike?" He answered, "Oh, yes, when do we go?" The
officer said, "Tonight." Well, as we went over that bridge the last
time, I yelled "Good-by, Bridge."

We rode all night in a weapons carrier. It was a rough ride but
a nice one, leaving the front-line area more and more behind. We
got to Paris and were put up at the Ritz, which was more my
speed at this time of life.

Mike and I had a big suite with no heat and no hot water, but
it was sure great to be there. The Ritz was then under the A.T.C.
The officer in charge treated us wonderfully. I had had but one
bath in five weeks and that was in some ex-prison in Belgium.
We worked out of Paris for about five days, at hospitals mostly,
and I did the performance which was the main reason for my
being brought back to Paris. It was a big variety show held at
the Olympic Theatre, and we repeated it the following night. It
was the first American appearance since the liberation of Paris.

I ran into my old friend Bill Hearst, who was a war correspond-
ent at that point, and told him I was worried because I didn't know
whether Phyllis had ever received word that I had arrived safely.
He very kindly arranged for me to get a message to her. I was
greatly relieved at this.

Then came the big thrill. Paris was still under blackout regula-
tions but there were no air raids. The thrill was a message from
General Eisenhower inviting us to his headquarters, which were,
as we found out later, some twenty or thirty miles outside of
Paris. He did not specify any entertaining by us, and when I
asked about this, his aide said:

"No, the General just wants to entertain you and your group."
I suggested that Mike would bring his accordion anyway because
we would like so much to do some sort of a show. I was assured
that it was all right if we wanted to, but the General did not expect it.

When the time came, we were picked up in the official limousines with the three flags on the front and whisked off into the blackout night. I'll never forget our arrival at his place. It was plenty black outside as we drove into the courtyard entrance. The front door of the house opened and there, standing in silhouette, was the General. We got out of the cars and started up the few steps leading to where he was standing. As I arrived up there, he put his hand out and said, "Good evening, I'm General Eisenhower, it's very nice of you to come." Well, that did it; I could see myself voting for him then!

He was kind to all of us. I talked at length to him during the evening. At one point we sat on the steps of the staircase in the entrance hall for a good half hour.

I remember his saying to General Spaatz, "Tooey, go and get your guitar." We put on our show, and by that time General Spaatz had returned with his guitar. He performed for us and expertly too. Ike joined in the singing.

The General asked me if I would do a little dance for his kitchen staff, who were down in the basement and couldn't see our show. So he sent for them—four large colored men—and it was a joy to dance for them there on the marble floor of the entrance hall.

The house was an attractive one, with pictures of racehorses all over the walls, and had recently been the headquarters of General von Runstedt. Hoping not to overstay our welcome, I asked one of the aides to give me a signal when we should leave. He said, "No, not yet, the General doesn't seem ready yet."

Finally, about 11:30, I made the move and someone asked if he would sign our "short-snorter" bills. This he did with seemingly great pleasure. He sat at a table as we lined up. We all then said, "Good night," and were off into the blackness again.

We got out of Paris in a day or so. My little group disbanded there. They stayed on as members of a regular U.S.O. unit. They were great kids and I was lucky to have been with them. Our breaking up was rather a sentimental event. We had become accustomed to each other and got along so well.

I ran into Crosby again and we had some laughs relating our experiences. Arriving in London, we were loose for a day or so awaiting the alert to embark for home. I had chosen the boat trip and so did Cros. We were shipped on the *Queen Mary* and it was loaded, but loaded. The boys were sleeping in the halls, on the stairs, and every place. It was a good trip, with several deviations to avoid submarines.

There were a great many bomber boys on this trip. They were being transferred from the European to the Pacific area mostly, as they told me. Some were just going on long leave. They were dead tired.

Cros and his group and I entertained on the boat a number of times in a special setup in the main dining hall, also in the hospital sections for the many returning wounded.

We got in to New York in good time and once more I was back with Phyllis. I, of course, hadn't heard from her, but she did get a couple of letters from me.

Thinking back over that trip I was convinced of how fortunate I was to make it. We saw so much in a short time. The desolation and chaos almost everywhere were a revelation for somebody like me, who had never had any military experience. It was nothing to see a whole railroad yard transformed into a mass of twisted steel and iron with hundreds of freight cars strewn all over the place, piled on top of each other, the outcome of having been blown sky high in bombing raids.

I kept a little book to jot down notes which I've just found after all these years.

Here are some jottings:

First night St. Marie Dumont—Second night Le Mans prisoners . . . Back ache . . . Food lousy . . . French fans . . . Shows out doors . . . Little Colonel five feet high . . . Got souvenirs . . . Show on truck lighted only by GI audience flashlights . . . Watched spy on way to hang at Veaux de Cernay . . . French fans Champs Elysées . . . P-38 buzzing Champs Elysées about thirty feet off ground then barely over top of the Arc de Triomphe . . . Entertained M.P.'s at prison camp . . . Truck loads of Germans . . . All look alike . . . Germans well treated in hospitals . . . Medical unit show fine, 10:20 A.M. . . . German officer captured with broken wooden leg.

Little French girl, shrapnel in head . . . GI bought cow for $70, made steaks, sold to soldiers at 3,500 francs apiece . . . All GI's wanted to live in Calif. . . . Belgian house marked with swastikas by retreating Germans . . . German prisoners building our stage . . . German sergeant salutes me, asking autograph . . . Saw movie, Sinatra in "Step Lively" . . . Welcoming crowds in streets of Holland . . . During show outdoors on platform, bomb explodes nearby while English girl singer entertains . . . When she came to dressing tent afterwards said, "Did something go off while I was on?"

Just heard Jock Whitney escaped German prison camp . . . Hospital with little German boys twelve years old prisoners . . . One five-year-old captured forward spotting allied positions . . . One captured Storm Trooper slapped nurse, refusing transfusion of American blood . . . Rumor Eisenhower leg in cast hurt in forced landing muddy field . . . Wrenched knee . . . Elliott Roosevelt . . . Savoy Grill saw Jack Dempsey, Doug Fairbanks, Jr. . . . Glasgow fan mob . . . Driving rain . . .

Aboard ship for home wear life belts all times . . . Paul Gallico on board . . . Danced in hospital quarters, up and down aisles of beds . . . Big show with Crosby in mess hall . . . Big last night show . . . Glad it's over . . . Hope Phyllis can meet boat.

Phyllis did not meet the boat. There was no way for her to know when it would arrive. I had sent a cable before leaving saying we would soon be on our way, but I could not indicate any specific time.

Many ladies from the various auxiliary forces were on hand to welcome the war-weary passengers, and although I could not be classed with the lads on that boat, I got the same treatment. We were showered with hot coffee and doughnuts and kindnesses. It embarrassed me a little.

I went straight to the Ritz and waited in the room for Phyllis to arrive from the country where she had been staying with Fifi Fell.

At last we could resume our life again. I was so thankful.

Phyl said the children were in excellent shape. We would be off by train the next day and see them very soon.

I asked if anything new had happened with our horse business and found that Clyde had bought several more for me. They were all in California, having been shipped a few weeks back. Triplicate was coming along well and would be ready to run soon.

It looked promising for our stable, said Phyllis, and she added, "We need another ranch. Valley Center is too far away with this traffic. We can sell it. I have my eye on one in Chatsworth. Don't you think we should get some brood mares?" It all sounded fine to me.

Getting back home to California was, as ever, a joy. Everything was normal again and the youngsters curious, as I unpacked my load of souvenirs. And I had plenty of them, everything from a set of German false teeth to an Italian automatic pistol which had been taken from a German prisoner by an American M.P. who gave it to me. Fred, Jr., grabbed it; Pete grabbed it from him. Ava found some parachute silk which she promptly put over her head.

Although I had taken civilian clothes along on that trip, I never wore them. It was so much handier and enjoyable to work in uniform and avoid all the changing of clothes under difficult circumstances. I wore that one suit the entire time and it seemed strange to doff it.

Chapter 25 The Gold Cup

In a few weeks I was back at M-G-M for *Yolanda and the Thief*, the Bemelmans story which Arthur Freed had carefully planned. Much care was being taken to make this one outstanding in every respect. Vincente Minelli, directing, injected many novel color and camera effects. Gene Loring did the choreography. Lucille Bremer played Yolanda. Frank Morgan and I worked together all through as thieving buddies. We all tried hard and thought we had something, but as it turned out, we didn't. There were some complicated and effective dances which scored, but the whole idea was too much on the fantasy side and it did not do too well.

Edwin Schallert in the L. A. *Times* hit it on the head:

" 'Not for realists' is a label that may be appropriately affixed to 'Yolanda and the Thief.' It is a question, too, whether this picture has the basic material to satisfy the general audience, although in texture and trimmings it might be termed an event."

This verified my feeling that doing fantasy on the screen is an extra risk.

Next on the roster for me at Metro was *Belle of New York*, due in a few months. I didn't like the thought of it too much—there was some difficulty getting a script in shape. The fact that *Yolanda* had turned out to be a weak one worried me. I didn't want to do another light-weight right on top of it. Two "weakies" in a row can reduce you.

Phyl and I went away to relax and worry about it later. That holiday lasted no time at all. I had a phone message that I was needed badly at Paramount for *Blue Skies* with Bing Crosby. This sounded like a good one to me. M-G-M went about arranging the loan-out as soon as I had agreed.

Skies, another Irving Berlin epic, proved to be a big one. Many showmanship angles helped make this a box-office wallop. Sol Siegel produced, Stuart Heisler directed, Hermes Pan was on choreography.

I made up my mind during the shooting of this film that I wanted to retire on it. *Skies* measured up to the requirements I considered essential: It looked like a hit.

It looked perfect to me as I thought about this rounded-out movie career of mine. I had made my entrance with Joan Crawford and Clark Gable—now coming up was the exit, with Bing Crosby. Of course, I had to ask to be released from my M-G-M contract and prevailed upon Leland Hayward to get me out of it. At first there was a definite opposition to the idea because of some preparation already under way on *Belle of New York*, but they finally agreed to release me with the understanding that if I decided to come back I would be obliged to fulfill the remainder of my commitment with them. That was entirely satisfactory. I liked M-G-M and had no desire to go elsewhere in the unlikely event of my returning. That was it. I announced it to the press department at Paramount.

There were many numbers in *Blue Skies*, as is always the case in a Berlin picture. It took a long time to prepare and shoot it, especially with my solo specialties to be done at the very end.

Cros and I worked together a lot and I enjoyed it all, especially our number "A Couple of Song and Dance Men." We threw everything but the doormat into that one.

I had numbers with the beauteous Joan Caulfield and Olga San Juan which turned out well, and I was also fortunate in coming up with one of my most useful trick solos, for "Puttin' On the Ritz." This one was done with a series of split screens to produce the effect of me dancing in front of a chorus of eight images of myself . . . very complicated stuff, but it worked. My assistant on this, Dave Robell, along with the excellent special-effects department at Paramount, proved helpful in planning the technical job.

This was widely publicized as my "last dance" in a world-wide display. I did a special series of "last dance" still photographs for various magazines. It was all serious. I meant it and never had any idea that I'd be back to do any more films.

The idea of retiring was really suggested by my mother when I was about twenty-five. She said to me one day, "You started working at such an early age and I think you should retire when you're about thirty-five. You are entitled to it. After all, most young people don't start to earn a living until after they get out of school and college when they are about twenty-two or twenty-four. Here you are twenty-five and you've been working for twenty-one years already. Yes—in about ten more years you should retire. That gives you about thirty-one years of strenuous work and then you can do something less apt to put a strain on your heart, or perhaps take it easy and not work at all."

Well, it so happened that things just began to pop for me at about thirty. The movie career took over—and now, twenty-nine years later, I'm still at it.

The retirement announcement brought out all sorts of reactions —much to my surprise. I received a lot of mail asking me not to do it. Some wanted to know if I was ill. Others simply objected, taking the attitude that I was shirking my duty. It was all very flattering and gratifying, of course, to know that so many people cared.

One letter predicted that I would not go through with it and

what's more I was meant to dance until I was at least seventy-
five!

Help!

One lady wrote, "My children cannot understand why you
should want to quit with all the fun you are having."

Still another one said, "You should not do this at your age, it
is not setting a good example for the young people of the world."

Then came some inquiries from the press as to why I was
quitting.

I explained that I felt I had gone about as far as I could, and
did not want to run out of gas—go dry. Actually, I guess I needed
a complete mental relaxation from pictures at that moment. I
wanted to devote my entire time to being with Phyllis and my
family—to do just as we pleased. Also, there were a number of
interests which needed my personal attention. We wanted time
to establish my dance schools. We had recently acquired our new
ranch.

My racing stable was getting hot as a pistol. I had finally seen
a horse of mine win. It was the afternoon of June 7, 1945, at Santa
Anita, and I was able to be present when Triplicate picked up the
seventh and feature race of the day.

I liked what I saw.

With *Blue Skies* completed, I literally washed show business
right out of my hair. We went east to Aiken for the winter and all
the while Triplicate was doing his stuff at Santa Anita. That was
1945. Clyde wired me: "You better come out and see this horse—
he might run good in the Santa Anita Handicap."

We were back in California to see the $100,000 contest and he
ran a creditable race, fourth ($5,000 was his share of the purse).
That performance indicated something special. He was improving, and Clyde said, "There's no tellin' just how good this horse
might be."

I lost interest in movies and show business for some months,
other than going to see a few pictures. I didn't miss it a bit and

had no thought of returning. We were very busy with our plans, Phyl and I—everything was working just right.

Again I thought, "I must be the happiest fellow in the world."

We were trying to establish the dance school chain but so far had not found the right partner. I wanted someone to take over the business responsibilities in New York.

Eventually I ran into Charles Casanave, whom I talked to for days about how to go into the business and really do it right. I had known Charles for some years before, when he was connected with the motion-picture business as head of National Screen Service, a publicity and display company. We often saw each other in the old days at RKO. He was interested in the idea and was keen about going in with me. We decided to do a little research and resume negotiations as soon as we had some basic plans.

The horses continued to do well all through that year, even the minor members of the stable grabbing a heat now and then, or at least getting in the purse money. This, incidentally, is a handy thing to have—oat earners.

Triplicate kept improving and knocking at the door in top company through the Hollywood Park meeting, but it wasn't until the 1946 Santa Anita season that he really asserted himself.

We were back in Aiken visiting the family as usual when the wires from Clyde would arrive such as: "Trip got the job done again today," etc.

We returned to watch him run a close-up sixth in the blanket finish of the Santa Anita Handicap 1946, beaten no more than two lengths in the biggest of all Santa Anita Handicap fields (twenty-three runners). He ran a hell of a race. Jockey J. D. Jessop thought he would have won easily had it not been for being drawn number twenty 'way on the outside and getting shut off and pushed around. He asked for the mount on him in the San Juan Capistrano, $50,000 mile-and-a-half stake coming up the following week.

Jessop got his wish and so did we. Triplicate won the San Juan by five open lengths and established himself as a tough handicap contender. There were sixty thousand people there that day, and as I fought my way to the winner's circle I got slapped on the back so many times that I was more beat than the horse. What a day!

Trip was a rather moody sort, sometimes disappointing his followers, but he went on that year to win the major portion of his lifetime earnings of around a quarter million dollars. I had learned by now that owning a successful racehorse takes on the proportions of big business, with all the nerves and jitters that go with it. I had retired to rest. This was rest?

At Hollywood Park, Clyde timed him just right with sights set on the $100,000 Hollywood Gold Cup. We engaged Jessop to fly out from New York for the ride but he was set down by the stewards a few days before, and lost the mount. We were frantic for a jockey and hated to lose Jessop, who was riding tops then and knew the horse so well. Clyde made an effort to get Arcaro and several others but without success.

Finally, we secured Basil James. This was a real-life drama, tense with excitement, as flying conditions in the East were unfavorable that day and there was some doubt whether or not James would be able to make it in time. Howard Hughes kindly sent word to my house that he would do all he could to help see that James got through.

Well—the jock made it in time.

This was a good horserace with a great ride by James and a close finish with Trip coming from pretty far back to nail Louis B. Mayer's fine filly Honeymoon by a neck at the wire, equaling the track record. When his number went up there was a great roar from the crowd of over fifty thousand. That was it. Randy Scott sat with us in our box to watch the memorable proceedings. I tried to get Phyllis to come down to the winner's circle with me but she preferred not to.

Again I had to take a beating on the way there, but it's such a nice kind of a beating to have to take.

Governor Warren's lovely wife presented me with the Gold Cup and it was an indescribable thrill, the whole thing.

Clyde Phillips was a happy man that day as we stood there while the cameras were clicking. He had trained many big-time winners but he told me this one gave him extra special satisfaction. I walked back with him to his box, where his Mrs. was waiting. We sat together for a while absorbing all the happy circumstances that come with such a windfall. There were wise-cracks and congratulations from the racing mob. Lots of laughs all around.

Clyde and his wife Kate having been deep in my affections for so many years, this was more than just another winner. It was the height of something.

Clyde had been a sick man for several years. I knew that he had a lung ailment but he was such a tough man that it was hard to figure him anything but strong. He faltered that Gold Cup day as we walked together to his box. I had to hold his arm.

A few months later he died, after a short stay in a sanitarium. Aged fifty-three. This loss was, of course, a blow. Clyde was my good friend.

Triplicate went under groom Laurence Campion's handling from then on. Campion took full charge as trainer. He won another big one at Golden Gate Fields that fall, the $75,000 Golden Gate Handicap. That was his last big stake win.

In 1947 and '48 he won more races but had a recurrence of his old ankle trouble, and I retired him to stud in Kentucky at the age of seven. Owning a stallion is no cinch. Racing is not easy. So many things can happen to a horse in a split second somewhere during a race. That's what makes it fascinating.

Many owners don't bet at all. The purse money involved is what I rely upon to pay my operating expenses. If I have a bet it is for fun and I have rarely bet more than a few hundred dollars on a horse of mine or on any others, in recent years.

I had a nice touch on Triplicate in the Gold Cup. There was a good reason to bet that time. In the first place, I thought he had a good chance and I wanted to give a lot of presents. The winner's share of that purse was $81,000 and I won about $6,000 in addition for my $400 across-the-board bet. (He was a little over seven to one.) That put me about even for life on betting.

Triplicate, after his retirement from racing, sired a good many winners but none of outstanding class. I think that was because he never had much of a chance. It is not easy to get the right kind of top brood mares booked to a stallion, with so much competition, and I didn't have any mares of my own at the time. After a few years I sold him to a Japanese breeder and he is now in Japan doing and looking very well, I hear.

Many people have asked me how I could sell him after what he had done for me. I've learned never to fall in love with a horse. When it becomes economically unsound to keep one, it must go.

Trip's attitude always fascinated me. He was a real snob. He looked down his nose at me—always. I paid him a visit at the stable after his Gold Cup win, with the intention of giving him a few fond and appreciative pats on the neck. When I reached out he grabbed the straw hat off my head and started to eat it. Good old Trip!

In summing up my racing experiences through some thirty years to date, I guess I've learned a little about it.

I often wonder how many people who go to the track really know what it's all about except to rush to the betting windows. I'm certain that only a small percentage understand the fundamentals and fine points. Many people think that every race is fixed and there are many others who are positive that at least a few every day are prearranged.

This is, of course, completely ridiculous. In all my fooling around the tracks I've never found a fixed race.

Once I was told to have a bet on a "shoo-in." If that was a fixed race they should find a better way to do it because the horse didn't win.

Racing is a lot of fun but an owner runs into a good many hazards and irritations at times. Some people can't understand why the horses they bet on should be beaten. They blame the jockey, the track, the horse—in fact, everybody but themselves—and often take it out on the owner.

One day I was leaving Hollywood Park after Triplicate had been beaten, and, as I drove by in my car, a man walking along the road said in a loud voice to be sure I'd hear, "There goes the son-of-a-bitch who owns Triplicate."

I had a nice little gray filly called Witch Wooky who won plenty of races. One day when she was beaten a fellow yelled at me,

"Hey, Fred—what happened to that pig of yours?" Did I burn?! "Pig!"

Charlie Casanave had been working on the dance-school project and our meetings went on until the early part of 1947, when the deal was closed. We launched it that year by taking a heavy lease on some space at 487 Park Avenue.

Then started the publicity and inquiries as to why I wanted to go into such a commercial thing as the dance-school business.

My answer was that, while I had always been in a field of artistic endeavor, it nevertheless had its commercial aspects and I was sort of accustomed to it. I pointed out that the same thing applies to the horse business. I went into racing for fun and sport and became engulfed by a four-legged bonanza which had so far copped me close to a quarter of a million.

My inspiration to embark into the schools stemmed from one main source. Phyllis, with her keen business mind, thought it would be a good move because I had received hundreds of thousands of fan letters through the years, mostly from people of all ages seeking advice on ballroom dancing; where to learn? would I teach? and so on. I often answered their communications suggesting they go to Arthur Murray, whom I had known personally for many years.

Phyl and I plunged diligently into establishing our project about

January of 1947. We were told the studio would be ready by September.

I trained 150 teachers myself. The building decorations were late in getting ready. It cost much more than we expected. We had launching pains and "organizing agonies." At any rate, it started to assume the aspects of a circus by the time a few press announcements appeared.

After several delays, we had a flash opening. *Life* Magazine moved in, took about five hundred pictures and never used one. There were hundreds of people filing in and out all day and into the night. Most of them wanted autographs, not dance lessons. A number of people signed up for courses.

I don't know where those hundreds of thousands were who wrote me about lessons, but I do know they did not turn up for the first two years. It was rough sledding.

Phyl said, "I made you do this—it's all my fault."

I assured her it was not her fault and that there were promising indications.

The venture needed more capital, which I threw in, and we left for Aiken. After that holiday we returned to New York to find that the school was working and we agreed we would have to be patient.

After the previous year's experience with Triplicate and now this, I found my retirement was somewhat of a joke and that I probably should go back into the movies for a "rest."

Home in Beverly Hills a few months later, I was playing a record of Lionel Hampton's, "Jack the Bell Boy," one day and it "sent" me right through the ceiling. I thought to myself, "I might as well be doing this someplace where it counts." The urge and inspiration to go back to work had hit me.

Chapter 26 *Easter Parade*

There I was, full of ideas and ambition again, but no picture to do, and it would take at least a year to plan and get one ready, if I did tell Metro that I wanted to come back. I also was not sure the movies would want me back.

I let it rest, and two days later got an urgent call from M-G-M asking me if I'd consider returning to the screen. *Easter Parade* was in the middle of rehearsals; Gene Kelly had broken his ankle and could not continue. L. K. Sidney, vice-president, got me on the phone and asked me if I cared to come "home" again. He explained the situation, so I went to see him to discuss it. Arthur Freed was the producer, Chuck Walters the director. With Irving Berlin's score and the wonderful Judy Garland to play opposite, I was lucky. The part could be made to suit me. It was a mighty important setup with Ann Miller, Pete Lawford and Jules Munshin.

I called Gene Kelly to find out for sure whether or not he was so disabled that he really wanted to relinquish his role. Gene assured me that he could not possibly continue. His accident had put the studio in an awful predicament. Would I come back and take over? I told him I was ready.

Not having danced for nearly two years, with the exception of my ballroom teaching activities in connection with the dance schools, I became aware of the big job ahead. Suddenly I wondered if I could still do what was expected of me. Maybe the old joints would stiffen up in reaction to a strenuous workout. I had read so much in the papers about my approaching fifty, which seemed to be practically too late for the torso to take it, according to them.

Here I was forty-eight and I wondered if it was safe for me to kick forcibly without having a leg leave the body.

I took it easy for a few days and crept back into shape. Everything was all right. I couldn't find anything different from before. Nothing cracked or hurt any more than usual.

Quite a lot of revision was necessary in the film to suit me. I pitched in with choreographer Bob Alton on getting my dances in order and in about five weeks we were shooting the picture. My retirement was over.

The tramp number, "We're a Couple of Swells," "I Love a Piano," "Snooky Ookums," "Waiting for the Robert E. Lee," "Easter Parade," all with Judy, remain with me as high spots of enjoyment in my career. Judy's uncanny knowledge of showmanship impressed me more than ever as I worked with her. She was, of course, wonderful in the picture and I was elated when Arthur Freed told me he had already started work on another one, *The Barkleys of Broadway,* to follow *Parade.*

Ann Miller and I drew one of Irving's new songs, "It Only Happens When I Dance with You." That was my first opportunity to work with her. Annie is a terrific performer.

Two solos turned out well for me, one "Drum Crazy," and the other "Steppin' Out with My Baby." In "Steppin' Out" I utilized the slow-motion camera again for a bit, with the ensemble dancing in normal speed while I was superimposed working in front of them in slow motion part of the time.

Parade was a big hit picture and drew plus reactions all over the world. It was a lucky break for me just when I wanted it. My comeback had been completed.

A pleasant surprise came to me in a letter from Bing. He wrote: "For a guy who had retired ostensibly, your comeback represents the greatest event since Satchel Paige."

The Barkleys of Broadway, next on the list for Judy and me, was due to start in a few months. We liked the story by Betty Comden and Adolph Green. When they read their original script to Judy and me in Arthur Freed's office, we flipped with delight and said we'd have a hard time following them in the parts. They are noted for their brilliant readings of their own material.

With the dance schools still in their formative stage there were many things to check and attend to as we were gradually overcoming various difficulties. The operation began to take shape.

The stable was doing well. My racing luck held on and we gathered our share of minor winners with a few new acquisitions.

Phyl and I dropped in at Aiken for a short stay on schedule. Young Fred, Jr., was then a pupil at Aiken Preparatory School.

Phyl distinguished herself by winning the mothers' race at the school athletic meet that year. She trained by running up and down the porch of the Bulls' residence and occasionally around the gardens.

I never knew about this prowess of hers until the day of the race, when I watched her win by about ten lengths from a tough field. It was a hotly contested heat of fifty yards but Phyl went to the front at the gun and stayed there. Very impressive. There was much cheering as I sat proudly with my little Ava on my lap, loving it all. One youngster said to Freddie, "Say—your mother can fly."

I found out afterward that she had worked rather seriously at track in her school days at Fermata. We teased her about keeping things from us.

Those were wonderful days.

When it came time to start *Barkleys of Broadway* at M-G-M, I was disappointed to find that Judy Garland could not make it on account of illness. Although we decided to wait as long as possible in hopes that she might recover, we were bitterly disappointed as she advised the studio to go ahead and replace her.

The whole show having been written with Judy in mind, this situation presented a major problem.

Luck was with us, however, and Ginger Rogers happened to be available. Gin and I had often discussed the possibility of getting together for a rematch and here it was out of a clear sky. Up to then, no vehicle had presented as favorable an opportunity. The old team was hooked up for one again and this gave the publicity department a little something to work on. We were pleased that there was still so much interest. Oscar Levant and Billie Burke were prominently cast.

Harry Warren and Ira Gershwin did the score for *Barkleys* with one interpolation, "They Can't Take That Away from Me," from one of the early Gershwin films.

Our rehearsals brought forth a new set of gags and jokes and we had fun working with director Chuck Walters. There were a whole slew of dance numbers with which we hoped to top our past performances. It was hard for Gin and me to realize that nearly ten years had passed since our last show together.

When we finally got around to shooting our first dance, I thought Ginger for some reason seemed taller than usual. I asked Hermes Pan, "Am I crazy or is Ginger on stilts?" He said, "I know—something is different." I went to Ginger.

"Hey—have you grown or have I shrunk?" She laughed and confessed that she had snuck some higher heels over on me.

One of my favorites was the Scotch number we did in that film, "My One and Only Highland Fling."

I had a solo in which hundreds of pairs of shoes became involved. This was a dream-fantasy idea taking place in a shoe-repair shop scene, on which Hermes Pan worked with me. The shoes came to life, jumped off the shelves, and danced with me in all sorts of eccentric ways—another complicated special effect. Everything was going along fine through the rehearsals of this thing, but I had no finish.

For days I couldn't figure out how to end this number. It was then I deviated for a change from my steadfast rule of not listening to suggestions. On this particular occasion I got great help from my friend Harold Turburg, M-G-M prop man of long standing. Harold was assigned to many of my pictures and was always around during rehearsal periods to supply any props or gadgets I might want while I scratched around experimenting with ideas for various trick dances.

As I mentioned, for days I couldn't figure out how to end this number. Harold came up with: "Why don't you just shoot the plate-glass window in the background and go nuts with shoes falling from above and all over the place?"

That was it. At this point in the number I was holding two guns but I never thought of shattering that plate-glass window in the shoe shop. Harold did. Thanks again, Harold!

Barkleys made it. We were pleased that the press reception was extremely favorable. Mr. Crowther, Mr. Guernsey, Mr. Schallert, Miss Creelman and Miss Cameron were among the unanimous approvers.

That film is now on TV quite often.

Frankly, I can't remember what happened after the completion of *Barkleys* except that our normal and rather simple existence at home went beautifully on. We still avoided going to parties. Phyl and I had plenty to keep us busy. The children and all the family were fine. Life was perfect—all plans for the future were materializing.

I had committed myself to Paramount for a picture with Betty Hutton, for which the script was not completed. A delay developed and was more or less welcome. At that point I wasn't too anxious to plunge right into another dancing melee. M-G-M had nothing ready for me. I planned a six months' respite.

That plan was short-lived. I received a script of *Three Little Words* from Jack Cummings at M-G-M, which he had scheduled for the near future. How it happened to fall into my lap so suddenly, I don't know, but I sure liked it and told Jack I could hardly wait.

This was the life story of two friends of mine from my vaudeville days and I felt it was a natural. My part was that of Bert Kalmar, the former vaudeville dancing star. Red Skelton was cast for the role of Harry Ruby. Kalmar and Ruby became an ace songwriting team and their story was loaded with material which George Wells' fine script captured completely. In addition, I was to have the brilliant dancing star Vera Ellen opposite me as Bert Kalmar's wife.

It promised a great deal and nobody was disappointed. Under our director Dick Thorpe we coasted through in easy fashion.

Vera and I had a good time with a combination tap dance and pantomime number called "Mr. and Mrs. Hoofer at Home," and with "Where Did You Get That Girl?" "Thinking of You" was another type of dance which showed Vera at her best. Again Hermes Pan worked with us.

There were numerous high spots and Red Skelton hit one of his utmost peaks both in comedy and on the more serious side at times.

I enjoyed singing the old Kalmar and Ruby hits with Red, such as "Three Little Words," "So Long, Oolong," "Nevertheless" and others.

Words was an outstanding film and one of my top favorites. I'd like to be doing it all over again.

Paramount was still not quite ready for me with the Betty Hutton picture so I found a little time to devote to the stable. Triplicate having been retired, Phyl and I decided to replenish the gap left by his departure, if possible. It was not easy, that task; in fact it was impossible and has remained so ever since.

We've had some good winners but no Trips. There was time

to visit Kentucky during the interim and we stayed with Leslie Combs and his wife Dorothy at their Spendthrift Farm.

"Meanwhile, back at the ranch," the horses were still at it and our thoroughbred breeding plans developing at the newly acquired establishment. I put in a lot of labor building paddock fences. Phyllis and I spent as much time as we could improving the lovely spot which became Blue Valley Ranch.

Arthur Freed notified me that *Royal Wedding* with June Allyson would be my next at M-G-M to follow the Paramount commitment. June had discussed working with me for some time and I was delighted.

The dancing schools now took hold and we had over forty new branches operating.

When *Let's Dance* finally got under way, it, like every picture I've done, felt like the best one of the bunch. Working with Betty Hutton keeps anybody moving. She's so talented and conscientious that if you don't watch yourself you feel you're standing still and letting her do all the work.

Harrison Carroll visited the set one day and asked me how a worrier like me felt about working with a worrier like Betty. I told him that I found it great because I knew she was going to worry about everything and I didn't have to worry so much.

There were many things in *Let's Dance* that I liked, particularly "Oh, Them Dudes," in which Betty and I portrayed a couple of scrummy cowboys. Another of Frank Loesser's songs which caught me was "Why Fight the Feeling." Hermes Pan, as usual, came through with help on the choreography and I had a couple of solos that worked.

Producer Bob Fellows and director Norman McLeod made every effort to get a good show. We all pitched hard.

I don't really know what happened to that film. It opened big and just seemed to come and go. Anyway, I liked it.

Arthur Freed was soon ready with *Royal Wedding* and I found myself obliged to kick off at rehearsals with only a few weeks to catch a breather. June Allyson and I started a few numbers with choreographer Nick Castle and were going along well when things began to happen.

First of all, little June (Mrs. Dick Powell in private life) arrived one morning, after about ten days, and told us she could not go on with the picture because she was expecting a baby. That settled that. I said bye-bye to June, much to my chagrin. Now, we had a problem. Who could we get?

Originally Chuck Walters had agreed to direct but he retired to take over some other assignment. The studio submitted the script to Judy Garland. Judy readily accepted, much to the jubilation of us all. We now could resume after a week's quandary. I was delighted that Judy and I could get together again after the false start of *Barkleys of Broadway*.

We went back to rehearsals. Although still without a director, we could go ahead with the dances.

After about two weeks, our Judy was taken sick and could not rehearse for several days. We waited and soon realized that it would not be possible for her to make it. There were five weeks gone and we had no leading lady and no director.

I began to wonder if we ever would get this picture made. After another week or so, Arthur told me that Jane Powell was available. All I said was, "Grab her—please."

While Janie was not primarily a dancer, I knew she could do what was required in this show. She surprised everybody by her handling of the dances—we were on our way.

Now, for a director. We could get Stanley Donen, whom I felt would be ideal for this film. He had co-directed with Gene Kelly but had never done one by himself. Stan started out as a choreographer, had recently graduated to straight direction. I was happy to be a part of his first solo effort.

Wedding turned out well. It played five big weeks at the Music Hall in New York and was rather well received by some of the critics.

There were potent values with Pete Lawford, Keenan Wynn

and Sir Winston's lovely daughter, Sarah Churchill, in the cast. She was delightful in the picture.

Light as the tale may have been, it was an excellent pattern for the numbers and very pretty to look at in color, with some of the actual royal wedding scenes of Prince Philip and Princess Elizabeth woven into the story line.

"How Could You Believe Me When I Said I Loved You When You Know I've Been a Liar All My Life?," authoritatively acknowledged as the longest song title in history, was written by Alan Lerner and Burton Lane for this picture. Jane and I with the help of Nick Castle got a crazy mixed-up hoke number out of this which clicked.

I found a spot in *Wedding* for my upside-down-on-the-ceiling-and-around-the-walls dance which I had planned for some time. This one involved tricky mechanical photographic and scenery maneuvers. Incidentally, it was another idea that hit me one 4 A.M.

Soon after finishing that picture I found that my next would be *Belle of New York*, the one I had avoided back in 1946 by retiring.

The less said about it the better, I think, because it never did get off the ground although plenty of money and pains were spent on it. For some reason or another, I liked making it, probably because Vera Ellen and I had some interesting dance ideas to keep us busy. There were five numbers of Harry Warren and Johnny Mercer's which stood out, but the element of fantasy which prevailed backfired on us. One trick which we hoped would prove effective was dancing on air and that above all failed to register.

The story thought was for us to be so carried away, in love, that we simply took off into space. I had one solo in which I wafted myself to the top of the arch in Washington Square. After much experimentation and testing, it neither came off photograpically nor story-wise.

Phyllis went to the sneak preview and overheard a remark

from some lady seated behind her, as she watched me walking on air: "Well! How silly can you get?" I knew then how we stood.

The 1910 period background was a bit tired at that stage—in fact, there was a musical picture calm setting in again too, and we missed—period.

The critics loathed the film and we, the principals, were gently patronized for trying, I guess, with no means of accomplishing our aim. It would have been nice if we could have known beforehand what they knew afterward.

The boys complained of the "thin story," which reminds me of a remark of Noel Coward's in England some years ago. When the critics lambasted a play of his for being "thin," he retorted with: "Very well—from now on I will write nothing but very fat plays for very fat critics."

I took off with the family after that for a complete change. It bothered me to think I could try so hard with enthusiasm only to realize afterward that everything amounted to nothing.

I was on *Belle* for eight months, beating my brains out, and all I got out of it was—a fortune.

There's one thing about having a flop movie at a major studio that has it all over a stage flop. You do get paid.

My faithful producer, Arthur Freed, didn't hold anything against anybody because of a situation like that. He had a splendid way of simply not thinking about it any more in favor of something new and better to come. He started planning immediately on *The Band Wagon* for Cyd Charisse and me. This was to be a new story. We used some of the Burton Lane–Howard Dietz score from the original Broadway show *Band Wagon* that my sister and I did in 1931, but otherwise the entire thing was new.

Cyd Charisse and I had not worked together since the *Ziegfeld Follies* at Metro in 1944 when she danced around me as a ballet girl while I sang one of the opening numbers in that film. Now she had developed into one of Metro's brightest stars. It was a big show Arthur had planned, with Jack Buchanan brought over from England, Oscar Levant, and Nanette Fabray. Again Betty

Comden and Adolph Green read their story to us and again they made it tough for us to follow them.

We all loved the setup with Vincente Minnelli directing and Michael Kidd doing some special work on the choreography.

There were something like twenty-four musical numbers, of which I was in seventeen. All, including the less important ones, required a lot of staging, and it took time.

Just before starting work on the film I was asked by Norman Granz, famed *Jazz at the Philharmonic* impresario, to make a special record album, under his direction, of some forty-odd songs which I had introduced in the past. I found this a most interesting and enjoyable job as Oscar Peterson, Alvin Stoller, Flip Phillips, Charles Shavers, Barney Kessel, Ray Brown and I cut these discs spontaneously on the spot without any prearranged orchestrations. This album, called *The Fred Astaire Story*, with limited printings, became prominent in the collectors' item category. Subsequent condensed versions called *Mr. Top Hat* and *Easy to Dance With* have been released.

The "Girl Hunt Ballet" in *Band Wagon*, patterned after Mickey Spillane's stories, I must make special mention of, because I liked it so much. Michael Kidd choreographed that one.

Cyd Charisse is a terrific dancer, a wonderful partner. She has precision plus—beautiful dynamite, I call it.

Funny, with all the hoofing I did in that picture, I remember at the big Hollywood première a kindly old lady shouted to me as we were all filing out of the theatre, "You didn't dance enough!" I had to laugh. Actually, four dance numbers were cut out because we had too much. That film was a bit unwieldy to get down to reasonable running time and we had shot too much stuff. I liked it although it had some flaws, I suppose. The New York critics raved about it but the Hollywood boys did not.

Bosley Crowther in the Sunday *New York Times* said:

There was some instinctive hesitation in the mind of this reviewer the other day when he came out and said "The Band Wagon" might be one of the best musical films ever made. Lofty comments of that nature sometimes have a way of popping up a few months later causing the maker's face to turn bright red. But another inspection of the picture which is now on the Music Hall's screen, and a hasty review of the record, emboldens us to let the comment stand. As a matter of fact we'll make it stronger: It *is* one of the best musicals ever made.

Whereas H. M. in the Los Angeles *Daily News* said:

But for all its 100-octane talent, "The Band Wagon" develops several knocks before grinding to a lavish Technicolored finish. Its chief source of engine trouble is a trite slow moving story.

We don't know how you feel about it but the back-stage perplexities of putting on a Broadway show (the stars fighting, the show flopping, the big switch, the inevitable success, etc.) are things that just don't excite us any more!

Our intention was more or less to rib the theatrical side of this story mercilessly in the playing.

I had a strange experience during the filming of that picture.

When you work with the brilliant Vincente Minnelli as your director, you want to come through with everything he asks for and sometimes the order is a bit difficult to handle.

In this instance, the scene was a small hotel room crammed with members of our show at a party immediately after our opening-night flop.

We were all supposed to be trying to forget the miseries of our flop and it was a difficult scene to stage with all those people in such tight quarters. Nothing seemed to play and Vincente kept changing lines and positions.

After about an hour of this confusion I ran into a complete mental block. I couldn't think of one definite thing of any kind, including my own name, and I shouted, "That's it—kill the lights—I can't think—I've got to get out of here," and walked off the set directly to Arthur Freed, who happened to be sitting there. I can remember the astonished look on everybody's face as I left. I had never done that in my life, and there was a strained silence.

I said to Arthur, "Come on, walk around with me for a few minutes will you—I've cracked." Arthur, amazed, looked at me. "What's the matter, kid, take it easy." I kept saying, "I can't think, I can't think," as we walked arm-in-arm. All I remember is that I wondered what Phyllis and the children would say when I was brought home a sort of maniac. Concentrate I could not.

We walked for at least fifteen minutes. Then, I called the script man over to feed me some dialogue cues. They meant nothing; I was mentally blank. After about five more minutes I sat down with my head in my hands and started to function again. I was able to resume work.

I went to Minnelli afterward and apologized, explaining my mental lapse, and Vincente said, "Oh, that's perfectly all right, Fred, I drive everybody crazy."

Chapter 27 *Stone Wall*

Around this time the various experiments on large screens began to take place. There were high and wide ones, medium-high and low-wide ones as well as the three-dimensional menace. I had a feeling the 3-D wouldn't last any longer than it did when I first saw it introduced over thirty years ago.

Television was moving in with such force that something had to be done, I'm glad to say. I am very much in favor of the big screens.

With no pictures scheduled to follow *Band Wagon* (that was my last one at M-G-M by contract) Phyllis and I talked about some extensive travel plans. By then young Pete had completed two years at the University of Nevada and was doing his bit in the service. Fred, Jr., seventeen, was at Webb School.

I had practically made up my mind to retire again as Mrs. A. and I weighed the situation and decided that nobody seemed too anxious or excited about getting me to do another picture so that was the signal.

This time I wouldn't tell anybody about it—I would just fade gently out of action for a while, return minus the old dancing shoes and possibly go into producing when I got the urge.

We made some pretty extensive plans about rebuilding the ranch house, hoping to live there as a permanent residence. The horses were holding up their end and we continued to win our share of races with trainer Ralph West.

After a pleasant swordfishing expedition at Guaymas, Mexico, we went east the summer of 1953 to stay with Phyl's family for a short time. It was at the Belmont Park races that she, for the first time since I had known her, complained of an illness of any sort. On this day she asked to be taken home early in the afternoon on account of faintness and a dizzy headache. Although I was naturally concerned, I cast it out of my mind next day when she assured me that there was nothing to it, that she was fine and wouldn't think of seeing a doctor.

There was no recurrence of the ailment and we returned to California after a pleasant holiday and some work on the dance schools, which were going well.

My mother had moved to California and it was a relief to have her back somewhere near us after so many years abroad. She was in splendid health and looking perfectly wonderful as ever as she approached her middle seventies.

My sister, now married to Kingman Douglass and living most of the time in Middleburg, Virginia, at her Mount Gordon Farm, was firmly settled, happy and enjoying her new life. Delly, I might add, had lost none of her punch; in fact she had more than ever.

I had a few horses ready for the Santa Anita meeting of '53-'54, so we planned to stay home for most of that winter. I was a secretly retired man, mainly because nobody invited me to do another picture, and I began to like the idea more and more. Life had designed itself that way for me, it seemed. The plan Phyllis and I had worked out was taking effect.

My agent, Harry Friedman of M.C.A., called me on the phone one morning and asked me how I'd like to do another picture.

I answered, "Oh no—no—not that. What is it?"

He then told me that Darryl Zanuck had seen me dining at Romanoff's the night before and got the idea for me to play a modern musical version of *Daddy Long Legs,* which they would write up for me if I was interested.

I was interested—and how.

I made the deal for the picture to start sometime the following September (1954). They were in hopes of getting Leslie Caron.

Fred, Jr., surprised me one morning soon after his eighteenth birthday with the news that he had enlisted in the Air Force.

When I asked him why he had not at least mentioned it or discussed it with me first, he answered quite casually, "Oh, I just had the urge and couldn't wait. I saw a movie and that did it. I got up early next morning and went down to the recruiting office."

I didn't blame him much. Those air pictures made it all very enticing. Anyway, he was in and had to report in a few weeks. Freddie liked to fly and had had his pilot's license since the age of seventeen. He was soon sent to Lackland Air Force Base in Texas for basic training. Phyllis and I made arrangements to go to San Antonio to spend Easter with him.

In the meantime Santa Anita was in full swing and we were enjoying our usual racing season there. Ever since its inception, twenty years previously, we had been faithful patrons. Phyl would bring her knitting and we looked after the interests of our small but active stable.

Suddenly one day, early in the afternoon, sitting in our box between races, she said: "I think I'll have to go home. I don't feel well. It's nothing—just that dizziness." So we left.

The recurrence of this ailment bothered me of course, but I could not induce her to undergo a physical examination. She was apparently fine next day and for some weeks after that there were no signs of disorder. Then one evening she could not attend some sort of dancing-class function of Ava's on account of this same dizziness.

A week later we were to dine with Cole Porter. She could not make it and asked me to go alone. We dined quite regularly with

Cole and she never would think of declining at the last minute like that. It alarmed me but she convinced me again that it could not be anything serious.

A few days later, without any questions, I drove her straight to our family physician. He found her in extremely fine condition subject to the outcome of some X-ray pictures which were taken.

When the pictures came through, they proved the necessity of immediate major surgery.

Our trip to spend Easter with Fred, Jr., in Texas was canceled and I asked for special emergency leave for him, through the Red Cross, to come to us.

We were to move into St. John's Hospital on Thursday, two days later.

Phyllis, as ill as she was, wanted to go to the ranch for the day, Wednesday, to see a new filly foal just dropped by her favorite brood mare, Over Anxious. As we went through the gates, I knew what was on her mind and told her not to worry. We would soon be back to resume our routine weekends and various stays there, as well as our plans for rebuilding the house, which we had been working on. We reached the end of one of the paddocks where the new foal and its mother were standing. Phyllis smiled and said, "Oh, isn't it a nice one," as she sat down to rest. She insisted upon seeing all the horses and animals on the place, which we did. She was having trouble breathing.

I took her into the house for a short while. As we got into the car for the ride home, she said softly, "I wonder if I'm going to die."

I still felt completely sure that nothing could happen to her, and I tried very hard to convince her so. My religious faith could not permit me to feel otherwise. "People do not die so easily," I went on. "It is hard to die. You have so much to live for, you are so important to so many people, you are very strong—this is not your time to go. Please dispel it from your mind. It could not be—I know it." And, I did know it.

We went into the hospital next day and the operation was

performed the following morning (Good Friday). It was successful but serious, and in about five hours complications prevented her from responding as expected and we called in some other specialists for consultation. It was decided that she had to return at once to surgery. They told me there was only a remote chance of her coming through this time.

Somehow, as they took her away, I knew that she could still stand anything they would have to do. I sat down in the waiting room by the elevator on the ground floor with my close friends, David Niven and Hermes Pan.

I felt numb. I couldn't even cry—it was impossible that this, the very worst, was happening.

She had gone up in that elevator at 4 A.M. and at about 6 o'clock the door opened and there she was, apparently safely through another ordeal—miraculously.

They said she was doing fine and that she would start immediately to pick up. However, she would require extensive further treatment.

Young Fred arrived from Texas, the Red Cross having done a magnificent job of getting him here so quickly. Phyllis was gaining her strength and indications pointed to complete recovery. Fred, Jr., returned to his Air Force base in Texas. That was our Easter weekend.

Phyl underwent a series of X-ray treatments. They meant trips to downtown Los Angeles five days a week for five weeks. She didn't even have to finish all of the treatments—the recovery was that successful.

I always went with her and could see the gradual progress. All of the attendants agreed that she was doing wonderfully and I was certain we had won our fight.

She came home with only one nurse and soon did not even need her. This was three months after the first surgery. Uncle Henry, Auntie Maud, Phyl and I resumed our customary visits, convinced that there was no need for further serious concern.

We went to the ranch weekends as before and I had such

pleasure in saying to her as we drove through the gate, "Now, you see—you never thought you'd be coming back here, did you?" She said, "I never would have if it hadn't been for you." I said, "Oh, now just because I stayed at the hospital with you. It was nice to be off by ourselves with only a few intimate friends visiting, occasionally. It was sort of like a holiday. I don't seem to remember any of the hideous side. It's all past and doesn't mean a thing any more." She replied, "Do you really think so? I wonder." (She even gave Ava an automobile driving lesson that weekend.)

Suddenly, a few weeks later, she had another setback and we had to return to St. John's for more major surgery. Again the Red Cross arranged emergency leave for young Fred. I still couldn't get myself to be anything but optimistic. The operation was again called a success. She came home with some slight improvement but she never regained her strength and the definite down trend set in. I saw it all—but still could not believe anything would take her away. It wasn't possible.

She lapsed into a coma for several weeks. I knew she would snap out of it. She didn't. She looked like a beautiful child. She never lost her sweet facial expression.

Phyllis slipped away from us at 10 A.M., September 13, 1954.

Chapter 28 Funny Face Again

I had started rehearsals of *Daddy Long Legs* in July, just before Phyl's second operation, and had to stop when things again became critical.

I tried to get out of my commitment but the studio (Fox) prevailed upon me to do the picture—they would wait until I felt that I was ready.

I resumed work early in October. It was fortunate that I had the work to do.

The first days of my return to the studio were given to the least exacting obligations I had in the picture. Producer Sam Engel and director Jean Negulesco kindly did everything to make it as easy as possible for me by rearranging the schedule.

Leslie Caron's ballet, staged by Roland Petit, had been started and there was little for me to do in it but appear in the background as was designed in the story point dream sequence.

After that I began to move again and we put in some hard work on "Slue Foot," "Something's Gotta Give" and "Dream" —our most important dance numbers.

Johnny Mercer wrote the music and lyrics for the picture. "Something's Gotta Give" was, to my mind, the perfect song for the spot required in our story. Johnny came through again when most needed. Mercer's song, "Dream," long a standard and favorite of mine, was one of the reasons I asked for Johnny to write the music for the picture. I had always wanted to do a romantic dance to that tune.

At lunch through that period I usually had a difficult time because my mind was temporarily unoccupied by work. Dave Robell, my dance assistant, sat with me and was helpful in keeping me straightened out mentally. Everyone at the studio helped me a great deal.

Henry and Phoebe Ephron's script for *Long Legs* was one of the best ever to come my way.

Leslie Caron is a fine artist, conscientious, apt, serious. She hesitates to attempt anything either in dance or acting unless she is absolutely sure of herself. Leslie will hold up production for many minutes (or hours), on some occasions, until she feels complete control of what she's about to do. I consider that a most commendable trait.

One day at rehearsals I asked her to listen extra carefully to the music, so as to keep in time.

Her reply, "Oh, I know, I know—I am so slow at learning. My mother used to send me to see all of your pictures to learn how to keep in time with the music." And then she laughed with a French accent in her own inimitable, unrestrained and attractive way.

The 20th Century–Fox Studio is much different in appearance from others I have worked in. It is open spaced and big in area. You feel that you can breathe. Mr. Zanuck was still at the head when I was there.

They have a fine musical department with Al Newman in charge. Getting to work with Al again, after many years, was a great treat, and with his sense of humor he had me well in hand at a time when I needed it. Same for brother Lionel, one of the funniest guys I know.

That was the only picture I did there. Another one was talked about and planned for me but it never materialized. I was rather disappointed because I liked the studio so much and was eager to follow up *Long Legs,* which did very well.

One can do a lot of things but it's the gems you look for. I liked *Daddy Long Legs* for many reasons, one being that I enjoyed playing the part of a guy with all that dough.

Daddy was a pip of a movie and I hereby give it a good notice.

I have often thought how lucky it was that I dined out at Romanoff's that night. Otherwise Mr. Zanuck might never have gotten his idea.

On completion of the picture I had my first experience at a television pitch to aid in promoting it. Appearing casually on three or four network shows, I found the medium enjoyable. I was not nervous or tense, even though it was a brand-new racket to me.

Appearing free of charge took the pressure off, I guess, and I found it like playing a game. It was a sort of "What do I do, and where do I go now?" approach: no script, no dancing to stage, everything more or less ad lib.

Ed Sullivan picked me up out of his studio audience and there I was making like a TVer before I realized it. My old friend Ed made it easy for me. He sure has a way of doing that with his extraordinary show.

I also appeared on *What's My Line?* and *I've Got a Secret,* with enjoyment.

These appearances mean that some fifty million people get a look at you and hear the name of your forthcoming picture mentioned, which is supposed to be vitally important from a promotional standpoint for movies. I wonder how much good it really does. There are two schools of thought about that. Anyway, appearing "for free" enabled me to enjoy it. I've done this in connection with my last three pictures.

All work in connection with *Daddy* was completed about July of 1955, after which I took a trip to Ireland with my mother and Ava to visit Adele, who had been given Lismore Castle for the month of July.

We were fortunate to get a solid month of perfect weather there, not one rainy day, almost unheard-of for that time of year in southern Ireland.

Ava fell in love with the entire place. She lived the imaginary life of a princess—waving from her top tower bedroom to the many sightseers who came daily by bus to stand gazing at the historic castle. The countryside was extremely beautiful that year in the abundant sunshine.

I still was not able to kill a salmon.

Ava went to Dublin, then over to London. I stayed at Lismore. My thoughts had not cleared and I preferred to remain quiet.

While there I received word that my stepson, Peter, wanted to marry Janet. I had never heard of Janet before, but I knew that Pete, at twenty-eight, was thoroughly capable of making his own decisions, so my blessings were with them. When I met Janet a few months later, I easily understood his eagerness. She is a charming and lovely girl and they are extremely happy.

Fox studios were still discussing that other picture for me to follow *Long Legs*, but no story turned up. Several ideas came forth but nothing was suitable and I found myself again wondering what to do next.

I wanted to keep busy, and on returning to California I went about investigating the situation.

I had just made one of the most successful movies of the year —it had rated as one of the top ten in foreign release, and it established a good record in the U.S.A. as well. Still, nothing was in sight for me to follow. I didn't like this lull recurring—but there it was. I waited.

After a few months I signed with Paramount for two pictures

to be made within the coming three years. One was to be done with Bing Crosby (the principal reason for my signing) and the other was a vehicle called *Papa's Delicate Condition,* a story written by Corinne Griffith. Don Hartman was then head of production and Paramount was keen about both projects. I never did make either of those vehicles.

Bing Crosby escaped from Paramount and was no longer available. The other was postponed at my request in favor of a coming project in which Audrey Hepburn was interested.

Now I found myself with two wholly new assignments, both ideally fitting my idea of something I wanted to do: the first was the aforementioned replacement at Paramount and the second was one for Arthur Freed at Metro with Cyd Charisse. Arthur wanted me for *Silk Stockings.* I accepted at once. It would follow closely on the heels of the Paramount picture.

The origin and the first contact pertaining to a big theatrical project always interest me. For instance, here's the way the news of my participation in the Hepburn picture reached me:

I ran into producer Roger Edens at a cocktail party at Clifton Webb's house. Roger stopped me with "What are you doing?" I told him I was about to start *Papa's Delicate Condition* at Paramount. He said, "You can't do it—you've got to do this thing of mine called *Wedding Day* first. Get the other one postponed. Audrey Hepburn likes the script and will do it if we get you."

I said, "Say that again, please!"

Audrey had asked for me to do the picture with her, her first major musical attempt.

This turned out to be *Funny Face,* the film version of the same title which I did with my sister on the Broadway stage in 1927 (with a totally different story, however).

Roger Edens, then at M-G-M, wanted to make the picture there. Negotiations went on for months among Director Stanley Donen, Edens, Paramount, Metro, Audrey's representative, Kurt

Frings, and Audrey's various foreign studio commitments and my representative, M.C.A. It was one of those things that could not be arranged, although Audrey was actually under contract at Paramount. The dates conflicted; Paramount could not handle it; Metro could not swing it; it was hopeless. I was repeatedly told that there was no chance to put the deal across.

However, I knew that Audrey wanted to make the picture and that sooner or later they would all come around—because Audrey is a lady who gets her way. So, I just told my agents to forget all other projects for me. I was waiting for Audrey Hepburn. She asked for me, and I was ready.

This could be the last and only opportunity I'd have to work with the great and lovely Audrey and I was not missing it. Period.

I guessed right. Within a few weeks everything was arranged and I was at it at Paramount. Audrey and her husband, Mel Ferrer, were due from Europe in a month.

I hadn't the remotest idea what sort of dances to put into the show at that point. Luckily, I ran into one useful thought while experimenting for a solo I was to do. Arriving at the studio one morning in a raincoat, I was improvising in front of the mirror, dancing in it, and noticed that the coat moved rather well. I kept on for some time as my friend Walter Ruick ad libbed some Spanish music on the piano, for which I took off my raincoat to use it as a bullfighter's cape. From that was born the mock bullfight dance solo for the "Let's Kiss and Make Up" song.

Some of the Gershwins' songs from the original show were used and also some added numbers by Roger Edens and Leonard Gershe.

Stanley Donen, Gene Loring, Audrey, Pat Denise, Kay Thompson and I had fun putting on our numbers.

Nearly half of the picture was shot in Paris, where we spent many extra days waiting for good weather. It rained so much that one of the fashion model scenes at the Tuileries was shot in the rain by force of circumstances. This lent an effective and unusual touch photographically which probably never would have been preconceived.

Audrey and I had an important romantic dance to perform at La Reine Blanche in Chantilly, a number we had rehearsed for some weeks in Hollywood before leaving for Paris.

The rain fell so steadily at our prospective location that it was impossible to shoot the dance until the very end of our stay in France. Finally, when we did manage to get to it, the weather had cleared but the soil had not dried out as we had hoped.

Rehearsing was difficult there. We had not touched the number for more than two months and were confronted with the task of recalling and fitting this tender romantic dance to scenic surroundings which covered a very large area on the grass, over a bridge, and on a small raft crossing a stream at one point.

It was cold one moment, hot the next; cloudy, then sunny, and the ground was never too reliable in its sodden state.

Audrey worked relentlessly and danced beautifully, never complained about anything. Finally, just as we were about to start photographing after many hours of rehearsing, she spoke up, "Here I've been waiting twenty years to dance with Fred Astaire —and what do I get? Mud!"

One night during an all-night session in a section of the Left Bank we were on a complicated dialogue sequence. It was about 3:30 A.M. and I spotted Hermes Pan in the crowd of visitors on the sidelines. Hermes had just arrived for a holiday in Paris and said he couldn't find his hotel. He happened to see our lights blaring out in the darkness a few blocks away and wandered over to find out what was going on. He spent the rest of the early-morning hours in an adjacent bistro, which we used as shelter, delighted that he had got lost. We then explained to the lost Pan where he lived.

That picture was such a complete joy that we all hated to see it end.

I went to New York for the TV and press pitch, accompanied by my friend and M.C.A. representative, Harry Friedman. As usual, those missions keep your appointments listed on an almost split-second basis.

I appeared again with Ed Sullivan, on Arlene Francis' show and with Art Linkletter on my return to California.

Funny Face proved a walloping success in the main big-city first runs and particularly at the Music Hall, where it broke several records. The critics were intrigued. *Time* gave it a bad review. *Life* gave it a good one.

When I returned to California, Ava was out of school on vacation and suggested that we go right back to Paris so she could see some of the locations where I had worked.

We set out a few weeks later by plane all the way, with a stopover in England to attend the Goodwood Race Meeting, where a horse of mine, Rainbow Tie, was scheduled to run.

A nice handy two-year-old filly, she had established herself by winning three races of good class for me so far that year. Jack Leach had picked her up at the Doncaster sales quite reasonably, thus maintaining his reputation as a genius at picking horse-flesh.

Jack and his attractive daughter Gillian (my godchild) met us, and we spent much time together.

At Goodwood, Queen Elizabeth graciously requested that Ava and I come to the Royal Box between the third and fourth races. The message was conveyed by her equerry, Lord Plunkett, and he accompanied us to the Royal Box.

Ava was presented, and we chatted for some fifteen minutes about the movies, racing, the beauties of Goodwood and dancing. This was my first meeting with the Queen since I had seen her years before as the tiny Princess Elizabeth at the home of her mother and father, then the Duke and Duchess of York.

In conversation I mentioned that I had danced with her mother some years ago. With her fascinating smile she topped me with, "You mean she danced with you!"

As we left, Ava was not quite sure about whether or not another curtsy was necessary and she gave a sort of half-hesitant dip. Neither of us backed away as we should have, either. Later we teased each other about our clumsiness. It was such a long time since I had had any meeting with royalty and I had forgotten. I guess I was also nervous.

Anyway, we discussed it with Plunkett afterward. "How did we do?"

"You were perfect," said he tactfully.

Then we watched my horse run. She looked sleek, shiny and sharp. Did she win?

No!

A few days later, back in Paris, I was retracing many of the steps recently covered. Only this time it was on a sight-seeing tour with my daughter: the Louvre, the Eiffel Tower, the Tuileries, Notre Dame, the Ritz, the Champs-Elysées, the Bois, the Palace at Versailles and the Opéra. They all looked so different.

At some of these places I had recently spent all-night sessions getting the job done. It was strange to realize suddenly that I was back there, with the weather fine and nothing to do but loaf. Very pleasant, as a matter of fact.

When we returned to California all was well at home. Mother, nearing another birthday in excellent health, had consented to come and live with us.

Fred, Jr., now twenty, with another year to go in the Air Force, told me he wanted to marry Gale. This bit of news came as a jolting surprise.

I knew Gale, of course. They had been seeing each other a lot for some six months. I couldn't blame him a bit and I told him so. Gale, a most attractive brunette of eighteen, was destined to become my daughter-in-law.

Exactly that happened.

Now, I found myself with a whole new family and loving it, although I was a bit dizzy during all these quick changes.

Silk Stockings was cooking at M-G-M. The rehearsal dates were set for September, 1956, and I was anxious to start on it with Cyd Charisse.

I had wondered if I would ever do another picture with her or one for Arthur Freed. Also, the opportunity to work with director Rouben Mamoulian was something I had long hoped for.

Stockings, as a film, was an adaptation of the Broadway musical comedy, which was an adaptation of the screen success *Ninotchka.* Freed, Mamoulian and Leonard Gershe did wonders with the script, I thought, and all of us in the cast were much enthused about the newest version.

Cyd Charisse had no easy task following Garbo in that part but she did it beautifully, carrying a slight accent all through the piece. Her solo dances were outstanding. We had plenty of dances together, too, and they did not miss.

That Cyd! When you've danced with her you stay danced with.

I had an idea for a twist on the rock-and-roll craze which I presented to Cole Porter, asking for a song along those lines. Of course, Cole came through with the ideal piece of material, which he titled "The Ritz Roll and Rock."

I put this number on with some help from Hermes Pan and it filled a gap which worried me a lot. I needed a sock solo.

Janis Paige scored brilliantly in her role and the three commissars, Peter Lorre, Jules Munshin and Joseph Buloff, registered comedy wallop punctuations throughout. I enjoyed especially the Cha Cha Cha number early in the piece in which I danced briefly with the illustrious Betty Utti, dynamic Tybee Afra and the beauteous Barrie Chase.

Perhaps I sound like a critic getting his copy ready for the morning paper. This is undoubtedly presumptuous of me but I find it rather fun to give this one a review because it could be the last of my musical pictures. For several years now musicals have again been the forgotten cousins.

Stockings was a hit in Hong Kong. I happened to be there on a pleasure trip with Ava when it opened. Actually, the picture did pretty well generally in a sort of taken-for-granted way. It had a big six weeks' run at the Music Hall in New York, which keyed its status. Most critics praised—a few didn't.

Bosley Crowther in the *New York Times* said: "Somebody should declare a holiday to give everybody time to see this delightful musical." The New York *Daily News* gave us the coveted four stars, and Edwin Schallert wrote in the Los Angeles *Times* that "it is an amusing, colorful show." But George H. Jackson in the Los Angeles *Herald and Express* remarked: ". . . another detracting influence in the story is the May-December romance of the principals, a fact which destroys any romantic illusions." Couldn't he have made it May-October?

Although a number of scripts were sent to me after that by various studios, there was nothing I really wanted to do, so I decided that I had *had* musical pictures.

Chapter 29 Rideout

For about a year then I went through a period of indecision as to whether I should attempt something nonmusical or make an all-out approach to television. There were the usual suggestions for a weekly series, but I did not want to become involved in that sort of commitment. Even three or four specials a year of a dance program would be too much. I waited until I had a conception for a single show before considering any definite step. In the meantime, I appeared as a guest on Oscar Levant's show in California which stands out as one of my most enjoyable experiences.

During this year of cogitation I played a lot of bad golf, took a few pleasure trips, one to the Orient with Ava. We were captivated by Tokyo and Hong Kong. I had plenty of time to think over the past and to try to visualize the future.

My interest in the horses had waned a bit in the preceding two years. Racing luck had completely abandoned me. I could not get an animal to run anywhere near a winner. When mine did seem fit and ready it was often impossible even to get one in a race because of the large number of horses at the California tracks. Several of my brood mares lost foals at birth, and other foals were not even qualified to put in training. The only thing to do in a situation like this is to wait for your racing luck to return. I'm waiting.

The first nonmusical, non-singing-and-dancing thing I tried was for television, a half-hour comedy film called *Imp on a Cobweb Leash* for the *General Electric Theatre* Sunday night series. I got away with that one: nobody seemed to mind that I did not sing or dance, and *Imp* also played a successful repeat run. So I made another for G.E. called *Man on a Bicycle*. Now I was somewhat established in straight comedies and eager to put both feet forward in a live dance special for television.

I went about planning it, and made a deal with the Chrysler Corporation which put the entire package in my lap. I agreed to produce through my newly formed Ava Productions, and appear in a one-hour special, a live telecast in color sometime during the month of October, 1958. Now I could enjoy taking this step, doing it exactly the way I wanted to.

Shortly after signing for the Chrysler show I received an offer from Stanley Kramer to play the part of Osborne, the scientist, in the film from Nevil Shute's best-seller *On the Beach*. This appealed to me, an opportunity to try a straight, serious role as one of a powerful cast headed by Gregory Peck and Ava Gardner, and including Tony Perkins and Donna Anderson.

My professional outlook suddenly became interesting—everything new. The experimental things I had in mind were now all matters of fact. I planned to start rehearsing the television show at least three months ahead of its performance date and signed to leave for Australia to make *On the Beach* in January, 1959. These were challenges. I don't like challenges, but I suppose they keep you from getting stuck in a tired groove.

Time was on me to start the television venture.

I had half a dozen ideas and a definite conception for the show, including several choreographic notions. One came from a Jonah Jones album called "Muted Jazz." Jonah's "St. James Infirmary

Blues" flipped me, and I began to block out in my mind the dance steps to go along with his singing and playing the number. The next thing to do was to get Jonah and his boys for the show, which I was fortunate in doing.

Another notion came from the lyrics of Irving Berlin's "Change Partners," a new dance version of that number. Still another inspiration came from a recorded composition of David Rose's "Man with the Blues."

With these ideas mapped out, I asked Barrie Chase to appear with me. Her work had impressed me in *Silk Stockings* and her individual style was part of the inspiration for these dances.

Everybody contributed much to the show, Bud Yorkin, David Rose, Hermes Pan and sixteen dancing boys and girls. Rehearsals with the company ran for seven weeks, in addition to about five weeks which I put in alone before that.

We had a dance bash putting that show together. Alvin Stoller on drums and Bobby Hammock at the piano brought out all that was in us. Before we knew it we were at the NBC studio in Burbank ready to cut loose.

Planning a big television show is an extraordinary experience. To me it's somewhat like launching a space missile. We had numerous run-throughs and several dress rehearsals at NBC, and then came the fateful evening, October 17. With the excellent assistance of NBC and its facilities, our show went faultlessly.

The response astounded me. At most I had hoped for and perhaps expected a success, but I could not have anticipated the kudos and awards that came our way. In all my years in the theatrical profession I have never experienced such a unanimous reaction of approval both from the audience and from the press.

Among the messages I received about the show was one from Irving Berlin, who said, "You have a whole new career if you want it."

I didn't want a whole new career, but I welcomed a different one.

Well, that about covers the activities of this hoofer up to now. "That's all there is, there isn't any more." Whatever happens from now on will have to be covered in my next book.

Oh, NO! Not that!

However, now that I have almost written a book, I glance back and discover that there are a few loose ends to tie up and some afterthoughts. For instance:

Fred, Jr., has completed his four years in the service and may become interested in theatrical production.

Pete is a sergeant in the Los Angeles County Sheriff's Department and firmly settled down with a lovely new baby daughter, Phyllis Maud.

Adele is busy in retirement, enjoying herself at her farm in Virginia, or in New York, or Jamaica, or wherever she chooses to go.

My mother is very well. She divides her time equally trying to satisfy both branches of the family.

Ava is approaching seventeen. She likes the theatre but has not yet made up her mind.

As for me: I look back and realize that I could go another thousand words merely thanking some of the people who have helped me. Cameramen, for instance, wizards all of them, patient and resourceful, which they have to be to photograph me; and Louella and Hedda, who have always been so kind to me; also Joe Niemeyer, in recent years my talented general assistant.

You'll recall that in Chapter 1 I was stuck for a title. And I stayed stuck until I was more than three-quarters finished. Then Noel Coward, who had come to Los Angeles on one of his tours, dropped in one afternoon and unstuck me with his usual quick perception. "Call it *Steps in Time*, and don't forget that, now," he said. And I didn't. Thank you, Noel.

Some people say that *Top Hat* was my best picture. But I think *Top Hat* was good for its period, just as our Broadway show

Lady, Be Good! was for its time. I feel that all branches of present-day entertainment are better than ever before.

I don't watch my old movies on television. I'm frequently asked about that, and people are astonished when I say I don't look at them. It's rather appalling to me to think that they may still be running a hundred years from now.

I am often asked to expound on the history and the philosophy of "the dance," about which I have disappointingly little to say.

Sometimes my work is referred to in terms of ballet, but I am not, of course, a ballet dancer. Ballet is the finest training a dancer can get and I had some of it, as a child. But I never cared for it as applied to me. I wanted to do all my dancing my own way, in a sort of outlaw style. I always resented being told that I couldn't point my toe *in*, or some other such rule.

I felt at the beginning that there should be no restrictions because, after all, I knew to start with that I would not devote my career to ballet or ever become a member of a ballet company. I felt that I was going to become a musical-comedy performer or bust and this meant that there should be no limitations.

In other words, I wanted to retain the basic principles of balance and grace but I did not want ballet style to be predominant.

When you come to the evolution of the dance, its history and philosophy, I know as much about that as I do about how a television tube produces a picture—which is absolutely nothing. I don't know how it all started and I don't want to know. I have no desire to prove anything by it. I have never used it as an outlet or as a means of expressing myself.

I just dance.

List of Performances

4. Roberta, RKO, 1935.
5. Top Hat, RKO, 1935.
6. Follow the Fleet, RKO, 1936.
7. Swing Time, RKO, 1936.
8. Shall We Dance, RKO, 1937.
9. A Damsel in Distress, RKO, 1937.
10. Carefree, RKO, 1938.
11. The Story of Vernon and Irene Castle, RKO, 1939.
12. Broadway Melody of 1940, M-G-M, 1940.
13. Second Chorus, Paramount, 1940.
14. You'll Never Get Rich, Columbia, 1941.
15. Holiday Inn, Paramount, 1942.
16. You Were Never Lovelier, Columbia, 1942.
17. The Sky's the Limit, RKO, 1943.
18. Ziegfeld Follies, M-G-M, 1944-45.
19. Yolanda and the Thief, M-G-M, 1945.
20. Blue Skies, Paramount, 1946.
21. Easter Parade, M-G-M, 1948.
22. The Barkleys of Broadway, M-G-M, 1949.
23. Three Little Words, M-G-M, 1950.
24. Let's Dance, Paramount, 1950.
25. Royal Wedding, M-G-M, 1951.
26. Belle of New York, M-G-M, 1952.
27. The Band Wagon, M-G-M, 1953.
28. Daddy Long Legs, 20th Century-Fox, 1955.
29. Funny Face, Paramount, 1956.
30. Silk Stockings, M-G-M, 1957.
31. On the Beach, Stanley Kramer Productions, Inc., 1959.

TELEVISION FILMS:

Imp on a Cobweb Leash, G. E. Theatre, 1957.
Man on a Bicycle, G. E. Theatre, 1959.

TELEVISION LIVE:

An Evening with Fred Astaire, Chrysler Corp., 1958.

MOTION PICTURES AFTER 1959

32. The Pleasure of His Company, Paramount, 1961.
33. The Notorious Landlady, Columbia, 1962.
34. Finian's Rainbow, Warner Bros., 1968.
35. Midas Run, Cinerama, 1969.
36. That's Entertainment, MGM, 1974.
37. The Towering Inferno, 20th Century-Fox, 1974.
38. That's Entertainment II, MGM, 1976.
39. The Amazing Dobermans, Golden, 1977.
40. Un Taxi mauve, 1977.
41. Ghost Story, Universal, 1981.

Index